Awakening Warrior

SUNY series, Ethics and the Military Profession
George R. Lucas Jr., editor

Awakening Warrior

Revolution in the Ethics of Warfare

Timothy L. Challans

State University of New York Press

Cover illustration: "The Sleep of Reason Produces Monsters" (Caprichos no. 43), 1796–97. Etching and aquatint. By Francisco de Goya (Spanish, 1746–1828). Used by permission, courtesy of Davison Art Center, Wesleyan University, Middletown, CT.

Published by
State University of New York Press, Albany

For information, contact State University of New York Press, Albany, NY
www.sunypress.edu

Production by Marilyn P. Semerad
Marketing by Fran Keneston

Library of Congress Cataloging-in-Publication Data

Challans, Timothy L., 1954–
   Awakening warrior : revolution in the ethics of warfare / Timothy L. Challans.
      p. cm. — (SUNY series, ethics and the military profession)
   Includes bibliographical references and index.
   ISBN 13: 978-0-7914-7125-8 (hardcover : alk. paper)
   ISBN 13: 978-0-7914-7126-5 (pbk. : alk. paper)
   1. Military ethics. 2. War—Moral and ethical aspects. I. Title.

U22.C49 2007
172′.42—dc22

2006023733

10 9 8 7 6 5 4 3 2 1

This book is dedicated to those warriors
emerging from their battle sleep.

Contents

Preface ix

Acknowledgments xv

1. THE UNREFLECTIVE LIFE: THE SLEEP OF REASON 1
   The Myth of Moral Progress 1

2. THE PSEUDO-REFLECTIVE LIFE: BATTLE SLEEP 29
   Reflection Deferred and Moral Error 31
   Moral Authority 38
   Lost in the Particulars 49
   The Vices of Virtue 60
   Is Moral Progress without Reflection Possible? 68

3. THE SEMI-REFLECTIVE LIFE: INSTRUMENTAL MEANS 73
   Instrumental Means and Moral Error 74
   Inadequate Decision Procedures 77
   A Philosophical Critical Method 82
   Disregarding Ends: When Means Become Ends 93
   Are Moral Means Possible? 101

4. THE QUASI-REFLECTIVE LIFE: INADEQUATE ENDS 105
   Inadequate Ends and Moral Error 106
   Disregarding Means: When Ends Eclipse Means 110
   Presumed Ends 116
   Deliberating New Ends 127
   Are Moral Ends Possible? 133

5. THE FULLY REFLECTIVE LIFE: AUTONOMY
   FOR AUTOMATONS   137
   Autonomous Modes and Methods of Philosophical Ethics   141
   The Ethical Principles of War   151
   From Heteronomy to Autonomy: Reformulating Moral Intuitions   157
   Moral Autonomy: Creating Better Understanding and Motivation   166
   Is Moral Autonomy Possible?   173

6. THE FULLY REFLECTIVE LIFE AND MILITARY ETHICS   177
   The Possibility of Moral Progress   177

Notes   187

Bibliography   215

About the Author   219

Index   221

Preface

The war machine lumbers along as the ghost in the war machine slumbers. The war machine is competent yet unself-conscious, confident of its moral character yet unvirtuous. The military institution in America—the war machine—is asleep at the wheel, and the individuals within it are deep in dogmatic slumber. The military mind is still stunned in the twenty first century that military success doesn't win wars, that the larger logic of human action in the social and political realms remains unpersuaded by the logic of pure military force. The moral slumber deepens as reason itself sleeps. This book examines the war machine's sleep of reason.

I finished the basic manuscript for this book in the summer of 2001. The ideas explored in this critique pre-date the military adventures of the past several years. My critique concerns the moral education of the military, and I argue that an inadequate moral understanding developed by an inadequate system of moral education can lead to moral error. The large-scale systemic moral error present throughout military operations in the last several years flow logically from this inadequate understanding of the ethical dimension of conflict and warfare. It is important up front to understand the basic logic of my argument. I am not deducing that moral education is lacking based on the evidence of moral error. If I were to do so, I would be committing the formal fallacy of *affirming the consequent*. Nor am I inducing such. Instead, I offer a philosophical critique of the system of education. If the education is lacking, then moral error can result. Current evidence does not falsify my argument.

Reason buoys progress. Progress is properly an Enlightenment ideal, and philosophers often associate Descartes' *Meditations* with the dawn of the Enlightenment and the spirit of those times, a spirit of reason that animated new possibilities for progress. Before Descartes, it was difficult to engage in any inquiry without first establishing or presuming the nature of reality. Metaphysics was the master discipline, the first philosophy. And in that time before the Enlightenment—perhaps an era of *endarkenment*—how could one gain an imprimatur on any potentially alternative reality while remaining subject to a regime of metaphysical truth? Descartes' innovation was to assert that epistemology, not metaphysics, was the first philosophy. This declaration enabled him to explore the nature and limits of knowledge, unbounded by metaphysical presumptions. Guided by the primacy of reason and the valuing of free inquiry, modernity enjoyed the growth of science, an increase in the understanding of our universe, and the first viable vision of global peace and justice. In the spirit of the Enlightenment, I begin with the notion that ethics can be pursued as a first philosophy, too, dependent neither upon metaphysics nor upon epistemology. As such, this book is not a search for moral truths, ethical foundations, or fixed notions of human nature or psychology.

Moral progress? The possibility of progress was a feature of Descartes' time, but more importantly the idea of moral progress signals a debt owed to Kant, a chief architect of and principal contributor to the Enlightenment. Kant talks in his historical writings of the vagaries of evaluating moral progress, reminding us that we could interpret moral change any number of ways: as progress, decline, or even cyclical change. Kant nevertheless gives us his assessment of moral progress. He argues that people as individuals have made little if any progress; however, progress is possible through the improvement of our institutions. Concomitant with Kant's penchant for systemizing is his large contribution of insights to what we call today systems theory. This book explores many aspects of moral progress in one particular institution, the American military—it's past, present, and future. Has the American military made any moral progress? Is it progressing right now in moral matters? How can the military best facilitate future moral progress? To answer these questions, we can turn to moral philosophy. My critique focuses on the institution and the institutional conception of morality and its relationship to the moral agency of the individual and the moral responsibility the individual has for the military institution as a whole. Moral error will of necessity be the result of individual human action—error, though, that is enabled, nurtured, sustained, accelerated, magnified, and multiplied by the not-so-obvious systemic nature of a large institution.

Our ideas about morality matter. These ideas come from our moral training and education. These ideas set the conditions, establish the parameters, and provide the possible solution sets for our actions. I do not attempt any systematic evaluation of moral progress based on empirical description, sharing Kant's skeptical view of such a project. So the reader should not expect an empirical project. A descriptive causal analysis, beginning with a search for correlations between moral thought and moral action would be quite overambitious. Since this project is not an empirical one, the reader should not mistake the examples I use as a basis for making inductive generalizations. Mistaking the project as an empirical one will lead the reader astray into thinking that I am simply relying on my own perceptions, impressions, personal experiences, and anecdotes to form the basis of my generalizations. The examples of moral error I use are not simply token anomalies that are exceptions to a sound, coherent, and legitimate system of moral training and education. These examples are evidence of wholesale systemic failure. But I think I can posit the much more modest commonsense claim that moral thought and action are connected. There are very likely connections between our thought—our moral perceptions, beliefs, judgments, explanations, interpretations, and theories—and our actions. And if this connection exists in the midst of systemic failure, then the moral error is not anomalous yet rather results from the old paradigm.

While drawing upon ethical theory and philosophical argument, this work contains examples from historical, psychological, sociological, legal, and literary sources. Yet it remains primarily a theoretical work of moral philosophy that surveys and evaluates sources of moral normativity. Let me qualify further how this book as a work of philosophy differs from an empirical work. If it were an empirical project then I would be inferring from the effect of moral error to the cause, which would be a bad moral education. Aristotle defines a paralogism—a mistake in logic—as the truth of an antecedent inferred from the establishment of the consequent. To infer a cause from an effect is to commit a paralogism. Kant famously challenges Descartes' cogito (I think therefore I am) in his refutation of idealism. According to Kant, Descartes commits a paralogism when he infers his existence (I am) from his thinking (I think), because thinking is an effect of his being, his existence. His existence is in reality the cause of his thinking: I am, therefore I think. Likewise, I do not want to argue that the military commits moral error, therefore its system of moral education is bad. This kind of logic would be paralogistic. My argument is the reverse. I argue that, how, and why the system of moral education is bad. Because it is bad, therefore, it will lead to moral error.

Most philosophers use imaginary examples to illustrate their theory; I am using real examples to illustrate theory because real examples are more interesting than imaginary ones.

The *critical* nature of this book (from "critique" connoting analysis and synthesis as well) may seem to some audiences to be gratuitously negative. The purpose of honest critique is to pave the road to progress. The military progressed tremendously in the training arena over the last two decades because it was willing to endure honest critique. It is perhaps now time to apply honest critique in the moral arena as well. While I fully admire the important philosophical tradition of political and moral activism carried out by such courageous public intellectuals as Bertrand Russell and Noam Chomsky, my work remains within the less risky but equally important practice of social and moral critique, more in the tradition (albeit deep in the shadows) of such great luminaries as Rousseau and Sartre. Principles of academic freedom demand that we carry out an honest dialogue about institutional ideas and practices. Such self-critique is *especially* valuable when it comes to current operations, for if we wait for the postmortem analyses, then the casualty rate will be too high for both the body and mind (the ghost) of the war machine. My arguments seek to explore the moral domain without moralizing, by suggestion not decree, in an attempt to explain rather than convince through the course of a short book—one that is contemplative not didactic. The reader should realize that my arguments are my own and do not reflect the opinions or attitudes of any military school or organization. My personal experience in the military motivates these meditations, but my argument is not merely the universal extrapolation of my singular experience. Philosophical thought can help us transcend our particular experiences, for, indeed, reflection has this benefit.

The dismal present is that bright future we dreamed of in our youth. More than a dozen generations of war-making should perhaps be reason enough for one to wonder if the United States can ever make good our forefathers' implicit promise that their children could study something other than war. Now that America has established over the past half-century a record of perpetual fighting, engaging for the most part in one unwinnable war after another, it is time to face the possibility that the American war machine may be doing something wrong. I am retired from the Army now, and after a career of experience and reflection I am left pondering some very painful questions about recent generations. Where did we go wrong? Many people will no doubt wonder what I mean. How did we help to make the world a worse place? We certainly did not intend to make it worse. Intention is not the only moral measure. How did the recent and current generations of leaders with good character who strove to do their duty with every good intention pass on a more dangerous world to our children? Actions and intentions together are not sufficient, either. For starters, a rigorous moral exploration and evaluation will suggest that character and values may not be enough if we really want moral progress. Consequences are important, along with actions and intentions, when evaluating morality. This book will explain what is necessary if we want moral progress in our military institutions for future generations. I am inspired by my own son, Chris, now in college, who through his intelligence and humanity has chosen to study something other than war (philosophy). I am happy about his lack of interest in things military, given America's new militarism and war's continued unnecessary excesses of inhumanity.

More than a decade of teaching more than a thousand military students from the rank of cadet to colonel has provided me invaluable insights. I like them (well, some of them), and I fully sympathize with the moral challenges laying wait in their future. My students have challenged me to clarify the problems as well as to justify the claims for their solutions. I have spent three decades being involved with the military. During that time, many of my juniors, peers, and seniors through their words and deeds have demonstrated the need for moral reform, but many others through their intelligence and humanity have given me the hope that a revolution in the ethics of warfare is possible. Possibility is neither probability nor necessity, though. By revolution I mean a complete overturn, a new paradigm. My long association with this topic has led me to think the problem is systemic. Trying to repair the old system will not work. This book will be another critique among many. But this book is different because it is a systemic critique. Under the old paradigm, the solution would be to simply adjust the content of moral education: better stories, clearer rules, more relevant case studies. This won't work. My critique is not about content—what they should think. I am challenging the very structures, the methods, employed by ethics educators. This revolution will empower the warrior to know how to think about ethics, not just what to think. To paraphrase Michael Walzer, if moral progress is possible in the military institution, given its charter, then it is possible anywhere. This critical book ends with guarded optimism for the moral progress of the military, for some warriors are waking up, and the awakening warrior is the vanguard of the revolution.

Acknowledgments

M any thanks go to my academic professors, colleagues, and students, from Johns Hopkins University, the Military Academy at West Point, the United States Naval Academy, the United States Air Force Academy, the U.S. Army Command and General Staff College, the School of Advanced Military Studies (SAMS), Israel's Operational Theory Research Institute (OTRI), the U.S. Army War College, U.S. Naval War College, National Defense University, The Center for a New American Security (CNAS), and elsewhere for their counsel, assistance, encouragement, and inspiration, including Dave Barnes, Kevin Benson, Art Bilodeau, Al Bishop, Paul Blakesley, Tim Brotherton, Dave Burbach, Gordon Campbell, Chris Challans, Fred Chiaventone, Paul Christopher, Martin Cook, Ben Danner, Kettie Davison, Walter Dimmick, Glen Downing, Bob Epstein, KC Evans, Shannon French, Pete Fromm, Mark Gerges, Kate Goodland, Tom Grassey, Elliott Gruner, Cathy Haight, Tony Hartle, Michael Ignatieff, Aimee Jaskot, Fred Kennedy, Jake Kipp, Gary Krahn, Tom Lafleur, Sam Lewis, José Madera, Gary Mesick, Mike Mosser, Ed Mueller, Shimon Naveh, Johnny Oliver, Steve Parshley, Alan Penczek, Dave Pendall, Dave Perry, John Petrik, Al Pierce, Tony Pfaff, Mike Piro, Joe Popper, Judy Popper, Ethan Rafuse, Tom Rauch, Scott Ritter, Joe Ryan, Elizabeth Samet, Rob Schwartzman, Eric Shirley, Jim Schneider, Richard Schoonhoven, Forrest Smith, Jeff Smith, Gad Sneh, Roger Spiller, Rob Stanton, Peter Stromberg, John Suprin, Rick Swain, Max Thibodeaux, Pat Thomas, Karen Thoms, Paul Tipton, Emma Vialpando, Richard Wallwork, Jason Walk, Jeff Whitman, Carrie Wibben, Larry Yates, and Dan Zupan. Special thanks go to Susan Wolf, who challenged me considerably, allowing me to improve my argument throughout. Jerry Schneewind helped me the most and in more ways than he could know, not only by his invaluable guidance through the early drafts of this work, but also through his own important and inspirational work that has done so much to enable philosophers to take Kant more seriously. George Lucas helped me tremendously on all phases of this project, and without his advocacy as a distinguished veteran philosopher serving in the field of the ethics of warfare, this book never would have seen the light of day. Finally, I want to express my thanks to the editorial staff at SUNY Press, especially Editor-in-Chief Jane Bunker, Marilyn Semerad (Director of Production), Fran Keneston (Director of Marketing), Larin McLaughlin (Assistant Acquisitions Editor), Susan Petrie (Publicist), and all who were involved in the process of getting this work into print, *including* the anonymous reviewers who took me to task.

Cover: Goya's Sleep of Reason.
The inscription translates as "The sleep of reason produces monsters."

The youth in his battle sleep heard this as one who dozes hears.
—Stephen Crane, *The Red Badge of Courage*

1

The Unreflective Life

The Sleep of Reason

THE MYTH OF MORAL PROGRESS

As this book goes to print, there should be little controversy that the American war machine has failed to bring about the political, social, and economic transformation in the Middle East that the machine's operators thought it could achieve at the dawn of the new millennium. The little remaining controversy will most likely be kept alive by pretty much the same people whose group-think denied any negative conclusions despite the mountains of negative evidence. The damage done by this expedition is grave and indicates system-wide failure throughout all institutions associated with it. I want to focus on the moral failings of the war machine. In doing so, I may depart from the critique that things have gone bad only recently. This book is not about the rapes and murders that can be explained by slackened recruitment standards or criminal recruits who enlist with "moral waivers." I am interested in the wholesale systemic moral failure from the highest to the lowest levels. I believe that the system that helped bring about the current moral failure has always been there. I am going to shift the debate in another way as well. Most moral debate focuses on the failings of people; the solutions usually revolve around fixing people. This book will be about fixing the system, not fixing the people.

When ideas about morality are widespread throughout an institution, they can have a profound influence upon its practice, if even indirectly. These ideas affect practice because they affect judgment, and they affect judgment because they first shape the very understanding about morality. Perhaps we can better evaluate the military's practices by looking at its members' moral

1

judgments concerning these practices. In turn, we can then assess their judgments through an examination of their understanding of morality. All of this can be facilitated through a philosophical analysis of the ideas associated with moral practice, moral judgment, and moral understanding. Such an analysis can bring dark contradictions and shady inconsistencies into the light of reason. In addition to finding problems with the institution's ideas about morality, such an analysis can also suggest ways to improve these ideas. This philosophical analysis will challenge the perceived improvement in the moral domain that the military thinks it has already achieved. The analysis will also offer other possibilities for real moral reform. If the *ideas* about morality can be improved within the military institution, then its moral *understanding, judgment*, and *practice* can also be improved. While unpredictable, contingent, and underdetermined, the influence of our ideas upon our actions should not be underestimated. Our ideas are the substance of the propositional attitudes that make up our beliefs and desires, and our beliefs and desires together provide reasons for our actions. This book explores the ways in which some ideas we acquire may be misguided, amounting to moral error.

The vast majority of warriors within the American military institution want to be honorable and decent human beings. They navigate by their moral compass, defined at a minimum by their oath to support and defend the Constitution. Such support would entail a commitment to the rule of law. Respect for the law includes not only domestic law, but also international law, which becomes the highest law of the land by virtue of the second clause of the sixth article in the Constitution. At the same time, however, there is either a lack of awareness or a lack of concern toward constitutional principles that provide certain protections for all persons, especially our enemies, about which the Supreme Court reminded the executive branch and the military in two separate cases. The Padilla case upshot is that American citizens will retain their civil liberties of due process and judicial oversight. And the Hamdan decision is a move in the right direction to protect human rights everywhere. Pervasive are attitudes of disdain toward international agencies and institutions, especially toward the law-making bodies, judiciaries, and instruments—the very law itself. It is an outright contradiction for the military institution to disdain the very principles of that which they are sworn to support and defend. Is the military saying one thing and doing another? How did things deteriorate so badly to begin with? What was the reaction of the military when confronted with these contradictions? If there were widespread acceptance of these violations, that would indicate some sort of dismissal of the moral judgments that would be commensurate with their legal obligations. And if there are wayward practices and flawed moral judgments, then underneath it all lies a murky understanding of morality. The ideas surrounding the practices, especially ideas that support and defend illegal and immoral practices, are the central focus of this book. The military has engaged in some atrocious practices, and these practices have not adequately been examined; they have not been sufficiently *deciphered*, at either an institutional or a public level. Without adequate examination or sufficient decipherment, the moral quality of present and future practices may continue to be at times appalling.

Moral failure at the institutional level contains patterns, whether we are looking at the present or into the past. The world community recoiled when the undeniable cruelty of U.S. troops toward the enemy hit the news. Many Americans were aggrieved by the fact that American troops had committed what some were calling atrocities, but others were not apologetic regarding the mistreatment. This was war, after all, and everyone knows (or should know) that bad things happen in war. They were our enemy, so to speak. Or it was the fault of the media. Who are they to try and make America look bad? They always are reporting the bad news, never the good. No need to worry—the institution has it under control. It is just one of those anomalies that occur during war. And the bottom line: it's just a few bad apples near the bottom of the barrel, which may include a few bad leaders near the bottom. While some veterans spoke out against the mistreatment, others supported it, some even claiming that the practice was widespread and no big deal since these kinds of things happen all the time in a time of war—always have, always will. Those who were critical were asking questions. How could the American military do such a thing? They were supposed to be the good guys. To be sure, the enemy suffered; many died. What sounds like a description of Abu Ghraib is also a description of My Lai. The past may not repeat itself or even rhyme with the present, but the oblique resounding echoes compose haunting slant-rhymes. The atrocity itself was horrific, but the issue here that should also cause concern is that when they talk today about what went wrong at My Lai, few Army leaders can do much more than vilify Lieutenant Calley. For example, Colin Powell denigrates Calley as he recalls the incident by saying, "My Lai was an appalling example of much that had gone wrong in Vietnam. Because the war had dragged on for so long, not everyone commissioned was really officer material."[1] Major Colin Powell was the operations officer, the G3 of the Americal Division beginning in October of 1968, the division Calley served in. While Powell was not the G3 at the time of the massacre, he was the G3 during the investigation by the Inspector General of MACV (Military Assistance Command Vietnam). Even though Major Powell cooperated freely with the inspector, sharing the division's operational journal entries of March 1968, which showed the details of the incident, including body count, enemy weapons captured, and so on, he says, "I would not learn until nearly two years later what this visit [by the inspector general] was all about. . . . Subsequent investigation revealed that Calley and his men killed 347 people. The 128 enemy 'kills' I had found in the journal formed part of the total."[2] Why did it take two years for Major Powell to learn what this incident was about? Why didn't he understand what he was looking at? Why wasn't he better able to connect the dots, so to speak? Almost everyone approaches the moral failure of My Lai as a problem of the will, implying that the soldiers understood what was right, and all they lacked was the will. I argue that the issue here is not about moral problems of the will. The answer has to do with moral problems of the understanding. The subsequent Peers investigation focused a great deal of attention on the fact that the unusual details of the unit journal caused little concern for all who had access to the reports. They did not understand the systemic nature of the problem.

For example, the report to MACV headquarters that Task Force Barker had killed 128 Viet Cong (VC) and captured only three weapons should have raised some suspicions among the MACV staff. Rarely was one weapon captured for every VC reported killed in action, but a ratio of forty-three enemy dead to one weapon captured was completely out of line. The operations section should have noted the disparity and called it to General William Westmoreland's attention, and an inquiry should have been initiated. Instead, a message of congratulations was sent to the unit.[3]

At the systemic level of ethics for the institution, past and present merge. Troops will do whatever those in charge lead them to do, for the most part. Those in charge can lead troops to do worthy things; they can also lead them to do despicable things. Troops take cues from the leaders, and they learn very quickly the kinds of things their leaders will condone and the kinds of things they won't. Orders are orders, commands are commands, and leaders have a grave responsibility to communicate very clearly to their troops during a time of war to ensure that the line between acceptable and unacceptable actions is as clear as possible. Dozens of the enemy, perhaps even hundreds, have died during the detention and interrogation operations in the war against terror. Hundreds, thousands, have been mistreated in order to gain intelligence. At the same time, it is a matter of public record that the post-9/11 majority of those in detention does not belong there, but were rounded up carelessly or wound up there through unreliable line-ups or by the offering of generous bounties. It is clear that leaders from the White House through the Department of Defense condoned a relaxation of legal procedures. It will take years for many to draw the linkage between this illegitimate relaxation of standards and the manifestly illegal practices that ensued at the tactical level, but much has already been revealed in the *Torture Papers*.[4]

There is a corresponding illegitimacy at the strategic level of this war against terror. The current war on terror includes all operations, domestic and international, military and otherwise, related to security matters after 9/11. There are members of Congress who clamor for accountability. The

Center for Constitutional Rights is building a case for impeachment based on the grounds of torture, domestic suveillance and an illegal war in Iraq, Dave Lindorff and Barbara Olshansky, *The Case for Impeachment* (Thomas Dunne Books, 2006). Detailed accounts of wholesale failure and illegitimacy are now widely available in books such as *Cobra II* (Pantheon, 2006) and *Fiasco* (Penguin Press, 2006), far exceeding anecdotal observation. It will take years for the public and the military institution to be able to admit the illegitimacy of the current conflict in Iraq, brought on by the political leaders yet also condoned by the top leaders of the military institution, largely because the war continues. There is neither a legal nor a moral justification for the war. Legally, there is neither a domestic nor an international basis for the war. Domestically, the two stipulations in the *provisional* Public Law 107-243 were never satisfied. This was the congressional instrument that allegedly provides the domestic legal basis for war. President George W. Bush has yet to support the assertions that would make that law valid: 1) that Iraq possessed weapons of mass destruction and 2) that Iraq was connected to the attack on American soil in the fall of 2001, as John Dean lays out in his book *Worse than Watergate* (Warner Books, 2005). And there was no international basis at all. The United Nations rejected the American rationale for war and neither at this time nor any time previously made any declaration or resolution that would sanction an invasion of Iraq. It was the same Major Powell, swept along with the *injustice of* The (false) War against Communism in Vietnam, who was also swept along with the *injustice of* The (false) War against Terror in Iraq as the Secretary of State. People are not quite sure what to do now that they know that the rationale presented by Secretary of State Powell has turned out to be false. Were the political leaders lying to the American public, or did they just make a mistake? Colin Powell to this day blames the bad intelligence. Is that all he can or should say? Is that all any of us can say? Yes, the intelligence was wrong. But the bigger issue is how the leaders misused the intelligence. Even worse, the American resort to war was unjustifiable even if the intelligence were true. Preventive war is not part of law. After the American misadventure in Iraq and the Israeli misadventure in Lebanon, chances are very slim that the law will change to favor or allow preventive war or even pre-emptive war. Perhaps the rationale for the war was bullshit, as the philosophical analysis in Harry Frankfurt's book, *On Bullshit* (Princeton University Press, 2005), may suggest if applied to this situation. Because the truth of the propositions is not as important as the effect achieved, bullshit is something other than a mistake or a lie. Did Powell really believe the conclusions he was presenting from the evidence: drawings of chemical vehicles and pictures of trucks at a facility there one day and gone another? We may never know. When someone is bullshitting, the link is broken between the truth function of the state of affairs and the

belief represented in the propositions about that state of affairs. The consequences of being caught when bullshitting are less severe than when lying. In
very significant ways, the truth of the rationale did not matter, for the rationale was enough to get us there, and now once we are there it is all too easy
to deflect any criticism of the rationale because of the attention drawn to the
problems now at hand. More of the American than the world audience
bought the rationale, for most of the rest of the world called our bluff, which
is another term Frankfurt uses for bullshit.[5]

There was no legal basis for the war with Iraq; neither domestic nor
international law sanctioned the war. I will argue throughout this book that
it was neither legal nor moral to invade Iraq. The weapons of mass destruction rationale would not likely have been a legal justification had they
turned out to exist. But after this rationale evaporated a new rationale
emerged—pro-democratic intervention. Such rationale, even if it were legal
could not be employed retroactively. Prohibitions against pro-democratic
interventions have only been strengthened by precedent whether they be
covert or overt. For example, the International Court of Justice condemned
the U.S. support of the Contras in 1986. Pro-democratic interventions are
still prohibited. The same can be said for rationale based on humanitarian
intervention. NATO intervention in Kosovo has only worked to strengthen
the prohibition against humanitarian intervention. This legal reality challenges any U.S. narrative that justifies current realities. *As a result, the military presently has widespread contempt for international law.* When there are
moral problems at the strategic level in a conflict, there very often are correlative moral problems at the tactical level as well. For the most part, legitimacy either runs all the way through a conflict or illegitimacy runs through
it. Is it possible to prosecute a war in a just manner if the war itself is unjustified? And conversely, is it possible for a war to be just if it is prosecuted in
an unjust manner? Michael Walzer famously argues that *jus ad bellum* and
jus in bello can be logically and practically distinct, in parts one through
three in his book *Just and Unjust Wars* (Basic Books, 2006). He also caveats
that argument by exploring the ways in which the justness of the war and
justice in the war coalesce, in parts 4 and 5 of the book. I will argue
throughout that the ethics of warfare is much more connected from the
highest to the lowest levels (and back again) than traditionally thought, and
more connected than Walzer thought. There are legal and moral problems
at the highest levels of The War against Terror in Iraq and the same goes for
The War against Communism in Vietnam. There are also legal and moral
problems at the lowest levels of the two wars. There are similarities that
make the two very closely related, even though the *Torture Papers* are very
different from the *Pentagon Papers* and Abu Ghraib is very different from My
Lai. Both My Lai and Abu Ghraib, while horrific in and of themselves, are

symptomatic of widespread systemic moral failure. The systemic failures begin with an insufficient understanding of the moral domain. These similarities have to do with the moral cultures of the military institutions, the institutional responsibilities of the leaders, and the ideas surrounding the ethics of warfare. These relations within one conflict resemble the same relations in the other. No doubt many will reject any analogy between Vietnam and today's conflict because of the many differences between the two situations. Here is one way in which they differ that should cause us to take pause: The world we helped create after leaving Vietnam to the Communists was not in any way as potentially dangerous as the world we are helping to create now. Some think we will be lucky not to have started World War III. My Lai and Abu Ghraib are visible twin peaks of the same iceberg.

I want to use the phrase *ethics of warfare* instead of *military ethics*, following the more polymathic historians Sir Michael Howard's and Roger Spiller's use of *history of warfare* instead of *military history*. The adjective *military* restricts the broader relevant domains of interest in wartime: political, diplomatic, social, cultural, environmental, economic, and human dimensions. The ethics of warfare, therefore, considers the interaction of the military with these other important domains. It has a much broader, systemic view of warfare than military ethics. We should examine the ethics of warfare at the strategic, operational, and tactical levels of war. The moral evaluation of the military includes its function, so the examination of the political dimension and the strategic employment of the military should not be avoided. The military is an instrument of foreign policy, so for its function to be moral the military depends upon the government to employ the military legitimately, by means of a legitimate process, according to the rule of law and the moral norms of international conflict. Did the U.S. government legitimately comply with the rule of law in this current "Global War on Terror?" Did the executive and legislative powers of the United States follow the constitutional and international processes to legitimate this current war? Just to review, America has constitutionally employed its armed forces overseas only a few times out of the several hundred military actions in its history (with many of these being unknown to the general public). The rule of force has predominated over the rule of law in American history. America today appears to be in a perpetual state of undeclared, unconstitutional war. There are pockets of goodness that should be highlighted, given the overall dark conditions. In the book *Fiasco* (Penguin Press, 2006) for example, Thomas Ricks goes out of his way to praise the good work of individuals such as General Dave Petraeus and Colonel H. R. McMaster. These are two in the group of awakening warriors, who by thinking for themselves have improved their situations rather than worsened them.

War is necessary for the warrior; the warrior cannot exist without war. Roger Spiller, in his excellent book *An Instinct for War*, refers to what he calls the "military ethos" as a "pseudo-philosophy, a pastiche of militarism and romanticism that appealed to the immature mind."[6] This pseudo-philosophy has many names: military ethos, military ethic, warrior ethos, warrior ethic, or warrior spirit. There is much ado about the warrior spirit these days. But if I were to name the components of the warrior spirit, it would be composed of equal parts adrenaline, testosterone, and bullshit—bullshit in the philosophical sense as Frankfurt describes it, propositions indifferent to any truth value. Infinite war is the strategic consequence of political leaders being suffused with the same warrior spirit as the military leaders. Preemptive or even preventive war?! Regime change operations?! When engaged in military action, the political goal should be a legitimate goal, a goal that can be endorsed ultimately by the people, for, after all, a well-ordered democratic republic should engage in war and can sustain a war only with the informed consent of the people—especially lengthy and costly wars. Were the people informed? Do the people consent? According to the Enlightenment political philosophy of those who founded the United States, America has a democratic form of government to the extent that its policies are endorsed by the informed consent of the people. And America remains a republic to the extent that its governmental powers remain divided. What of the international community? Since the people in the United States make up a very small part of the world's population, it may become increasingly harder to ignore a world citizenry that has little sympathy for American global influence and military belligerency. The current moral and legal conception places responsibility with those in charge. However, those in charge—both political and military leaders—continue to refuse to take moral responsibility, or to even admit fault when they are wrong. Since our leaders have always and perhaps will always continue to fail us morally, and since the current conception leaves us to depend upon morally failed leaders, perhaps one potential solution is to change the conception—we need a moral revolution to bring about moral progress in warfare.

The military today is one element of power that provides the means for attaining American political goals. Our commander-in-chief asks who could possibly disagree that we are better off without Saddam Hussein. Not only should the goals, or ends, be legitimate, but the means used in attaining those ends should be legitimate as well. I will argue that the current National Security Strategy and National Military Strategy are at odds with morality and require revolutionary thinking to change in a positive direction. A state of perpetual war in which Congress abdicates the legitimizing power of war-making to the commander-in-chief is unconstitutional and is de facto illegal as well as immoral. There is strong legal and philosophical consensus for this view, with the exception of John Yoo, perhaps, and his fellow apologists. So, at the strategic level, American war making is currently morally questionable. Operationally and tactically, it is equally questionable. Preemptive war is at best only marginally justified and only if the danger is *clear and present*. Preventive war (different from preemptive war) is fought for *vague and distant* danger and introduces new levels of moral error on a huge scale. The governing doctrinal principle for the military as it moves into the new millennium is that of manipulating the national will of an enemy through preemptive (or preventive) action with overwhelming "shock and awe."[7] The details of this method include attacking the infrastructures of a people, of the civilian populace. The mindset that the military adopts under such a method is that their job becomes simply that of servicing a set of targets for maximum effect while offering at the same time the greatest force protection possible with the maximum standoff. The idea is firmly embedded in the military's emerging doctrine known as Effects Based Operations (EBO). This doctrine features the use of military might to shape the *behavior* and the will of the enemy, through force, to use a military operation to bring about desired effects. However, the associated indiscriminate destruction that ensues from destroying enemy centers of gravity, including the infrastructures—industrial, electrical, economic, and information infrastructures—works directly against any legitimate political end that should follow combat. These two emerging watershed developments working in tandem—*perpetual war* against terror as political ideology and the *warrior ethos* (warrior spirit) as ideology for the warrior—have connected an inadequate end with illegitimate means through the operational medium of Effects Based Operations. But in order for the military to be judged favorably in the ethical arena, which can be judged separately from the arena of victory, both ends and means have to be legitimate. If the warrior ethos is a military axiom, then preemptive war is its political corollary.

My argument holds true for the military institutions of today, but it also holds for previous decades, regardless of the moral error present at any particular time. Since I argue that the problem lies with the ideas we have about morality, these ideas will influence our actions and create moral error. If there were no moral errors right now, then that may affect the argument. My book, which delves into the processes of moral education themselves, is not dependent upon the degree of moral error present. Even so, there is an overabundance of evidence of moral error and there is more revealed in both academic presses and popular presses every day. As such I am not going to chronicle this catalog of moral error—I could not do so in a short book. To reiterate, I will use real world examples, though, because they are more interesting than the imaginary examples that philosophers usually use.

Much of moral philosophy deals with practical moral problems, and many philosophers work to solve some current problem.[8] There are many moral problems in the American military institution, but I want to focus on the problem of moral understanding and its connection to moral practice in the context of its public charter, wielding deadly force. The American military continues to act unethically at times, and it commits moral error whenever it engages in some immoral practice.[9] But it also commits moral error if beliefs are immoral, if there is error in perception, understanding, or judgment. And many warriors hold moral beliefs that are suspect. In the military, for example, many people, perhaps even a majority, still try to justify the bombing of Japan, our involvement in Vietnam, and the "certain victory" of Desert Storm or the justification of its follow-on, Operation Iraqi Freedom. These beliefs, rife with moral error, and many more are backward, or at least they do not cohere. The institution sustains many incoherent ideas that conflict with one another, incoherent because they are inconsistent; they do not cohere. For example, the requirement in the Code of Conduct to escape "by all means available" lures most warriors to want to justify the killing of one's captors. This impulse to kill one's captors—a pre-theoretic intuition of the warrior—is expressly forbidden by the laws, principles, and customs of war. In so many ways the warrior's moral sentiment remains counterintuitive to law and morality. That war apologists want to justify invading Iraq because of Iraq's disregard for the rule of law—while the invasion itself is a blatant disregard for the rule of law—rates pretty highly on a scale of unself-conscious irony. American exclusionism is a central tenet of U.S. foreign policy.

The current rhetoric of military ethics—the pursuit of the warrior ethos—has become important to the military institution over the last several decades, largely due to some significant moral problems, some new and some old. The incredible power of modern warfare brought with it new ethical challenges, but the savagery of modern militaries among civilized societies revived the old moral challenge of barbarity. The nightmarish potential of nuclear war brought into sharp focus the idea that there may be moral limits to man's destructive potential, but destructive war, indiscriminate war, persists, a type of warfare that considers all nationals to be combatants and features the intentional targeting of civilians. The horrific genocide in the last century—spanning several continents involving several peoples, including Jews, Armenians, Tutsis, to name a few—demonstrated that renaissances and enlightenments are no guarantees against romantic reversions to earlier days of brutality and barbarity. And the debacles at My Lai and Abu Ghraib showed that anyone, even an American, is capable of committing atrocities. Examples such as these give students of the ethics of warfare important paradigmatic examples for moral reflection. But these paradigmatic examples (paradigm is Greek for example) are in each case symptomatic of widespread practice. Massacre was commonplace in Vietnam, and torture and abuse in the current war is more widespread and commonplace than most people realize. As the global exercise of military power continued to evolve over the course of the last century, however, one should have expected a parallel interest in the ethics of killing. But by ignoring the ethics of killing, the military misses this important dimension. They missed it because the warrior ethic does not examine the ethics of killing. The warrior ethos is really about a special kind of work ethic, one that centers on mission accomplishment and potential self-sacrifice, not on moral restraints and law-abidingness. So the pursuit of the warrior ethos is perfectly consistent with a lack of interest in the ethics of killing.

The rhetoric and appearance of interest in the ethics of warfare is waxing while the substantive interest in the ethics of killing (the central essence of the ethics of warfare) is waning. Something is amiss. Over the last decade, the American military has emerged as the world's *military* superpower. The United States continues to be the most militarily engaged power in the world, leaving its heavy footprint wherever it goes, from Europe to the Far East, from the Fertile Crescent to the Hindu Kush, with the sun never setting on America's military presence and activity. The United States has long been involved in regime change operations. Stephen Kinzer names more than a dozen over the last century in his book *Overthrow* (Times Books, 2006). Another book to examine in this regard is Michal J. Sullivan's *American Adventurism Abroad: 30 Invasions, Interventions, and Regime Changes since World War II* (Praeger Publishers, 2004).

Apparently, the moral problems that consumed the American military in earlier decades—nuclear holocaust, genocide, and massacre—are problems of the past. Instead, a new moral theme consumes the military imagination. The emerging theme in the military ethic accompanying this advent of American global military superiority is that of American moral clarity and superiority, the moral superiority of a professional military that putatively *sets the example* and does *the right thing*. Moral superiority is one of the key features of the warrior ethos.

For years after Desert Storm I wanted to believe, like many Americans, that the U.S. military had completed a moral transformation. Those of us who had been duped by our own propaganda wanted to believe that the indiscriminate killing in Vietnam had been replaced by precision munitions in Desert Storm and beyond, that the repugnant crimes of war so prevalent in the degenerate destructive fighting in Indochina had been replaced by consciously clean conventional fighting in the Gulf, and also that the psychotic psychologies of a bankrupt former generation had been swept away by a reformed professional military that fought with moral clarity and certainty. But the progress that I and many others had imagined was a myth. The story that we told ourselves in the last quarter of the twentieth century was as follows: The American military had arguably reached its historical nadir in the

Vietnam era, a military bereft of most social or moral qualities. After much introspection and soul searching, the *prodigal* American military transformed itself over the next few decades and reformed and renewed itself in every way; the least respected institution in the 1970s became the most respected institution in the 1990s. Such is the plot line of the widely read and universally admired book by James Kitfield, *Prodigal Soldiers* (Potomac Books, 1997). Okay. By many measures, the American military has met with much success of late, if those measures focus on efficiency, professionalism, or the raw, uncontested application of deadly force, considering Gulf I, Afghanistan, and Gulf II. This aura of success, even if it is only the appearance of success, often entails attitudes of progress in every dimension, including the social and ostensibly even the moral. In their process of renewal over the last several decades, all services of the military—led by the Army—have resurrected for their institutions the cult of the warrior. They cloak this largely ineffable aspect of their cultures in respectability, by referring to it as the warrior ethos, or the warrior ethic. However, today's American warrior is a construct with a collection of attributes that is inspired more by myth, legend, and superstition than by actual history or sound philosophy: never give up, death before dishonor, win at any cost, etc. This book considers every branch of military service in the United States. I will talk specifically about soldiers when referring to the Army, marines when referring to the Marine Corps, and so on. However, there is no single generic term in the English language when referring to any member of the military. Given that this book critiques the advent of the new warrior ethos in relation to members of every branch of service, I will use the term "warrior" as a generic member of any of the branches of service. The term warrior by itself is morally neutral—a warrior could be morally good or morally bad. Even so, contrary to the predominant view among warriors today, I will argue that the warrior ethos with its ubiquitous yet unexamined influence on the moral culture in the American military is one of the main impediments to moral progress.

Is the current moral understanding and practice consistent with the notion of moral progress? This book is a critique of the military's system of moral education, a critique of the methods, structures, and processes used to impart an understanding of ethics. I emphasize again that this book is not primarily a moral evaluation based on our historical past. Such an empirical project could lead to any conclusion. I could stack the deck with my data and present nothing but positive moral examples and claim progress, or I could do the opposite and claim moral recidivism. Instead, if I can present enough examples of moral error—moral error that is significant—then I can put forward the modest but important claim that we have a lot of work to do to get better and that any declaration of victory in the ethical arena would be premature. We can never make moral progress if we cannot face our shortcomings. While I survey an evaluation of *actual* moral progress, I am more interested in the *possibility* of moral progress and what that possibility may entail: what we may have to change in order to improve. The possibility of moral progress in the American military over time could in principle be enhanced only if moral understanding and practice were improved upon, over time. This claim should be uncontroversial, but it carries with it some strict logical implications. Better moral understanding and better moral practice are necessary conditions for moral progress. And moral progress cannot occur unless there is improved understanding and practice. So, moral progress for the military cannot be accidental or happen unconsciously; that should not count as progress. Additionally, moral progress for the military would be independent of success or failure, victory or defeat. Separating military success from moral progress is more difficult than it may at first appear.

The national mood set by the executive branch and their supporters with their rhetoric and policies carries with it an air of moral superiority coupled with moral clarity.[10] A stance of moral clarity is a position of moral superiority in disguise, but in actuality it is moral naiveté. Language that hints of superiority is especially problematic since the current war on terrorism targets the Islamic world, and the rhetoric is essentially that of a crusade against Islam. There has been for centuries a Western cultural bias of superiority over the non-Western world. The United States has inherited this discourse of superiority from the former imperial powers that dominated the oriental world, mainly from France and Britain. The colonial goal was not an obviously malevolent one. The great powers thought of themselves as being altruistic, carrying out the "white man's burden," civilizing "lesser" peoples. Such was Napoleon's goal in Spain. Is our desire to benevolently democratize the Middle East just the contemporary version of carrying the "white man's burden?" Even the imaginary literary worlds of Tolkien and Lewis—Middle Earth and Narnia—portray the enemy as being oriental (in the Middle Eastern sense), living to the south and east. Americans today are so steeped in their cultural discourse of superiority over the non-Western world that they do not even recognize the linguistic conditioning of our cultural stance. What Americans need in this regard is "an understanding not so much of Western politics and of the non-Western world in those politics as of the *strength* of Western cultural discourse."[11] Now, members of the military, generally, want to believe they are moral people, and that desire is good. They also want to believe they belong to a moral institution, engaged in moral activities for a moral country: appropriate desires, every one of them. But it is enough of a task for the military to aspire simply to be moral; there is more than enough work to reach that modest goal. While working to reach the objective of being *moral* is noble, the military should not pursue *moral superiority*. The military now boasts both global and domestic moral superiority, but claiming the *moral high ground* leaves the American military vulnerable to attack (seasoned soldiers know it is dangerous to remain on high ground). Military moral doctrine boasts global moral superiority over any enemy: "There is no moral comparison between American Soldiers and their adversaries in wars throughout our history."[12] And military moral doctrine claims to have domestic moral superiority over American society at large, due to the supposed values gap between presumed pure martial values and the alleged impure societal values, for "the country still looks to the Army as a source of moral discipline."[13]

But these attitudes of *moral superiority* are misguided: The comparative nature of superiority conflicts with the substantive nature of morality. It would sound quite odd, for example, if members of other professions—police officers, fire fighters, professors, lawyers, and politicians—were to dwell on the notion of their moral superiority. Why does the military culture require it, then, or even desire it? Part of the problem stems from lack of linguistic and conceptual precision. Consider the terms "warrior ethos" and "warrior ethic," usually used interchangeably. The primary meaning of *ethos* from the ancient Greek is "character." The word "ethics" derives from *ethos*, since the ancient Greek philosophers located the subject of ethics in the character of an individual: character ethics or virtue ethics. Modern moral philosophy demonstrated the inadequacy of this ancient conception (discussed in later chapters); there are too many moral concerns that the ancient conception cannot accommodate. The secondary meaning of ethos is that of the spirit of a culture. When the military speaks of the warrior ethos, it is referring mainly to some combination of these two senses of ethos, but it is not referring to ethics in the modern sense. And by "ethic," they are simply referring to a work ethic, again, separate from ethics. Doctrinal language similarly confuses the term "moral" when it conflates "moral" with "morale," the first referring to the ethical, and the second to the psychological. Since the two referents are then used interchangeably, we have the unfortunate consequence of thinking that moral superiority flows from psychological dominance.[14] The fact that moral superiority is a feature of military moral doctrine, a highlight of the moral rhetoric of its leaders, and a cornerstone of many members' moral beliefs are all evidence enough that the system of moral understanding in the military requires some critical analysis and perhaps some revision. As in so many other areas, the military is hesitant to honestly and openly critique itself in the moral domain.

Not only has the military developed ill-formed beliefs concerning the ethics of killing, it has also misplaced its priorities regarding moral concerns. Instead of an interest in the ethics of killing, as one would expect in these more dangerous modern times, the military today is obsessed with private morality, especially sexual ethics. The energy directed toward matters of pri-

vate behavior, particularly sexual behavior, has completely eclipsed any dialogue about any substantive moral matters regarding the moral application of
military force. In other words, sex crimes are more serious than war crimes in
today's military. The military has openly discussed *ad nauseam* (normally after
an unsuccessful cover-up) the personal indiscretions of a few people over the
last several years,[15] but as an institution it has spent relatively little time publicly discussing the means, ends, limits, or implications of the moral dimensions of applying deadly force. Uniquely among people within the United
States, particularly in the military, there was much more concern over the
indescretion of an American president's private sexual life than over the
indescretion of his public acts of wielding military power, in actuality reversing
the theme of the film *Wagging the Dog*. And remarkably yet unsurprisingly
the military culture sustains an enmity toward political leaders who are dishonest about their sexual lives at orders of magnitude much greater than
toward political leaders who prevaricate about war. Outside of legal and
philosophical circles, the public dialogue on substantive moral military matters hardly exists. Imagine medical or law enforcement professionals who
focused exclusively on issues of sexual harassment and private sexual behavior to the complete neglect of any substantive public moral issues unique to
those professions, issues pertaining to the saving or losing of life and limb or
to the protection or destruction of human life. The military should pay more
attention to the moral questions concerning its public charter.

To evaluate moral progress requires a close examination of the ideas
behind the practice of the military. Improved moral understanding and practice together set the conditions for the possibility of moral progress. The current sources of moral understanding for the military consist of deference to
moral authority, indoctrination, and narratives that transmit the morally
questionable warrior ethos, which can be counterproductive to moral
progress. The current reality of practice is essentially the same as it always has
been—an application of instrumental methods that reach for inadequate
goals. While the military is comfortable with its moral thinking and practice
based on authority, indoctrination, and oversimplified instrumental methods
of rationalizing morally, I argue that the military should change completely
and move toward a more reflective model of moral autonomy that emphasizes
philosophical ethics yet still is compatible with good order and discipline. I
argue that we should not conclude that modern moral theory forces us to
choose between method and outcome—both are important; means *and* ends
should be moral. My argument challenges the predominant moral heritage
Americans have inherited—pragmatism. My argument also challenges principal approaches to our current conceptions of morality, consequentialist
approaches as well as virtue ethics (or character ethics). Drawing mainly
upon Kantian moral theory, I argue for an original set of moral principles to

inform ethical understanding and practice of the military enterprise, and I
argue that the military should seek a new moral end while exercising sound
moral methods. The current conception of the ethics of warfare should be
revised, a model that has caused demonstrable and significant moral error—
through unreflective appeals to authority and immoral doctrines, the application of instrumental means, and the pursuit of inadequate ends. This revision
amounts to nothing less than a revolution in the ethics of warfare. The revolution is to move toward philosophically informed normative sources for our
moral understanding and away from sources not philosophically informed.
This argument is a normative argument as well as a meta-ethical one, which
is what makes it moral philosophy. If the argument depended on a descriptive
analysis, an empirical analysis of cause and effect, then it would not be a
work of philosophy. While my professional philosophical audience will readily
understand this point, the non-philosophical audience may not be familiar
with this distinction. If someone reads this book focusing on the empirical
examples then they are missing the philosophical critique at the normative
and meta-ethical levels.

In significant ways, the American use of the military during Vietnam
was morally rotten, from the top down. The substance of indoctrination
within the culture was morally bereft. The means employed were often illegal
and immoral. And collective judgments after decades of national soul searching found the ends we were seeking and the means to obtain them in
Vietnam were at best morally suspect and at worst morally bankrupt.
Strategically and politically, we should seriously question how we became so
misled by a failed theory, the so-called domino theory. This false idea as a
feature of the Cold War and its Red Scare fueled a security strategy that
entangled America in Vietnam for twenty-five years out of fear that if
Vietnam became communist, then the whole region would follow, including
Indonesia, Japan, and even Australia. Our political leaders lied to the public
(or maybe bullshitted them) and with the complicity of the U.S. Navy staged
the phony Gulf of Tonkin Incident as a pretense to justify initial military
involvement. The Army and the Marines regressively reverted to fighting a
destructive, unconventional war, increasingly ignoring the conventions of
war and international law as the conflict continued, including the illegal
invasion of the neutral countries of Laos and Cambodia. The Air Force participated in illegal and immoral strategic bombing on an unprecedented scale.
From a moral point of view, Vietnam was an abysmal horror show, from the
Gulf of Tonkin at the beginning to the Christmas Bombings at the end, with
plenty of moral censure available for military and political leaders and participants. With few exceptions today scholars condemn American involvement
with Vietnam in hindsight. We misunderstood the nature of that conflict,
fighting what we took to be a war against communism when in reality it was a

civil war, fueled by anticolonialism and a desire to eject foreign influence. The wars against communism of yesterday have been replaced with the wars against terrorism of today. What will the wars against terror look like in hindsight? The proximate cause of the current war against terror was an attack perpetrated by terrorists, to be sure. Most of those terrorists were Saudis. Since that time, America's response has amounted to rearranging two nations, neither of which was Saudi Arabia. We are told that the nation is at war against terror. Is terror the new avatar to replace communism? Not only does this focus show a misunderstanding of the nature of the current conflict, but it also sets the nation on a path so that it can never succeed. Perhaps, as in Vietnam, today's conflict has more to do with a civil war, fueled by anticolonialism and a desire to eject foreign influence, but now on a much more global scale. We spent fifty years fighting the Cold War without understanding the nature of that conflict. How long will we fight the next Long War without understanding the nature of it?

Why, some may ask, would a more reflective, more robust moral understanding, as well as more informed practice, give the military greater potential for moral progress? The possibility of moral progress would improve because it would reduce the potential—and the actuality—of moral error. A moral error is simply an ethical mistake, a mistake that can exist either in theory or in practice. Why, one may ask, would a more reflective understanding of ethics present us with the possibility of reduced moral error and greater moral progress? One answer would have to be that some errors are worse than others—worse in kind as well as in degree. For example, it is generally accepted in legal and moral circles that using inappropriate means brings graver moral error than failing to bring about some good end. In fact, our legal system itself is one that favors method over outcome. It is considered a much graver moral error to punish innocent people in our legal system than it is to fail to punish guilty people. The first error (a Type I error) is of a graver type than the second error (a Type II error).[16] The Type I error—falsely judging something to be present that is not there (such as guilt)—is in many contexts referred to as a false positive. The error is in the misjudgment; to act on such error is also error. There are laws (or sanctions) that proscribe the commission of inappropriate means. Alternatively, there are no laws (or punitive sanctions) that punish the lack of bringing about good ends. Type I errors are worse than Type II errors. So, in principle, but perhaps contrary to the unreflective person's intuition, we commit worse errors when we use inappropriate means than when we fail to bring about desirable ends. In the American system of justice, we consider it a worse moral error if the police were to injure or kill innocent bystanders than for them to fail to apprehend suspected criminals at large. By a fairly strong analogy, we should consider it a worse moral error for the military to injure or kill innocents (perhaps hundreds or thousands of them) than to fail to apprehend suspected terrorists, or even belligerents. The same goes with torture. The military commits graver moral errors when it violates legal and moral norms, even if these inappropriate means are employed to bring about desirable ends, such as victory or national security. Pre-theoretic intuitions may lead people to disagree with this last claim in its military context; such disagreement helps to make my case that warriors are in need of a better theoretical understanding of morality. My argument will lay out reasons to show why the potential and actual moral errors resulting from less reflective moral conceptions are worse than those errors that may result from more reflective ones.

Problems of the understanding are serious moral problems. And following the theme that some errors are worse than others, errors resulting from moral problems we don't understand are worse than errors resulting from those we do. They are worse because when large segments of an institution do not recognize deep aspects of a problem through a lack of understanding, there can be little hope for meaningful reform. For an example of failed moral reform due ultimately to a lack of understanding, consider a closer look at the My Lai massacre. Today, after more than thirty years of reflection on the infamous incident, the moral beliefs—the perception, understanding, and judgment—of that massacre are still in error. For example, My Lai, one of the most iniquitous atrocities of Vietnam, did not cause any moral alarm or attention by its own internal review, other than the moral indignation that *righteous* officers held for Lieutenant Calley. Unfortunately, the moral problems associated with the My Lai massacre were systemic problems, cultural problems, primarily because of the badly formed and deeply held moral beliefs throughout the military institution during Vietnam. Certainly every person in the chain of command who condoned the massacre was morally culpable, and furthermore those who actively aided in its cover-up were also technically legally responsible. But the responsibility goes even deeper than that. The operational policies in the division, and throughout virtually every military organization in Vietnam, helped to set the conditions for the massacre. These operational policies routinely included *search and destroy missions*, wholesale *free-fire areas*, and the indiscriminate *mere-gook rule*. The combination of these policies set the conditions for soldiers to use deadly force excessively without discrimination, routinely causing more harm than necessary. Reports and informal investigations within the division following the episode proved to be fruitless. Nothing was done internally by the military chain of command about the My Lai incident of March 1968, in which several hundred noncombatants were slaughtered, until Specialist Fourth Class Ron Ridenhour went outside the military—off the reservation, so to speak—and wrote a letter in March 1969 that opened up an investigation.[17] Only external intervention, mainly in the form of investigative journalism, brought real scrutiny to the problem.

Very few recognize the culpability that the Army's leaders and the military institution itself have concerning the incident. While most want to chastise Calley for the My Lai incident, few are willing or want to face the possibility that *the Army as an institution in large part created Calley and those like him*.[18] The military has yet to acknowledge this problem, a problem that came from immoral doctrines that engendered inappropriate means to pursue illegitimate goals. Indeed Calley is culpable for what he did. But the responsibility does not end with the crimes of one individual. Besides the massacre and the cover-up, there has never been an adequate assessment of the background beliefs of the institution on matters of killing and morality. Colin Powell disturbingly adds,

> I recall a phrase we used in the field, MAM, for military-age male. If a helo spotted a peasant in black pajamas who looked remotely suspicious, a possible MAM, the pilot would circle and fire in front of him. If he moved, his movement was judged evidence of hostile intent, and the next burst was not in front, but at him. Brutal? Maybe so. But an able battalion commander with whom I had served at Gelnhausen, Lieutenant Colonel Walter Pritchard, was killed by enemy sniper fire while observing MAMs from a helicopter. And Pritchard was only one of many. The kill-or-be-killed nature of combat tends to dull fine perceptions of right and wrong.[19]

Kill-or-be-killed; if it moves, shoot it; if in doubt, wipe it out; get ugly early; if you hesitate, you're dead; shoot them all and let God sort them out—these still-lingering maxims of war and many more like them are no longer morally justifiable, not that they ever were. Alan Donagan says that "a graduate of Sandhurst or West Point who does not understand his duty to noncombatants as human beings is certainly culpable for his ignorance; an officer bred up from childhood in the Hitler *Jugend* might not be."[20] Even with thirty years' hindsight, the inability of the military institution to *see* the problem, let alone *understand* its complexity, is a problem of moral perception, understanding, and judgment—a problem of moral error. The realm of force appears to have its own logic, apart from higher reason: threat leads to response; response leads to escalation; escalation leads to conflagration; conflagration leads to aftermath; and aftermath leads to new, more numerous, and more dangerous threats. The logic of force is visceral, limbic. It escapes higher brain function and leaves one to wonder if war is a problem of arrested evolution of the human brain. Perhaps at the level of individual violence it makes more sense. But it does not make sense at the level of the entire system. At the systemic level, at the level of the military institution or beyond, the logic of force manifests itself in irrational practices, practices that defy higher-order reasoning but yet fulfill and perpetuate its own destructive course. Luckily human nature is not fixed; nor is war inevitable. But neither is peace.

A key reason for the aversion toward moral inquiry for individuals and institutions alike is the possibility of a judgment that we may be doing something wrong. What does one do when faced with the prospect of doing something immoral? Moral agency for those who work within an institution is more than simply private human agency. When individuals in an institution act, they act as individuals but they also act as agents of the institution. So, when a member of the military, or any institution for that matter, is confronted with the commission of an immoral action, they are doubly responsible—for themselves and for the institution. All members of an institution share in the responsibility for the institution's moral understanding and practice. All members possess and exercise both individual and institutional moral agency. The responsibility that a member has, in terms of institutional agency, is proportional to that member's rank and position, proportional to his or her ability to influence the institution. What does one do if he or she comes to judge an institutional practice as possessing moral error? As for individual action in such a case, there are several options. A person could rationalize the action to be moral and perform it willingly; perform the action quietly while knowing that it is wrong; perform the action under objection; refuse to perform the action altogether. There would also be an institutional responsibility, though. For the sake of the institution, the person could do something within his or her power for the institution to reverse the immoral practice. Perhaps the institution is unwilling to reform or recognize its immorality. In that case, the person could do something within his or her power outside of the institution. One option is to communicate disagreement to Congress, without fear of retribution, through the perfectly legitimate process called Appeal for Redress. Another option is to resign in protest. But this rarely happens. Many who consider resignation in protest rationalize that they can do more for the institution by staying and working from within. Perhaps it's time to walk away from manifest illegality toward a new and better institutional norm.

A distinction is perhaps helpful at this point. There is an important difference between those who perform immoral acts knowing they are wrong and those who perform immoral acts believing (falsely) that they are right (when they are wrong). Let's call the former a *knave* and the latter a *dupe*, based on their respective understanding or lack of understanding of the moral nature of their actions. Knaves understand they are doing wrong or harm, committing moral error. Dupes believe that whatever they do is right; they can't see or understand that they are committing moral error. Any person could be one or the other, or even both, under different conditions and circumstances. Take Colin Powell, for example. Insofar as Powell did not understand the wrongdoing in his unit, he was a dupe, as in the case of misinterpreting the unit log that described the My Lai massacre. But in another circumstance, Colin Powell's description of shooting MAMs on sight indicates that he was cognizant of the improper nature of the policy, even if regrettable and unfortunate. In other words, he was aware of the immorality of the policy, yet condoned and ultimately supported it anyway. In this sense, he had moments in Vietnam in which he acted as a knave, fully aware of the immorality of actions he condoned and supported. To his credit, he has more than most people spoken out with caution against questionable policies and actions, but in the end he goes along, remaining a knave—a pattern he has repeated to this day. How many times should one compromise his moral integrity in the hopes of improving the institution? None? Once? Twice? A dozen times? Will the major who knowingly goes along still be going along when he becomes Secretary of State? General William Westmoreland admitted that things were going badly, but he decided not to resign because he thought he could do more good by staying. The knave knows when things are wrong. The dupe, however, is in a much more despicable moral category than the knave because he does not recognize that things are wrong. Lieutenant Calley to this day believes that his massacre of innocents in My Lai was morally justified; he was and still is a dupe. I would argue that in general we would be better off being knaves than being dupes, for, as bad as the actions of knaves can be, the actions of dupes can be much worse. But how many times can one play the knave without becoming the dupe? In all fairness, Colin Powell has spoken up about the world beginning to question America's moral standing, in reference to the White House's pressure on Congress to revise the law so as to legalize torture. Colin Powell is half-right here. The world lost confidence in America's moral standing long ago. It is more accurate to say that America is beginning to question its own moral standing. It is refreshing to see Colin Powell speak out, even if he does so now without-penalty since he is retired.

If one comes to understand the wrong he performed or condoned later in life, then this graduates him to the knave category as well. For example, Robert McNamara came to admit that the policies, strategies, and tactics in Vietnam were immoral and mistaken.[21] And for all those who claim that his apologies are disingenuous, his position today may still be better than those who still believe that those policies, strategies, and tactics were morally justified. Henry Kissinger, for example, still believes that what he did in Vietnam was fully justified. Again, the knavery of Robert McNamara is arguably better than the dupery of Henry Kissinger or Al Haig, who both still praise the Christmas bombings and wish we had done more of the same. Why do I claim that? Their respective stances condition how they would move into the future. McNamara is active in reducing or eliminating nuclear weapons today, while Henry Kissinger stands by the first book he ever published in which he argues that limited nuclear war is winnable. I also argue that we would be better off as followers of knaves than as followers of dupes. Since knaves are aware of the harm they do, this awareness at least offers a chance of them mitigating that harm. And knaves may even do something to minimize or even eliminate the moral error institutionally, if even over time. In contrast, there are no limits to the moral harm that can occur at the hands of a dupe. There is one other logical possibility besides being a knave, a dupe, or both, and that is one could be neither. One could be a knight. Of course, it would be best if we could all be knights and work for knights. Knights would be those who would be aware of moral error, would refuse to commit moral error, and could change the institution so that it no longer practices moral error. But we know that taking such a stance is difficult at best. Hugh Thompson is a knight, for by interposing his helicopter to protect the innocents at My Lai from American warriors he was harassed throughout the rest of his military career, being rewarded publicly only on the thirtieth anniversary of My Lai. Daniel Ellsberg also was a knight, and he faced potential time in jail for going public with the *Pentagon Papers* over the government's duplicity concerning the true nature of our involvement in Vietnam. Scott Ritter is a knight, acting with integrity throughout his entire professional life. CPT Ian Fishback is a knight, one of the few warriors to publicly speak out against torture in the current Iraq war. Perhaps it is way too much to ask that members of the military become knights, which would ultimately guarantee their disaffection, censure, or resignation. Other branches of government have seen resignations in protest, but not the military—resignation in protest is not a part of the military culture. If that is too much to ask, then perhaps the most that could be hoped for is that we move away from being dupes and toward some level of knavery, moving as close as possible to knighthood if knighthood itself is impossible to reach.

Haven't things improved since Vietnam, many could ask? In 2000, West Point awarded Henry Kissinger its most distinguished honor, the Thayer Award, given for a lifetime of distinguished service to the nation, service that ostensibly reflects the values of West Point and the American military. Less than a year later, a book entitled *The Trial of Henry Kissinger*, by Christopher Hitchens argued for an investigation into Kissinger's past activities, which include his illegal use of the military as far back as Vietnam. The documentary version of the book aired in 2002. Roger Morris, the National Security Agency (NSA) scholar who, along with Anthony Lake, resigned over the invasion of Cambodia, says, "My own view is that if we held Henry Kissinger to the standards we have begun to hold other leaders, other policy makers, and the standards to which we held policy makers in Germany and in Japan after World War II, yes, Kissinger ought to be the subject of an international tribunal, ought to be the subject of a legal process in the United States and elsewhere."[22]

How can the military give such a prestigious award to someone who should be the subject of a very serious investigation? One answer may be that we are not descendents of the Enlightenment tradition alone. Our national and international legal conceptions and systems are certainly products of Enlightenment thinking. Ideas of universality, equality, reciprocity, internationalism, and fairness drove our Enlightenment legal tradition. But our foreign policy descends perhaps from another tradition. Nationalism, exclusionism, exceptionalism, and unilateralism all conflict with universal legal and moral principles. The historical reaction against Enlightenment thinking, the Romantic Movement, was motivated in part by the desire to accommodate nationalism. The Enlightenment era strove for peace and viewed war as a failure. The Romantic era viewed peace as unrealistic and thought of war as not only necessary but also noble, even glorious. American foreign policy today falls well within the spirit of Romantic thinking. And since the military is an agent of foreign policy, it is swept up in the realist thinking of the Romantics.[23] The warrior ethos lies squarely within the Romantic tradition, the tradition that views war as ennobling. America now has a National Security Strategy that premiers preemptive, or preventive, war, which at one time was the basis of crimes of aggression—crimes against peace—as a result of the Nuremberg Trials. So members of the military are conflicted. While they are agents of a morally bereft foreign policy, officers also take an oath to support and defend the Constitution and are responsible to uphold and enforce the laws of war. And the institution of the military and its political masters should come to realize this contradiction and work to resolve it. It should be resolved by moving foreign policy and military employment in line with the Enlightenment moral and legal tradition. I will argue that we have yet to fix the immoral understanding that led to the moral failures in Vietnam, debatably the nadir for the American armed forces.

In many ways, arguably, we are even worse off today than we were during Vietnam. Before Vietnam and for many decades afterward, the United States covertly, and at times with the assistance of the military, was actively involved in *regime change* operations: Iran, Vietnam, Nicaragua, Chile, Cuba, to name just a few. But in all of these examples, the regime change operations were covert because the policy makers and decision makers acknowledged the illegality, immorality, and inappropriateness of these operations, from the strategic all the way down to the tactical level. We still have immoral doctrines that encourage inappropriate means to pursue illegitimate goals. But we are worse off today because we no longer try to hide such operations; they have become part of our published policy. Until we understand and recognize this failure, and subsequently develop a new conception of moral understanding and practice, moral error will continue as it has manifested itself in regions such as Indochina, Latin America, the Balkans, and

Southwest Asia. The rhetoric in our security and defense strategies overflows with language of peace and the spread of democracy. The record does not match the rhetoric, however. The American government since World War II, often with the help of the military, illegally and immorally intervened at least thirty times, disrupting more than five hundred aggregate years of democracy throughout the world.[24] And for all the talk of improved moral practices within the military due to improved munitions, the record shows proportionally higher noncombatant deaths. At the beginning of the century only 10 percent of the deaths were noncombatants; noncombatants made up 90 percent by the century's end.

The vast majority of military students I have personally taught in the classroom have many malformed moral beliefs. For example, most justify the exhorbitant degree of collateral damage. They also justify harsh and coercive interrogation measures, even after understanding the manifestly illegal nature of such actions. They are more than willing to err on the side of excessive force or unnecessary harm over finding a balance between due risk and due care. In addition to believing in the basic tenet of *military realism*, they also believe in the doctrine of *political realism*. These beliefs are basic building blocks of their world view, which is contemptuous of substantive moral concerns. Their contempt for the United Nations or any other international institution is a manifestation of their political realism. Likewise, their dismissive attitudes toward customary and international law that would impede the application of their unmatched power is a manifestation of their military realism. The world view they hold impedes real moral understanding.

The main problem of the current system of military moral thinking stems from it not being fully reflective, and therefore it requires augmentation. Ill-formed moral beliefs indicate that the focus, content, and purpose of the ethics of warfare all require examination and revision. I will make many suggestions for the improvement of the ethics of warfare, significantly the inclusion of philosophical ethics. Many moral perceptions, intuitions, settled judgments, and priorities are in need of analysis and revision. This revision is largely possible by improving the moral thinking of the military. Philosophical reflection can aid in resolving the inconsistencies. The average warrior would not intuitively turn to philosophy or even to reason in general for moral elucidation. In the end, this book is an argument for a Kantian outlook, for Kant makes the strongest case for the role of reason in ethics. For a reflective military, a key feature of philosophical ethics is moral autonomy. Moral autonomy is a conception that Kant *invented*.[25] People are morally autonomous if they live as morally reflective people, if they live by beliefs based on rationale they understand, beliefs that are open to correction or abandonment in the presence of good reason. The purpose of introducing philosophical ethics to moral understanding in the military would be to add a principled way of thinking about ethics beyond indoctrination, authority, and simple obedience, beyond narratives, instrumental methods, and misguided ends. Failings in current practice at least in part may be due to failings in moral thinking, especially if that thinking leads to immoral practices. Moral thinking is also lacking if the beliefs lack moral perception, understanding, or judgment.

One of the reasons moral autonomy could help is that the institution has demonstrated time and again that it is not capable of significant moral reform from within, from the top down; significant moral reform has usually come from the outside, or from the bottom up, and sometimes from failure. Examples of significant moral reform include racial and gender integration, each requiring either executive or congressional intervention.[26] The military is given such wide discretion, even in judicial matters. Since external oversight is rare when it comes to military policy, unlike the oversight of other professions,[27] the moral autonomy of each military member can help to bring about the required changes, beginning especially with changes in some of the impoverished moral beliefs of the warrior. In Chapters 2, 3 and 4 I will critique the inadequate processes we currently use to teach ethics. None of these methods are fully reflective, and they all yield an inadequate understanding of ethics. In chapter 5, I outline a philosophical framework that would be fully reflective for understanding ethics.

In chapter 2, I will examine the ways in which authority and indoctrination can lead to moral error, beginning with the abdication of reflection. Then I will look at the nature of narrative, which is a major mode of moral indoctrination in the military. The failure is in the methods themselves. I am not arguing that we abandon moral doctrines or narratives altogether within the military; we properly teach many subjects through indoctrination, including rifle marksmanship or tactical drills, for example. But I am arguing that we should examine the way we reflect with principled reason about narratives. I am arguing that people in the military should balance the requirement for obedience with the requisite moral reflection necessary to prevent the simple, blind adherence to immoral or illegal practices—the doctrines and narratives have to be morally justifiable. The methods in this chapter yield a bad understanding of ethics, and I explain how and why these methods fail. If our moral understanding is bad, then this bad understanding can result in moral error. Chapter 2 examines the numerous ways we defer reflecting about ethics and asks whether moral progress without reflection is possible.

In chapter 3, I will critique the instrumental moral methods the military pursues to reach its goals. The failure is in the methods themselves. Methods are instrumental when they are driven by ends, and they can lead to moral error in the form of immoral practices and bad consequences for at least two reasons: The methods themselves may be faulty, and the ends they instrumentally and unreflectively reach can be inappropriate. I will examine less and more adequate decision procedures, arguing that a more systematic critical method of ends-means reasoning should be adopted. The methods in this chapter yield a bad understanding of ethics, and I explain how and why these methods fail. If our moral understanding is bad, then this bad understanding can result in moral error. Chapter 3 considers means and ponders whether moral means are possible.

In chapter 4, I will more fully analyze the inadequate ends that the military works so hard to reach, sometimes resulting in moral error. The failure is in the methods themselves. The ends may be inadequate and may potentially lead to moral error because we do not fully reflect upon them. I will argue in this chapter that the military has to augment its ends-means reasoning reciprocally with means-ends reasoning, thinking of means and ends as a chain that extends in both directions. Only after the military systematically revises its thinking about ends can it be fully reflective. I explain how and why the methods in this chapter yield a bad understanding of ethics through a detailed critique. As argued before, bad moral understanding can result in moral error. Chapter 4 examines ends and asks if moral ends are possible.

In chapter 5, I will argue for a fully reflective model of moral understanding for the ethics of warfare. This model will include philosophical ethics, particularly the notion of moral autonomy. Prior to Kant, moralists would divide moral reasoning between means and ends with reasoning about means belonging to the virtue of prudence and reasoning about ends belonging to the virtue of wisdom. Kantian theory bridges the gap between means and ends, between prudence and wisdom. Kant taught us that prudence doesn't have to be immoral. In this chapter, I will show how philosophical ethics and moral theory can help to derive and justify a set of moral principles for the military, principles that inform the military about the ethics of killing. These principles can be part of the military institution, an important part helping to ensure that the military is a just institution making up part of the structure of a just society. Moral autonomy is an important feature of this application of moral theory because of the requirement to justify these moral principles to the institution of the military, which means a justification to each member of the military as well as to the citizenry of the nation and ultimately of the world. The value of adding this philosophical inquiry to the ethics of warfare will be moral improvement in perceiving, understanding, judging, deciding, motivating, and acting, ultimately changing for the better the moral dimension of the military institution by enabling the pursuit of moral progress. Chapter 5 explains moral autonomy as a potential improvement in moral understanding and practice, thereby enabling the possibility of moral progress, but asks in the end if moral autonomy is possible in the military. Only after all of these questions are explored in all the chapters will it be possible to see another alternative that may better enhance the possibility of moral progress in the military.

Other books being profusely published are making the case *that* the United States is engaging in questionable or immoral actions as it prosecutes the current Long War. This book is different because it explains *how* and *why* these actions are questionable or immoral. In spite of mounting evidence and the case against such actions, the bulk of the War Machine believes these actions are justified. Most believe that regime change operations, pre-emptive, and preventive war are just fine. Most think that security, intelligence, and interrogation should trump civil liberties and human rights. And most still believe that the military should err on the side of excessive force and unnecessary harm. Such beliefs have resulted in illegal and immoral wars carried out by illegal and immoral means that include murder and torture. These bad beliefs have resulted in moral error. These bad beliefs are created and sustained by inadequate methods of moral instruction. Far from being anomalous within a sound system of ethics, this moral error is evidence of a crisis that calls for a moral revolution.

2

The Pseudo-Reflective Life

Battle Sleep

> I have two books at my bedside, Lieutenant: the *Marine Corps
> Code of Conduct* and the *King James Bible*. The only proper
> authorities I am aware of are my commanding officer, Colonel
> Nathan R. Jessop, and the Lord our God.
>
> —LT Kendrick, from *A Few Good Men*

And so Kendrick uttered an ideological military commonplace in his own
defense at the trial. In this fictional account, a marine officer draws
moral understanding from doctrinal teaching: a book of military doctrine and
a book of religious doctrine, military and religious authority. At the same
time, this narrative is part of popular culture and informs through example;
hence it is a particularist example of moral education itself in the real world.
In the story, Lieutenant Kendrick passes on an order from his commanding
officer to conduct a *code red*, which in this story is the name for a dangerous,
underground—yet tolerated and even secretly encouraged—practice among
marines to severely discipline those in their own ranks for displaying weak-
ness, a lack of the warrior spirit. This particular *code red* results in the tragic
and wrongful death of a marine. Kendrick's courtroom testimony pleads that
he was carrying out the orders of his commander and helps us understand
that he believed he was justified, that by following orders he had not done
anything wrong. The story presents to us an example of the moral error that
can result from morality being dependent upon indoctrination or a simple
appeal to authority. This cinematic representation of the story symbolizes illegal, immoral, or unsafe traditions that actually still exist in the military, from
garrison excess to battlefield excess, from excessive blood-draining peacetime
rituals such as blood wing ceremonies meant to enhance discipline and esprit
to excessive blood-draining practices in battle meant to enhance the chances

of victory. These practices can be carried out and sustained because they are condoned and encouraged by those in positions of authority.

They are also sustained through the stories used to indoctrinate and socialize the warriors. I begin this chapter self-consciously with a quotation from a story—a story that became a popular movie—that portrays the military as a morally wanting institution. And while I am sympathetic to the idea that the morality of the military is at times as the movie portrays, I do not want to propel this view simply by way of this story. Many people, including some philosophers, suggest that we can get moral truth and guidance not from abstract principle, but from particular circumstances, from particular stories or images portrayed in literature, history, poetry, art, or even film. Narratives can and do provide tremendous insights, and, as a great fan of good literature, film, history, and art, I am not claiming that we should never turn to these modes of expression. Joseph Heller captures much of the military's pathological sociology in *Catch-22* and Tom Wolfe depicts the psychosis of the flying culture, the warrior ethos, in *The Right Stuff*. Instead of suggesting that we discard particularist modes of thinking about morality, I want to suggest caution when looking toward these approaches while seeking moral guidance or drawing moral conclusions. A steady diet of unschooled or unreflective consumption of popular narratives may be soothing and satisfying for the psyche (the original Greek root for the word "soul"). Sometimes our souls, or psyches, can use a good cleaning rather than soothing. Perhaps instead of chicken soup for the soul people should use *Listerine® for the soul* or something even stronger, a purgative, an emetic, such as *epicac for the soul*. Consuming nonpalatable material, material that forces people to think, can be painful; it can burn or turn one's stomach inside out. Reflection is hard work and not often pursued outside of the classroom. Outside of the academic classroom, warriors are not reading Joseph Heller or Thomas Wolfe or others who powerfully critique the military. Instead they are reading the more romantic narratives that drive home the message that war is sublime and ennobling, enabling the warrior spirit to be sustained: *Once an Eagle, Killer Angels,* or *We Were Soldiers Once and Young.* The military's cinematic tastes have gravitated away from moral and cautionary tales toward romantic and patriotic films. The military embraces, for example, *Saving Private Ryan* because it brings lumps to people's throats and leaves them with a positive feeling by the end of the film.[1] But the military does not embrace *The Thin Red Line* because it brings painful introspection with the possibility that what many consider to be the warrior spirit in actuality hastens the death of honor, that war is not ennobling, leaving the viewer with a sense of nausea. The military audience could not get enough of *Band of Brothers* depicting the emotionally satisfying phenomenon of camaraderie, but they did not flock to see *The Quiet American,* based on Graham Greene's classic novel, since the film so artfully illuminates American naiveté in Vietnam as the United States so enthusiastically and damagingly proselytized Southeast Asia through a process of political, military, and economic evangelism. Since the military relies upon indoctrination as a method of moral instruction, particularly through narrative, I want to examine the potential shortcomings of this unreflective practice.

There are many ways in which warriors can act while deferring moral reflection; the deferral of reflection connects the various practices addressed in this chapter: different forms of authority, indoctrination, and particularism. In many ways, these different approaches differ greatly, but they share this important feature in common: reflection is deferred. They are also connected in unsuspecting ways: authority can be doctrinaire, doctrine can be authoritative, narratives can be particularist, and so on. For example, moral indoctrination can take several forms. The military imparts its *doctrine* to its members through the processes of *indoctrination*, whether that doctrine is tactical, moral, or otherwise. Doctrine is not necessarily bad, but at the same time it is never complete or even absolutely applicable at all times and in all situations. But if the military spends all its time and expends all its energy getting its warriors to understand and follow doctrine, then there is no time and energy left over to get them to think beyond doctrine, to consider when it is incomplete or to understand how or when doctrine may or may not apply. Carl von Clausewitz (1780–1831) referred to doctrine as the "tyranny of fashion" and was much more interested in getting military professionals to think theoretically.[2] Doctrines are ideas surrounding practices that are imparted through either the spoken or written word. Indoctrination can take the form of unreflective obedience to authority (a fundamental unself-conscious military doctrine in itself) or through written texts. I will explore the problems with and the relationships among these approaches of authority, indoctrination, and particularism in this chapter. These approaches leave their subjects quite susceptible to the phenomenon of bullshit, by the way. These approaches that defer reflection can have disastrous and overwhelmingly serious consequences of grave moral error.

REFLECTION DEFERRED AND MORAL ERROR

Simple appeal to any authority for ethical matters will be less than fully justified. The greatest problem with an appeal to authority is that once people submit to authority as the justification for acting "morally," then it is no harder for the authority to impose something immoral than something moral. When authority is the arbiter, it is just as easy to get people to do something bad as something good. Stanley Milgram's experiment demonstrating just how susceptible people are to authority should never disappear from our memories. Milgram's book, *Obedience to Authority* (Harper & Row, 1974), details and analyzes the infamous experiment in which test subjects willingly applied what they believed were harmful or lethal electric shocks to people when told to do so by an authority figure. Thankfully for the actors on the receiving end, the electricity was simulated. A provocative book by Christopher Browning, *Ordinary Men* (1993), makes the argument that any group of people, obedient and poorly led by corrupt institutions, can do what the Nazi exterminators did in World War II.[3] Ultimately, authority can have the potential to sanction horrendous acts through its power to create prejudice, engender bias, and promote questionable communitarian mores that are merely forms of moral relativism.

There are a significant number of people in the military who are simply mistaken about the extent of the power that those in authority hold over them. As Milgram explains, obedience is the default. And obedience is the expected default in the military, for reasons of good order and discipline. Military law allows prosecution for those who disobey legal orders. Enlisted members of the military take an oath to follow the "orders of the officers" appointed over them. Officers do not. Informal polls and class discussions with cadets and mid-career officers over the years have brought to light some alarming yet predictable attitudes about authority in the military. Many believe that the oath for officers requires swearing allegiance to the president, for example. In actuality, their oath requires officers to swear allegiance to support and defend the Constitution, not the president or any other person or entity. Officers believe, correctly, that they can be prosecuted for showing contempt for the president. But contempt somehow gets conflated with disrespect, and disrespect somehow gets conflated with disagreement. Sometimes the slippery slope is real, and in this case the military has an officer corps that mistakenly believes that disagreement with the president or seniors in general amounts somehow to disloyalty.[4] Authority thus becomes powerful and, in proportion to the power, potentially dangerous.

There is a strong attitude of religious moral authority as well. Based on teaching nearly a thousand warriors from the rank of cadet to colonel for over a decade now, I have found that many of them believe falsely that the "so help me God" clause at the end of their oath requires them to believe in God or at least acknowledge the existence of a supreme being. At the same time most of them are unaware of Article VI, Clause 3 of the Constitution, which guarantees that they are never subject to any religious test as military officers. The specter of religious authority in the military looms over most of them, haunting them to believe that religion and morality should be linked together for the military as a public institution. This belief is increasingly problematic in the military, even more so when the commander-in-chief, to whom they already defer to in the extreme, brings religion into the public, political domain and leads the country through its moral discourse into a quasi-religious crusade against terrorism.

Written moral doctrines are imparted to military members mostly through narratives, which have all the features, and limitations, of an approach referred to as particularism. Is particularism by itself an adequate approach? Narratives communicate moral ideas through the particulars of a story, through the concrete particulars of person, place, and time instead of the abstract principles found exclusively in a philosophical approach. Particularism is, most simply, the view that moral "principles do not exist; and all moral decisions must be made on a case-by-case basis, without the comforting illusion of general principles."[5] Many people—both philosophers and nonphilosophers—turn to some form of particularism as a method of moral instruction because, they claim, philosophers are lost in abstractions. One philosopher who is a critic of ethical theory claims that our "pluralist culture prepares a young person for moral skepticism, and a course or two in comparative moral theory (and application) is the perfect finishing school for such skepticism."[6] She goes further to claim that moral philosophy "breeds multiple and in the end frivolous systems and their less frivolous, more dangerous applications."[7] I will refer to this group of people, whether they are philosophers or not, as anti-theorists. I argue to turn their claim on its head: the anti-theorists are perhaps *lost in the particulars*. If there are holes and inconsistencies in approaches that employ theories, abstractions, and principles, then there are even bigger holes and greater inconsistencies in approaches that avoid principles and focus exclusively on the particulars.

The approach of particularism abounds in the military. Very few official documents discuss professional ethics without resorting to narrative. For example, the principled discussion on ethics in the Army's leadership manual is non-existent; however, there are fifty-three vignettes featured in the book to transmit the norms of the profession, including the ethical norms.[8] As for the Marines, they do not have a leadership manual; they transmit their ethical norms solely by recounting their own history. The Naval Academy has published an ethics book for its junior officers, which is a collection of narratives that are case studies,[9] and these cases help to sustain their particularist ethical norms. This practice of employing particularism has become a main feature of what makes up the current paradigm in professional ethics. This practice transmits the ethical norms of the institution in a dogmatic, non-principled way. Several interesting phenomena emerge in the practice of *professional ethics* due to the current paradigm.[10] Instead of practices that transmit morally relativistic norms, local norms of exclusionism or exceptionalism—moral and legal norms that apply to others just don't apply to Americans—the American military should seriously consider the benefits of thinking in terms of ethical interoperability, to have a common moral picture that the whole world can see. Moral thinking in the military should include principled, philosophical reflection, because unprincipled moral doctrines—largely transmitted through authority and narratives—can be an unjustifiable approach to ethics and lead to moral error.

People can and do see whatever moral or lesson they want to perceive whenever they read a narrative, view a piece of art, or watch a film. Most people approach narratives in a completely unstructured and unsystematic way; indeed, the ambiguities and free associations of ideas are precisely some of the virtues of literature and poetry. There are hundreds of details, hundreds of particulars, and different people attend to these details based on their different points of view, background beliefs, level of education, ability to reason, and so on. The Homeric hero looms large in the warrior's psyche and as such those narratives remain ever present in popular culture. Homer is the source of the heroic archetype and is the root of the master narrative of battlefield heroism. Many people, nevertheless, still think of Achilles as a hero, even after reading the epic. Those who do may stand in awe of his mystical beginnings, identify with his intense rage, marvel at his armor, covet his martial skill and strength, or sympathize with his vulnerable heel. Which particulars should we attend to? Which ones are morally salient? If he possesses ten good traits and five bad qualities, does he still have good character? Or does one moral failing mean that he has bad character? Are any heroes without a moral Achilles' heel? Without thinking about these in a systematic way, without reflecting, there is no way to answer these questions. But if we simply sustain our histories and narratives, mimicking our heroes unreflectively, we carry with us the potential for moral error, and the moral error caused by unreflectively following example is great. Shannon French in her splendid 2005 book on the morality of warrior cultures asks, "Is the lesson of the Iliad...that the greatest warrior would be a Hector who wins"?[11] The question demonstrates the importance on which warriors place the value of victory. We want the hero to win. And many want the hero to win so much that they are willing to give up much. Aristotle when speaking about the youth says that "While they love honour, they love victory still more; for youth is eager for superiority over others, and victory is one form of this."[12] Achilles was as much an archetype of a warrior in the ancient world as in the present one, for Aristotle adds that in the case of famous heroes, "because they are well known, the hearer usually needs no narration of them; none, for instance, if your object is the praise of Achilles."[13] Perhaps Achilles represents something of every warrior in war just as Odysseus represents something of every warrior trying to come home after war. But do the particulars of our narratives systematically transmit relevant continuities?

The potential for error is great when we consider that the particulars for any and every circumstance differ from any before it. Every war, campaign, battle, or peacekeeping mission differs from any that may precede it. The situation between the Serbs and the Kosovar Albanians differs in many respects from any peacekeeping situation before it, including the one preceding it in nearby Bosnia. Soldiers could study every detail from every peacekeeping mission in our history, and they would be hard-pressed to understand the moral concerns by simply reviewing the raw data, without some kind of principled speculation. They may not be paying attention to the right particulars, or may not even be paying attention to the right stories. Where did the soldiers of the 3rd battalion of the 504th Parachute Infantry Regiment get the idea that mistreatment of civilian Kosovar Albanians was all right? This battalion's motto was "shoot 'em in the face," and the soldiers operated under the maxim that they were to "get ugly early." Where did Lieutenant Colonel Allen West get the idea that he should personally use heavy-handed interrogation techniques in Iraq (notwithstanding the fact that battalion commanders are not interrogators anyway)? Were they taking pages from the book that Roger Trinquier wrote on the French para unit dealing with similar problems in Algiers? General Paul Aussaresses to this day believes that the approach used in the Battle of the Casbah was the correct one.[14] Does the General just not understand that his alleged tactical victory at the Casbah was illusory, or that it created the conditions for the embarrassing strategic French defeat later? This is not a rhetorical question. The 4th Infantry Division in Iraq requested dozens of copies of Trinquier's treatise on counterinsurgency (the book is regularly taught as part of the staff college curriculum, not always in a negative or ironic sense).[15] After decades without adequate reflection on counterinsurgent warfare, the American warriors launched late in 2003 Operation Iron Hammer, designed to crack down on the "terrorists," to fight fire with fire, perhaps more accurately described as fighting terrorism with terrorism. To be even more accurate though, it is not correct usage to call the belligerents who attack American armed forces "terrorists," since that crime is reserved for those who conduct attacks on noncombatants. The American warriors are regrettably looking to Aussaresses' experience against the Algerians or Ariel Sharon's experience against the Palestinians for guidance and insights, following their models, which will eventually have disastrous results. Is the prisoner abuse scandal, of which Abu Ghraib is one of the global network of sites, merely a matter of a few ignorant or wayward soldiers? Or does the mentality that enables abuse echo throughout the force, as represented by West's unapologetic mistreatment of prisoners in order to get information? There was a lot of sympathy for LTC Allen West's actions among active duty and retired officers here at Fort Leavenworth, but this incident occurred before mistreatment at Abu Ghraib hit the news. Was the predisposition toward mistreatment that pervaded the military in the months prior to the scandal in any way connected to the actual mistreatment? We have yet to see the full record on the extent and degree of abuse once our military went into action since the attack on American soil.

Lack of reflection can lead to moral error. Traditional societies and institutions transmit customs, practices, and norms, and these norms can include ethical norms. Bernard Williams describes "hypertraditional" societies as those that are "homogeneous and minimally given to general reflection."[16] The particularist approach contributes to an unreflective transmission of ethical norms, whether they are good or bad. One theme that persists in the narratives, stories, memoirs, and biographies in the military culture is that of *military realism*, the doctrine that "war is hell." General William Sherman wrote when defending his actions in razing Atlanta and much of Georgia that "[w]ar is cruelty and you cannot refine it; and those who brought war into our country deserve all the curses and maledictions a people can pour out."[17] Sherman is dead wrong, of course, for war can be refined. In fact, it had been refined and limited under Enlightenment precepts, but the American Civil War in many ways signals the decline of limited, conventional war. Sherman's doctrine presumes that realism in war—unavoidable cruelty—is somehow a "necessity of nature." He is not the first to invoke this doctrine of realism, and he is not the last. The Athenian generals allude to the necessities of war in the Melian dialogue in Thucydides' *Peloponnesian War*. The Athenians tell the Melians, "Our opinion of the gods and our knowledge of men lead us to conclude that it is a general and necessary law of nature to rule whatever one can."[18] General Douglas MacArthur hinted at necessity of another kind when, in his famous speech at West Point, he cited Plato as saying that "only the dead have seen the end of war."[19] The idea that war is necessary is different from the idea that cruelty in war is necessary. Some may wonder if cruelty is not the point of war, if cruelty is domination and submission by physical force. If so, then, there is no distinction here. But cruelty, even in its ordinary sense, is excessive and gratuitously unnecessary. My fellow philosophy professor LTC (Ret.) Pete Fromm interprets the film *The Thin Red Line* as a cautionary tale warning us that cruelty is the death of honor. Perhaps neither is necessary, but resignation from the possibility that neither is necessary helps to make both war and cruelty in war inevitable, for "from the Homeric account of the sacking of Troy to the conquest of Dienbienphu, Western literature is filled with descriptions of soldiers as berserkers and mad destroyers."[20] Linking war with the idea of necessity presumes a psychological disposition about human nature that is not necessarily true. I must emphasize here what I stated in the preface, that I do not share the same notions as many do, of human nature or psychology being fixed. Both are contingent.

Military realism remains one of the biggest challenges we face in having a moral military. A prominent Air Force general in a speech about the Gulf War makes the same case for military realism when he proclaims, "war is a horrible, horrible, horrible thing. There is nothing good about it. But it is sometimes necessary. And so somebody better be good at it. I am...you better be." He is justifying his actions after he participated in the slaughter on the "Highway of Death." He describes the killing: "I've killed people before, during this war, but this time I saw 'em. I saw the vehicles moving before the bombs hit. I saw people getting out and running and then I aimed at 'em with CBU. And dropped hundreds of bomblets on their head to make sure they wouldn't get away."[21]

But there seems little question that gratuitous destruction was wreaked upon individual soldiers and groups far off the road and well away from the vehicles and weapons. If reports of the use of cluster bombs against soldiers on foot are true, there seems to be little justification indeed.[22]

Grant and Sherman fought the Civil War with a type of warfare known as annihilation, and annihilation is the essence of the "American way of war."[23] The nature of some limited conflicts has restricted commanders from engaging in this mode of warfare, such as in Korea and Vietnam, but the American commanders in the Gulf War returned to this form of warfare, and they are very proud of that fact. The Powell Doctrine of overwhelming force in Gulf I or Desert Storm, the effects based targeting of shock and awe in Gulf II or Operation Iraqi Freedom, an abandonment of Enlightenment ideas of limited war, is a direct descendant of Grant's doctrine of annihilation and an endorsement to the return of destructive war. Current thinking in the military echoes ancient thinking in that it endorses the notion that cruelty in war is a "necessity of nature."[24]

There are of course important differences among historical narratives, journalistic reports, and imaginative literature. They are all important in the process we use when we employ particular stories, whether real or imagined, to our own moral lives. Mythic narratives can be more influential than historical narratives. Biblical text means more to the Zionist settlers in Israel than does the Balfour Declaration. A dangerous suicidal mythos has evolved from the Masada Myth. I call it the Masada Myth because of the epic and legendary narrative that has grown out of proportion compared to any historical event that may have occured on that plateau. An equally dangerous mythos surrounds the Al Aqsa Mosque. The visit of an insensitive Ariel Sharon to the mosque triggered an intifada that has resulted in thousands of deaths (albeit most of them Palestinian). Political decision makers and military commanders employ these particular stories. Achilles is still here. Plutarch tells us that Alexander carried the *Iliad* with him on campaign. Patton memorized large chunks of the *Iliad*. America's interest in the warrior archetype helped the production and success of the recent cinematic releases about Achilles and Alexander, both within the same year. Particularists enjoy all modes of narrative. Narrative can transmit norms in ways that are not well reasoned. Richard Dawkins suggested in *The Selfish Gene* (1976) that cultural norms are replicated and transmitted in information packets he coined "memes," to be roughly analogous to genes, which are biological information packets. These memes evolve slowly, and their great inertia would help to explain how cultural evolution of hypertraditional dogma retains great stability. Some irrational memes remain and work like viruses—parasites that live by destroying the host—which have adapted and survived because of irrational self-protective dogmas that continue to defy reason. If these hypertraditional dogmas are viruses, then logic in particular (and philosophy in general) is the vaccine (to use a biological metaphor) or the anti-virus program (as a machine metaphor).

MORAL AUTHORITY

Paternalistic authority is the operative concept. Much empirical research on the subject of ethics in organizations concludes with the idea that organizations should decide what is right and wrong for its members; moral deliberation should not even be a concern for the individual.[25] Even though no single academic discipline is singularly suited to handle the complex subject of leadership, the social scientists have virtually monopolized the academic study of leadership within the Army. The Army sees ethics as being merely a part of leadership, so ethics is therefore largely subsumed under the dominion of the social scientists as well. Cognitive science has replaced behavioral science over the last half century within the university. This transformation has shifted paradigms, as Bernard Baars details in his book, *The Cognitive Revolution in Psychology* (The Guilford Press, 1986). And even though cognitive psychology has eclipsed behavioral psychology in the academic world, the Army has not yet caught up to this revolution, and the social scientists who have contributed to the subject in the Army and Air Force are still operating on behaviorist assumptions, worrying only about input and output. Behaviorists rely on the assumption that behavior simply can be shaped, either through operant conditioning or Pavlovian conditioning. Stimulation (in the form or reward or punishment) occurs after the behavior for operant conditioning, and stimulation is given before the behavior for Pavlovian conditioning. The key point here is that the technique is conditioning in both cases. Behavioral conditioning disregards what actually occurs in the mind—

the mind remains a black box. Philosophers who work on action theory, and, more recently, cognitive scientists, think seriously about what goes on inside the black box, and it is messy. Even after many decades of work, they have not improved upon the folk-psychological understanding of intentionality, which comprises two major categories of things: beliefs and desires. Even so, they have done some great work by focusing on just these two ideas. Disregarding intentionality (why people do the things they do) greatly simplifies the work of the behaviorists, for all they have to do is worry about input and output. To get different output, all that is necessary is to adjust the input. Control of people is easier under this view because "reasons do not explain behavior; causes do."[26] While the rest of academia has replaced behavioral studies with cognitive studies, behavioral science with cognitive science, the leadership departments at the academies for the Army and the Air Force are still named Behavioral Science and Leadership (BS&L). Military training and education are stuck within the behaviorist paradigm. General (Ret.) Walt Ulmer, a well-respected leader and academic theorist of leadership—told me that he did not care *why* soldiers behave morally; he cared only *that* they behave morally. His research and work is firmly planted within the behaviorist paradigm. Those who share his approach today are still there, too.

Of course, the major problem with any moral system based on authority is that something is not right or wrong just because of some edict or because of some interpretation of some edict. For example, disrespecting people is bad because it hurts people, not because some authority says it is forbidden. Ben Franklin suggests in *Poor Richard's Almanac* that something is not bad because it is forbidden; it is forbidden because it is bad. Likewise, something is not good because it is permitted; it is permitted because it is good. Franklin's statement is no doubt a gloss on Socrates' question posed to Euthyphro: "Is the pious loved by the gods because it is pious, or is it pious because it is loved by the gods?"[27]

According to all of the official and popular accounts, the first Gulf War, Desert Storm, was supposed to be one of the American success stories. It was supposed to be successful not only because it succeeded tactically, thereby vindicating the American military living for so long in the shadow of tactical frustration during the protracted Vietnam conflict, but it was also supposed to be a moral victory, in that it was supposed to show how the American military can fight morally, again, to shine a light that would help remove the immoral shadow from Vietnam. General Norman Schwarzkopf says that the killing of those retreating from Kuwait on the "Highway of Death" triggered General Colin Powell to tell him, "We ought to be talking about a ceasefire. The doves are starting to complain about all the damage you're doing...the reports make it sound like wanton killing." These reports were generated when pilots reported that the attack was a *feeding frenzy* or a *turkey shoot*, and that they were simply *shooting fish in a barrel*. Schwarzkopf was convinced "that wasn't the case."[28] Ever since the killing along the Highway of Death occurred, though, many have questioned the legal status of that engagement, and if not the legal status at least its moral status. In his 1994 book *The Fire This Time*, Ramsey Clark makes the strong claim that many aspects of that engagement make it a war crime. "Many of those massacred fleeing Kuwait were not Iraqi soldiers at all but Palestinians, Sudanese, Egyptians, and other foreign workers. They were trying to escape to save their lives."[29] Others conclude that there were no civilians.[30] The moral status remains ambiguous but the legal status does not because the destruction on the Highway of Death occurred before the ceasefire—legally it was just fine. But even if the legal status is retained, the moral status of the American military in the Gulf War is perhaps diminished. The propensity to continue to use force and inflict harm when it is not necessary—even against combatants—harkens back to the excesses of Achilles. It amounts to cruelty, and cruelty is the death of honor. If our conduct in the Gulf War based on this engagement is not immoral, then it could not be more marginal. And our hypertradional military culture sustains this suspect practice through its particularist narratives and histories, through memetic replication. Most warriors will err on the side of excess.

Clark writes, "The *New York Newsday* reported yet another slaughter of Iraqi soldiers that was approved by General Schwarzkopf two days after the ceasefire."[31] General Schwarzkopf reports that on "Saturday morning, March 2, two days after the shooting supposedly had stopped, I came into the war room to discover that we'd just fought a major battle in the Euphrates valley." He goes on to say that the Iraqis on a couple of occasions "had opened fire with antitank missiles....McCaffrey had replied with a full-scale tank and helicopter counterattack, smashing the Iraqi columns and taking three thousand prisoners without suffering a single casualty. To me this wasn't altogether bad news."[32] Major General Barry McCaffrey had his 24th Division completely *destroy* an entire Iraqi Republican Guard unit as it was retreating to Iraq. Not everyone is convinced that the Iraqis fired on the Americans first. Many people think that McCaffrey was "spoiling for a fight," and that he was intent upon fighting a major engagement in this war. It was not a counterattack; he initiated it. His division had not been in a firefight at all up to this point in the war. There is a great deal of evidence and testimony that should at least warrant an investigation. For example, while American troops could fix their positions within twenty-five feet, General McCaffrey's division was twenty-five miles in front of their reported position, twenty-five miles in front of the ceasefire line, and he happened to be positioned right in the way of a major route that the Iraqis were using for their orderly withdrawal. The Iraqi tanks were on flatbeds with their gun tubes locked down and turned to the rear.[33] As the commander, McCaffrey bears both individual and institutional responsibility, since he exercised both individual and institutional agency. The details transmitted in our stories and narratives have the potential to mislead us morally. The potential is even greater in an institution that practices censorship, disinformation, and propaganda, rampant in Gulf I yet reaching even new height in Gulf II. For example, few are aware that independent satellite photos do not show the buildup of the Iraqi Army at the Saudi Arabian border before Desert Shield as the JSTARS photos show. It is quite possible that the threat of Iraqi invasion was faked to justify the war.[34] The military and the nation have completely ignored this disturbing episode due to the "victory" and the resultant patriotic fervor. Little doubt remains that the Americans used excessive force—violating on a huge scale one of the most important moral principles—during the Gulf War. Every American in the Gulf War understood that his task was to *destroy* the Iraqi Army. Many warriors may have understood that to mean to destroy virtually every person, weapon system, and vehicle, if they understood the task to destroy literally. The excessive rhetoric may have in this case led to excessive measures on that battlefield. And those in authority are responsible for the immoral cultures they create as well as the immoral orders they give. Excessive force is evident in the second Gulf War, Operation Iraqi Freedom, but it will take years to fully appreciate this excess, since we are still fighting there. The government has never had greater control over the media than it has today. The military puts great effort into what it calls its information operation—the control and manipulation of information as part of the overall operation. Somewhere along the way within this information operation, the psychological operation merged with public relations, so the media now views every bit of information as part of the war effort. The media has, in effect, censored itself. Truth and objectivity are no longer goals; victory is the only goal. Honest critique and bad news are becoming scarcer as the war continues because honesty can damage morale and war resolve. What is right and what is wrong are being defined by those in charge to a degree never before seen. We now know that the rationale for the current war was manipulated, that intelligence was fixed around a policy of illegitimate invasion. Those in charge want us to appeal to them for moral justfications—moral authority has never been more in vogue.

Religious authority is one type of an "appeal to authority," which in logic is known as an informal fallacy because the chain of reason ends when it runs up against the authority. And many warriors link religious authority to morality. The two major philosophical problems that would exist if the Army based its professional ethic on divine command would be 1) metaphysical (does God exist?) and 2) epistemological (if God did exist, how would we know what God is telling us?). The metaphysical problem is one of begging the question due to the presumption of a supernatural being. Any attempt at promoting a religious, or a spiritual, foundation would presume the existence of something supernatural. There is a wide array of ideas among religious communities about the existence and nature of the relationship between a supernatural being and the nature of morality. The epistemological problem compounds the metaphysical one. While the metaphysical problem revolves around the nature and existence of things supernatural, the epistemological problem revolves around our being able to know the nature of the relationship between things supernatural and morality. The indefinite variety of religious doctrines and interpretations leaves no chance of any kind of agreement, which would be necessary for a professional ethic. Even if people could come to some kind of agreement, which is impossible due to *religious relativism*, there is no requirement in a governmental organization to adhere to any supernatural tenets.

Robert Audi, among other philosophers, argues that religion should be separated from morality in general.[35] All of his reasons are even more applicable to professional ethics, especially a profession that is part of the government. His argument is based on the principle of separation of church and state, a principle that made the United States unique at one time. Simply stated, the principle guarantees that the government does nothing either to hinder or to promote religion. Religion is a matter of individual conscience, and it is too important for governmental meddling. Audi discusses six principles: 1) libertarian principle, 2) equalitarian principle, 3) neutrality principle, 4) pluralism principle, 5) secular rationale principle, and 6) secular motivation principle. The libertarian principle guarantees that every person has the liberty or freedom within the nation to choose a religion. The equalitarian principle prevents the state from favoring one religion over another. The neutrality principle goes beyond the notion that people have freedom in choosing a religion because it includes the notion that people are also free to have no religion whatsoever. The pluralism principle aims for toleration in the public sphere among peoples of many different faiths. The secular rationale principle maintains that state-sponsored activities have secular rationale, and the secular motivation principle is similar in that the motivation is secular. These principles are important, but religious authority in the military threatens every one of them.

For example, the place of worship for those of the Jewish faith at West Point is called the Jewish *Chapel* (instead of *synagogue*). If places of worship for those of Buddhist or Shinto religions were ever built at West Point, would they be called *chapels* instead of *temples* or *shrines*? An Islamic chapel instead of *mosque*? Or does Christianity so pervade the American military that it must violate Audi's second principle in the most obvious ways? The chaplains in the Army have long espoused in their own doctrine (which applies only to them) that it is their job to ensure the spiritual fitness of the Army. Now this same language of "spiritual fitness" has made its way into the leadership doctrine (which applies to everyone in the Army). One of the parts of the Lemon Test, a legal test that is used to help keep church and state separated, features the idea that any governmental initiative must be secularly motivated, another one of Audi's principles—otherwise church and state have become entangled. Army doctrine has chaplains giving commanders moral advice, and Army schools appoint chaplains in teaching billets to specifically teach ethics. At the Army's Command and General Staff College where I teach, the chaplains design lessons on ethics and do the ethics instruction. The examples I use here were cause enough for alarm, when I first laid out the claim and argument in the late 1990s. The alarm I felt years ago was more than fully warranted, given the encroachment of religion since the turn of the century upon politics and war, pushing its roots deep into America's military institutions. For a frightening look into the abyss of religious fundamentalism at the heart of political power, see Kevin Phillips' *American Theocracy* (Viking Press, 2006). For a long time, though, the apocalyptic horse of war has been saddled with a steadily increasing load of religious baggage.

The chaplains should get out of the ethics business in the military. A Supreme Court case, *Katkoff v. Marsh*, 755 F.2d223 1985, tested the constitutionality of the mere existence of the chaplains in the military. If this sounds odd, consider that the Japanese Constitution, written by Americans during the American occupation after WWII, forbids the existence of chaplains in the Japanese military. Also consider agencies in the business of attempting to build a liberal democracy in Iraq are emphasizing the importance of the separation of church and state there. Why is the separation of church and state a good idea for other countries but not our own? The Supreme Court decided that the existence of the chaplain's corps was constitutional as long as it merely fulfilled its function of providing religious services for service members, especially when they are deployed and would have less access to places of worship. The teaching of ethics in a pluralistic society cannot safely be left to denominational teachers. Morality is a topic for public reason. John Rawls also argues that religious doctrine cannot be a part of a public morality, so the principle of separation of church and state remains fundamental.

> The reasons for the separation of church and state are these, among others: It protects religion from the state and the state from religion; it protects citizens from their churches and citizens from one another. It does this by protecting the freedom to change one's faith. Heresy and apostasy are not crimes.[36]

One of the principles that Audi talks about is the principle of religious neutrality, the notion that people are free to have no religion. This principle is important, for it guarantees that the government is not favoring being religious over being nonreligious. Draft versions of the 1999 leadership doctrine covered this principle of neutrality. The book at one time in draft form even included a clause from the Constitution (from the original document, not one of the amendments), from article vi, clause 3, which says that "no religious test shall ever be required as a qualification to any office or public trust under the United States." When the book went to print, the important principle of neutrality was removed and replaced with language that highlights the importance and utility of religious belief in the Army: "The commander delegates staff responsibility to the chaplain for programs to enhance spiritual fitness since many leaders and subordinates draw moral fortitude and inner strength from a spiritual foundation."[37] This description in doctrine is then misread as a prescription. Religion suffuses the ethical discussions in a very influential book, *The Future of the Army Profession*.[38] In this book of twenty-five chapters, in its first edition, three are dedicated to ethics and the Army profession, and only the one by Martin Cook, "Army Professionalism: Service to What Ends?," gets to ethical concerns of killing in a substantive way without religious prescriptions. The chapter by Mark Mattox, "The Ties That Bind: The Army Officer's Moral Obligations," contains at least a *dozen* biblical references, and the chapter by James Toner, "A Message to Garcia: Leading Soldiers in Moral Mayhem," contains almost *seventy* biblical or theological precepts, references, or citations—all of which amount to moral prescriptions that rest on a religious foundation. What does it mean that so many warriors want to spread the instrumental application of religious belief while at the same time almost none of them are aware of the *no religious test* clause of the Constitution? The irony here of course is that their oath of office is all about supporting and defending the very Constitution of which they know so little about.

A dangerous recent trend in military ethics is the merging of ethical thinking with religious thinking, a kind of moral fundamentalism evolving from the twin roots of political and moral authority. Religious neutrality has shifted to that of religious foundation. The military over the last decade has become more and more openly religious, and this open religiosity in the workplace is becoming more and more accepted, partly due to the current interest in indoctrinating morality.[39] The recent publicity over General William Boykin's grandiloquent religiosity is instructive in at least two ways. First, we should seriously challenge the idea of having a person in such a strategic position during an interminable war against terrorism whose religious fundamentalism rivals that of those with whom we are allegedly at war against. Should someone whose perceptions, beliefs, conclusions, and judgments are conditioned by millennial apocalyptic presumptions be making decisions about actionable intelligence? With General Boykin, religion has made its way into the strategic level of politico-military affairs. Sam Harris reveals interesting insights and analysis on this topic in his award-winning (2004) book, *The End of Faith*:

> Lieutenant General William G. Boykin was recently appointed deputy undersecretary of defense for intelligence at the Pentagon. A highly decorated Special Forces officer, he now sets policy with respect to the search for Osama Bin Laden, Mullah Omar, and the rest of America's enemies in hiding. He is also, as it turns out, an ardent opponent of Satan. Analyzing a photograph of Mogadishu after the fateful routing of his forces there in 1993, Boykin remarked that certain shadows in the image revealed "the principalities of darkness...a demonic presence in the city that God revealed to me as the enemy." On the subject of the war on terror, he has asserted that our "enemy is a guy named Satan." While these remarks sparked some controversy in the media, most Americans probably took them in stride. After all, 65 percent of us are quite certain that Satan exists.[40]

The second insight from Boykin's notoriety comes from the fact that his religiosity is no secret to those who have worked around or for him. He has gotten away with an egregious public display of religiosity because so many in the military welcome it. But I would argue that every time he has made such a public display, he was engaging in undue influence. This public approval of religious identification amounts to the endorsement of religion, and a specific religious tradition, which ultimately entails governmental establishment of religion. The Department of Defense now looks toward "faith-based intelligence," which clearly violates Audi's principles of secular rationale and secular motivation. Religion has made its way not only into the moral affairs of the American government but into the political affairs as well. This phenomenon has never been as prominent as it has become during the administration of George W. Bush. Religionists are making headway symbolically and substantially as well. Christian symbols will become more prominent in our governmental and educational spheres. Christians enjoy political financial support and incentives as well as a level of influence never before seen. The "Vatican of the West," Colorado Springs, headquarters the most powerful political lobbies in American politics. The Dominionists—with a Christo-fascist agenda that falls nothing short of creating an American Taliban—were "fundamental" in the last presidential election. President Bush employs the same irrational rhetoric that Osama bin Laden uses: apocalyptic code that conveys a Manichean struggle between good and evil, invoking an inevitable clash of civilizations. In reality, we are faced with a "clash of fundamentalisms." And the military chaplaincy has become more evangelical every year.

For a long time, the Christian church has had a loud voice in moral matters throughout America, surprisingly even in its governmental institutions. The Army looks to the Chaplain's Corps whenever the topic of morality comes up.[41] An Army chief of staff published a booklet on values in which he states that the Chaplain's Corps is instrumental in helping the Army to understand its values. If the chaplains are employing reason, then why do the Army's ethicists have to be chaplains? And how are the chaplains who have forsaken reason going to communicate an understanding of values to the Army? In fact, there are several problems with ethical conceptions if they are informed by notions of a religious foundation. Moral theology posits theories of false reality. Religionists tend to think of moral precepts in terms of absolutes instead of universals. Those who confuse universality with absolutism are painting themselves into a corner; they create a moral system that puts one in a quandary even before anything happens. There will be more on this subtle but important difference between absolute and universal precepts in chapter 5. A moral system that has a quandary, perplexity, as a starting point, even before someone does something wrong, is called perplexity simpliciter. According to Alan Donagan, "hence it does not follow, simply because a moral system lays down a plurality of exceptionless precepts, that perplexity *simpliciter* is possible in it, notwithstanding that a surprising number of Christian moral theologians have disarmed themselves against the onslaught of 'situation ethics'..."[42]

Even more problematic is that "there have been movements in Protestant moral theology to repudiate the doctrine that natural human reason can generate any moral laws at all."[43] This would not be so problematic if churches kept their doctrine confined to their own faith communities. The military should not ground morality in religion or religious precepts. To do so would mean to impose some metaphysical assumptions upon people who are not required to accept those assumptions. The religious basis for ethics in the Army is perhaps even responsible for the reversed priorities in military ethics. Sex usually is a much more salient ethical matter in religious doctrines than violence, and this inversion of priorities is also reflected in the military. Theologians and believers have routinely been more concerned about the seventh commandment than the sixth.

Appeal to any authority for ethical matters will be unjustified. If something is good because the gods command it, then we are faced with the possibility of obeying immoral orders from the gods. And if the gods command something because it is good, then the gods become irrelevant since we can reason the good for ourselves. The first section of Paul Christopher's book

The Ethics of War and Peace (2003) could be interpreted as demonstrating each of these two states of affairs that are entailed by Euthyphro's question.[44] Chapters 2 and 3 detail many of the actual war crimes and atrocities scriptually commanded by God, demonstrating the first untenable consequence of basing military ethics on religion. The Bible is one of the most genocidal books ever written. The necessary illusion propagated currently is that the Islamic faith is somehow more dangerous and violent than the Christian faith. Others may take a different approach and claim that the current rash of Islamist extremists is a perversion of peaceful religion. I would argue that all of the Abrahamic religions are equally dangerous because they are all based on faith, which by definition is the lack of reason. Islamic suicide bombing is a recent phenomenon, roughly only two decades old. The first suicide killer was Sampson, and Christianity is laced with ideas of sacrifice and martyrdom. Kant gives us cogent rationale for being wary of divine moral guidance.

> For if God should really speak to man, man could still never apprehend it was God speaking. It is quite impossible for man to apprehend the infinite by his senses, distinguish it from sensible beings, and recognize it as such. But in some cases man can be sure that the voice he hears is *not* God's; for if the voice commands him to do something contrary to the moral law, then no matter how majestic the apparition may be, and no matter how it may seem to surpass the whole of nature, he must consider it an illusion. We can use, as an example, the myth of the sacrifice that Abraham was going to make by butchering and burning his only son at God's command (the poor child, without knowing it, even brought the wood for the fire). Abraham should have replied to this supposedly divine voice: "That I ought not to kill my good son is quite certain. But that you, this apparition, are God—of that I am not certain, and never can be, not even if this voice rings down to me from (visible) heaven."[45]

And chapter 4 in Christopher's book demonstrates the second untenable consequence: that meaningful just war reasoning was accomplished only through secular reasoning. Many would want to argue that the church fathers have contributed to the just war tradition, and I do not disagree. They have contributed, but their contributions to the just war tradition are largely based on the philosophical reasoning they were engaged in, not through theological edicts. There is nothing that resembles just war thinking in the Bible. However, there is just war thought in the Koran. The just war tenets of jus ad bellum have a heavy scholastic influence, so they have aspects that can be traced back to church doctrine. The language of "innocent" instead of non-combatant is an example. We don't need the ten commandments to reason that killing is wrong. In fact, we need reason to understand why it is wrong or under what circumstances or conditions it may be justified. God may tell some people *that* something may be wrong but not *why* it is wrong. We need reason for that. Indeed, "even if recent Christian ethical theorists capture the essence of Christian ethics, it is unclear what of significance they add to secular ethics."[46] Sam Harris argues the same general point more strongly when he says, "the pervasive idea that religion is somehow the source of our deepest ethical intuitions is absurd. We no more get our sense that cruelty is wrong from the pages of the Bible than we get our sense that two plus two equals four from the pages of a textbook on mathematics."[47]

Additionally, a religious morality can even be harmful for the warrior. Following the psychological archetypes for two mental disorders, psychosis is a result of the development of the id, and neurosis is a result of the repression of the id. Warriors become psychotic as they indulge themselves in appreciating, becoming skillful at, and enjoying the art and science of killing. When religious morality is added to the warrior's training, then religion's attendant neurosis is piled up on top of the warrior's psychosis, making a very harmful mixture, and causing the warrior to become actually schizophrenic: both psychotic and neurotic. Faith-based morality is no more reliable than faith-based intelligence. Fixing conclusions around anything believed only through faith is logically flawed, unreasoned. Bertrand Russell referred to faith as being a vice, since it amounted to believing in unjustified propositions, with one proposition being adhered to through faith just as easily as the opposite of the same proposition. Religious faith equally endorses peace or war. Anything follows from a contradiction. Such a practice of faith-based morality is an example of Dawkins' memetic virus, a virus protected by self-destructive subroutines. Logic is the antivirus program (and one of the enemies of faith). Daniel Dennett, in his book *Breaking the Spell*, (2006) said that good people will do good things and bad people will do bad things, but to get good people to do bad things takes religion. I would add that any unreflective dogmatic ideology, whether it is religious, political, or cultural, can get good people to do bad things. The world is on fire right now, fueled by religiously informed political action. Rarely a day has gone by in the last six years that I have not been reminded in some way that non-state actor Islamic fundamentalist extremists killed three thousand Americans. And I am consistently reminded of the dangers of an emerging Islamic threat that is a state actor—Iran. I would like to see a single acknowledgment that a fundamentalist Christian nation with a fundamentalist president has been responsible for the deaths of potentially one hundred times that many. The government can never make this acknowledgment, though. Their attack was "unjust;" our response "just." The Americans who died were "innocent." This scholastic language is religiously informed. We are good, and our enemy is evil; there can be no comparison. But evil is in the eye of the religious beholder. Endarkenment returns.

LOST IN THE PARTICULARS

In the 1990s, Americans viewed with horror the image of Somali soldiers dragging a dead American soldier through their streets. Since antiquity the Just War Tradition has eschewed the defiling of the dead on a battlefield; such a proscription has loomed large in the consciousness of civilized combatants. At the same time, though, this immoral act has been immortalized by one of the arch heroes of the Western canon—Achilles, who dragged Hector from his chariot in the *Iliad*. What was the point of Achilles dragging Hector? Achilles "was bent on outrage, on shaming noble Hector."[48] To shame Hector, he "pierc[ed] the tendons, ankle to heel behind both feet, he knotted straps of rawhide through them both, lashed them to his chariot, left the head to drag and mounting the car, hoisting the famous arms aboard, he whipped his team to a run and breakneck on they flew, holding nothing back."[49] But Achilles did not drag Hector through the streets, defiling the dead, until after he had killed him ignominiously. What he did was immoral, by most conceptions of chivalric codes, rules of war, or moral customs. Some would argue that it was not immoral, and even if they did accede to his immorality, they might offer that Achilles is still a hero because of his great courage and battlefield prowess. But was Achilles really courageous? Only reflection and inquiry can produce an answer to these questions. We can have moral error if our understanding and practices lead us to perform immoral actions, whether these actions are considered to be immoral because of their consequences, their motives, their principles, or through defects of moral character.

Some people see great courage in Achilles and applaud him for dispatching his foes, regardless of the circumstances; "there is no substitute for victory"—everyone loves a winner. Those who read this narrative unreflectively and buy into the myth of the Homeric hero, simply responding to the particulars, can walk away with the wrong lessons or ideas. Achilles is often touted as possessing great courage, and such an unreflective reading can lead one simply to follow Achilles' example. Following the example of others is one of the primary maxims of almost everyone's concept of leadership in today's military; they often proclaim, parodying Vince Lombardi, that *example isn't the most important thing—it's the only thing*. It might do one well, however, to closely look at Achilles' motives and the myth of the Homeric hero. These motives can play a part in the moral evaluation. If one simply follows the example, unreflectively, then particularism can lead to moral error.

Even if we put all of our moral hopes into Achilles' courage, we still have a problem. He may have demonstrated the appearance of courage, but Achilles is motivated by anger every time he is moved to action. He enters the conflict motivated by his anger over Agamemnon's abduction of Briseis. He is motivated to fight Hector only after Hector kills his friend, Patroclus. The motives (vengeance), means (treachery), and ends (shaming Hector) of Achilles' actions would be hard to defend by any conception of morality. The immoral example of Achilles in an epic narrative is likely the kind of stuff that motivated Plato to warn against the moral example set out by the poets in the *Republic*. Eric Havelock argues that Plato's rigorous modes of philosophy were his attempt to correct the hapless, rhetorical, and dangerous methods of the poets. According to Havelock, Plato thought that "poetry as an educational discipline poses a moral danger, and also an intellectual one" in that "it confuses a man's values and renders him characterless and it robs him of any insight into the truth."[50] Perhaps poetry has its Achilles' heel as well.

The Homeric hero, the warrior archetype, lived on. Alexander the Great, who viewed Achilles as a great role model, killed one of his dearest friends and most trusted commanders in a fit of rage at a banquet. Clitus had grown up with Alexander and had been a soldier in Alexander's father's army; Clitus' sister had even helped to raise Alexander. The accounts of the specifics differ from source to source, but the incident occurred when Alexander and Clitus had exchanged differing viewpoints over whose exploits and victories had been greater, Alexander's or Philip's. Clitus had been drinking and had been harsh in his choice of words. "Alexander could stand no more drunken abuse from his friend. Angrily he leapt from his seat as if to strike him, but the others held him back."[51]

> At this, Ptolemy and Perdiccas fell to their knees and begged him not to persist with such hasty anger but to allow himself time to consider—he would settle the matter more equitably the next day. But, deaf with anger, his ears took in nothing. He stormed into the vestibule of the royal quarters in uncontrollable fury. There he grabbed a spear from the guard on watch and stood at the doorway by which his dinner-guests had to exit. The others had left, and Clitus was the last to come out, without a lamp. The king challenged him, and the tone of his voice testified to the appalling nature of his criminal intent. Clitus thought now not of his own anger, but only of the king's. He replied that he was Clitus and that he was leaving the banquet. As he said this Alexander plunged the spear into his side and, bespattered with the dying man's blood, said to him: "Now go and join Philip, Parmenion and Attalus."[52]

Alexander spent the next two weeks mourning and trying to regain his self-respect after his regrettable act. "But sorrow is the companion of anger."[53] He may never have completely recovered from this incident. "Would any one want to stab an enemy with such force as to leave his own hand in the wound and be unable to recover himself from the blow? But such a weapon is anger; it is hard to draw back."[54]

Achilles is a military archetype, an archetype that has been transmitted to the present day. Alexander fashioned himself after Achilles. General George Patton fashioned himself after both Achilles and Alexander. Many in the military today view all three as having an important place in the pantheon of warrior-heroes. If one were to judge the level of hero worship among warriors today, attested to by the popularity of such books as the widely touted *Leadership: The Warrior's Art* (2001), edited by Chris Kolenda, then one would think we were still in the Romantic era along with Thomas Carlyle, not yet aware of the world of men, just gods and heroes. These warrior-heroes are role models, for good or ill. Homer himself did not necessarily intend to write for the purpose of moralistic instruction. However, many who indulge literature are particularists, and even though they may view narrative and poetry to be devoid of philosophical principle, they would hold that narrative and poetry can still inform moral understanding. Let's explore why Plato believed that poetry corrupts the soul. I will critique the very process, and my argument is based on the philosophical analysis of this process. My anecdotal experience of teaching with particularists matches Plato's critique and bears out my own argument. As a point of logic, to reiterate, I am not arguing from my experience to the conclusion that particularism is morally corrupting. My philosophical argument is separate and stands alone. However, I have spent six years teaching alongside literature professors and two years along side history professors, both of these disciplines being generally anti-theoretical and anti-philosophical. While there were exceptions in both camps, I found in general that backgrounds in literature or history can have a corrupting influence. Faculty in these disciplines had less developed moral intuitions than philosophers, and their warrior disciples would sooner embrace immorality in war. Plato's attack on poetry was slightly redirected by Shelley's riposte:

> Poetry strengthens that faculty which is the organ of the moral nature of man, in the same manner as exercise strengthens a limb. A poet therefore would do ill to embody his own conceptions of right and wrong, which are usually those of his place and time, in his poetical creations, which participate in neither. By this assumption of the inferior office of interpreting the effect, in which perhaps after all he might acquit himself but imperfectly, he would resign the glory in a participation in the cause. There was little danger that Homer, or any of the eternal poets, should have so far misunderstood themselves as to have abdicated this throne of their widest dominion. Those in whom the poetical faculty, though

great, is less intense, as Euripides, Lucan, Tasso, Spenser, have frequently affected a moral aim, and the effect of their poetry is
diminished in exact proportion to the degree in which they compel
us to advert to this purpose.[55]

   Particularism is the pursuit of ethical understanding motivated by the
notion "that we *should* not 'search for a set of principles'"[56] and "claims that we
will do better morally in everyday life if we look carefully at each particular decision as it arises and give up the search for a complete moral theory."[57] One of the
manifestations is the pursuit of ethics through the use of a particularist understanding found in the narratives in literature, poetry, history, art, and film. Many
of those who embrace the current paradigm, and therefore do not employ philosophical ethics, are motivated at least in part by accessibility: many practical ethicists are intentionally avoiding the difficulties of philosophical ethics and are
turning to a popular, accessible mode of particularism. Particularists hold principle in contempt. Those who are drawn to particularism are motivated by the disdain or distrust they have of ethical theory. This position shuns theory, for "the
antitheory position is motivated by the perception that when moral agents think
about moral questions, they do so not in terms of abstract principles with an aim
to systematize some large chunk of moral experience, but in terms of concrete
relationships with other people within the context of their understanding of
those relationships, histories, and the institutions in which they are embedded."[58]
   Since particularism avoids theory and principle, the ethical ideas
themselves (justice, honesty, courage) and the relations among these ideas
are not made explicit. The lessons, ideas, and relations of these ideas remain
tacit, or what could be considered "tacit knowledge."[59] That is, the ideas
remain at a preverbal or nonverbal, sublimated, unarticulated stage; they
remain inchoate ideas if they exist as ideas at all. Since the ideas remain at
the preverbal stage, there is no deliberate reflection. An exploration of tacit
knowledge can shed light on the mechanism of acquisition of basic and
unreflective moral beliefs. This way of doing ethics is what R. M. Hare
describes as the intuitive level of ethics, to be distinguished from the second
level, which is the critical level.[60] Intuition, or even trained sensibility from a
particularist education, can be good only if it has been well trained; moral
intuitions and sensibilities can mislead us as readily as linguistic intuitions.
Age and maturity are not factors here. Anyone who reads *Aesop's Fables* and
abstracts the relevant principles—the morals of the stories—is engaged in
moral reflection. We have to look beyond the parable to the principle. If
these beliefs have been informed solely by amassing the particulars from narratives, then this set of beliefs is potentially a jumbled mass of incoherent,
inconsistent beliefs that come from a bewildering array of narratives. A possible outcome of the reliance on particulars is to engage in an ethical prac-

tice that merely perpetuates immoral practices. The narratives, histories, anecdotes, unrelated maxims, and case studies may contain immoral practices—normally at a deep, implicit level—that are not articulated. These deeply held morally suspect beliefs can directly impede our ability to be moral, as individuals or as institutions.

In any event, by focusing on particulars the antitheorists will in the main be forced to rely on intuition or perhaps trained sensibility, and there are many critiques of intuition as a source of morality.[61] Mill's extended critique of this type of reasoning deals with the limitations of what he calls *reasoning from particular to particular*. Mill thought that reasoned deliberation on a philosophical level was important to understanding ethics, and therefore intuition-based morality would not be philosophically deliberative. "Even Mill's strong objections to all forms of intuitional moral doctrine may have had one root in the fear that the general public could not make the discrimination, which a philosopher might, between a kind of intuitionism which allows for, and a kind which excludes, improvement in moral beliefs."[62] One reason the military as an institution relies on methodological particularism is that the approach supports its interest in making it a matter of training. Particularism is consistent with the military's methods of indoctrination. The imparting of the military culture through its narratives is easy and straightforward. But intuition will only be as good as the training that shapes it. And, unfortunately, the military does not always train correctly when it comes to moral matters, even today, after centuries of evidence showing moral error. In reality, it is a problem of education, not training. Having soldiers understand principles of respect and protecting noncombatants, avoiding excessive force, and preventing unnecessary harm are matters of education and are not ideas that the organization can "train" people to understand and then be motivated to act according to that understanding.

Dealing with the logic of particularism necessarily involves the way particulars may exist in the world as well as how we may know or even think about them. There are many ways we can err in reasoning when we employ particularism as a method of seeking moral understanding. Particularism can employ bad reasoning in that we can use the stories inconsistently. Additionally, reasoning from particular to particular can be improperly or unconsciously applied. And we can also err if we don't consider different interpretations of the stories and take into account that many forms of particularism are works of art. There are many ways that particularist narratives can mislead. Until the ideas in the narratives are compared at the level of principle, it is possible to imagine consistency when it is not there, to see differences when there are in fact similarities, or similarities where there are in fact differences. Consumers of narratives can unknowingly be misled in a variety of ways. One way narratives can mislead is that they can contain contradictions or contraries, thereby being inconsistent. Another way is that they can view two narratives as completely unrelated when they are related in significant ways. An extreme version would be the case in which narratives can even appear to be exact opposites, yet be significantly similar. Yet another way would be where two different narratives can appear to be the same, but are different in important ways. Finally, while coherence is extremely difficult to achieve when using only two narratives, incoherence increases as people use many narratives, perhaps a fourth way narratives can mislead. Regardless of the ways in which narratives can mislead and cause problems, it is instructive to employ principled thinking in order to at least perceive and then perhaps reflect upon possible solutions that these problems may cause. Let us consider some of these possibilities.

A single narrative may transmit inconsistent moral features. Take the history and the narrative of Henry V at Agincourt. Shakespeare's narrative of Henry V contains perhaps the most inspiring speech in all of his plays—or perhaps anywhere else for that matter—when Henry addresses his soldiers on the morning before the battle. The speech inspires his soldiers, and they courageously fight outnumbered and win. William J. Bennett includes this speech as a motivational piece in his *Book of Virtues*, and he adds that he believes that this speech is the model for all half-time talks given by all football coaches every autumn in America.[63] By the way, Bennett is one of the very few philosophers who still justifies the current Long War. But while Henry may have been courageous and may have inspired courage among his men, he was not completely virtuous or completely moral. People may want to be careful in putting Henry forth as an example in all ways. Henry, upon fearing that all of his French prisoners posed a threat due to their numbers, ordered them all to be killed, which is against the "rules of war." Captain Fluellen, one of Henry's confidants in Shakespeare's account says of the actions by the French, "Kill the boys and the baggage! 'Tis expressly against the law of arms. 'Tis as arrant a piece of knavery, mark you now, as can be offert." What is important here is the awareness that killing noncombatants even at that time was against the rules of war. Michael Walzer gives at least three different accounts of the narrative of this episode. Hollinshed says that Henry, "contrary to his accustomed gentleness, commanded by sound of trumpet that every man . . . should incontinently slay his prisoner." Shakespeare is not so charitable on this point and omits in his account Hollinshed's "assertion that only those who resisted were killed."[64] Hume in his histories is more charitable than Shakespeare and claims that Henry "thought it necessary to issue a general order for putting them to death; but on discovering the truth, he stopped the slaughter, and was still able to save a great number."[65]

However, no matter how charitably one reads the actual account, his actions and his character are thrown into suspicion because of his violation of the principle to protect noncombatants. This makes the single narrative of Henry V a good model and example of an inconsistent narrative whose inconsistencies cannot be rooted out just by paying attention to the particulars. The inconsistencies are rooted out only by considering the principles, something the particularists do not want to do. The proponents of virtue would have us simply ask, "What would Henry do?"[66] It is not so important to rely on what he did, but rather why he did it, and this is possible only with principled deliberation, invoking philosophical inquiry. Looking to example as a feature of acquiring virtue can still be particularistic if there is no principled reflection.

Two stories that appear to have little resemblance can in actuality be more similar than different in morally significant ways. Homer's *Iliad* is a narrative history of some of the Western World's greatest heroes. Within military circles, when soldiers invoke Achilles as a hero, they do so proudly and vauntingly. On the other hand, Stephen Crane's *The Red Badge of Courage* is a novel about the courage not of a hero, but of an ordinary soldier. Achilles is a respected warrior and leader with resplendent armor, weaponry, and fighting skill. In contrast, Henry Fleming is an ordinary soldier who comes to battle with great fear and trepidation, with no reputation or fighting skill. The epic verse of Homer makes the narrative extremely popular because at least in part it romanticizes the glory of warfare and is replete with themes of patriotism, valor, and courage. Crane's novel was not a romanticization of warfare and was in the opinion of his editor not likely to be successful because a story is only good for an institution if it "casts an aura of glory over the soldier, the army, the cause, and the country."[67] Crane's novel through its irony was critical of notions of courage and cowardice present at that time in the military. Yet, even so, many people—especially in the military—did not read it ironically, and so then and now they look to it as an example of an ordinary person meeting the trials of combat, getting bloodied, and becoming courageous. Military people today look to both Achilles and Henry Fleming as examples of courage, yet in very different ways. While people see Achilles as always being courageous, they see Henry Fleming as being an example of the initiation and transformation myths, transforming his character from cowardly to courageous. These two books are part of our intellectual heritage, and most of us read them or become aware of them in high school or college. They help to form deeply held beliefs of heroism and courage. They help to create and sustain the mythos surrounding heroism and heroic transformation. In this sense, they are archetypal and worth examining.

So, on the surface, they appear to be quite different narratives whose particular moral features are quite different. But, they have some relevant features that are the same, at least in principle. Significantly, both Achilles and Henry have a morally relevant feature in common: their courage in battle is motivated by anger. And in many ways, one could argue that it was not courage that they were displaying, but the simulacra of courage—false courage. Henry Fleming does get wounded, but not by the enemy; he gets hit by the rifle butt of a friendly soldier. Achilles is angry with both Agamemnon and Hector; this anger motivates him to fight bravely, or what appears to be bravely. Henry Fleming "began to feel the effects of the war atmosphere—a blistering sweat, a sensation that his eyeballs were about to crack like hot stones. A burning roar filled his ears. Following this came a red rage. He developed the acute exasperation of a pestered animal."[68] Virtue theorists will claim that the exercise of virtue has to be more than unconscious, even if it is formed by habit.[69] The two narratives have at least this feature in common, that the main characters are both motivated to courage by anger. And while some may contend that there are significant differences in what causes their anger, it is quite conceivable to draw out the similarities as well. One philosopher describes the features of the emotion of anger when he makes the claim that all cases of anger possess the structure of having what he calls a "'wish-frustration': a belief that something is the case together with a wish that it weren't."[70] Achilles and Henry both have the belief that they have been wronged, have somehow experienced some kind of injustice, and they both have a wish that this injustice had not occurred. So both cases of anger, while quite different, have essentially the same structure of the emotion of anger.

The narratives may have even more in common. It is quite possible that Crane in many ways was retelling Homer's *Iliad*, at least in some ways, and maybe even in an ironic way. Both books have twenty-four chapters, and the themes roughly follow the same patterns. Crane uses Homeric language, which means if nothing else that he was quite familiar with the ancient text.[71] Yet, even without a more intimate connection between the two texts, they at least have anger in common as the motive of courage. If the particularists use the two texts as completely different cases with completely different applications, then they are being misleading because of the similarity of the two narratives. Warriors may look to Achilles as a born warrior. Or they may look to Henry Fleming, who they believe (wrongly) lives the transformation myth. Warriors look toward the different narratives for different insights. Whether born or made, the simulacra of courage is unjustifiably motivated by anger. Anger can be legitimately employed, but it takes principled reflection to determine if the circumstances can justify it. Achilles' rage does not make the appraisal of courage morally justified.[72] Nor does Fleming's.

When particularists do not recognize the similarities of any two seemingly disparate ideas, there is a problem of inconsistency. In the twentieth century, most countries and nation-states were proud of the fact that they no longer waged warfare for religious reasons. But crusades have made a comeback. The wars for country in the last century are reinforced now in this century; now warriors fight for both god and country. West Point still carries as its motto: "Duty, Honor, Country." There is no difference in kind between god and country. Morally, they have a significant feature in common. Both god and country have a moral object that is something other than humankind. Before soldiers would fight and die for god; now they fight and die for country. Both are motivated by abstract ideas, ideologies. Sidney Axinn describes this connection when he says that patriotism makes it "seem quite natural to describe nationalism as the religion of the age. When people are willing to sacrifice anything, including their lives, for their nation or their nation's principles, we must call their attitude religious."[73] The war against terror has often been cast as the result of Islamist extremism. Many are drawn to Huntington's thesis that we are in a clash of civilizations. Western civilization is according to this thesis under siege by Islamic civilization, or vice versa depending on the perspective. Tariq Ali challenges this premise in his book *Clash of Fundamentalisms* (2002).[74] Ali does not interpret world events to be driven by this split between the West and the rest, between one civilization and another. Instead, he argues, the clash is between the extremists on both sides. Religious fundamentalism is playing a role on both sides of the conflict, and the religious fundamentalists are a vast minority. The clash of civilizations is a myth for Ali, because the vast majority of people in the world are moderates. Fundamentalists are a problem for Sam Harris, but so are moderates. Moderates sustain the irrationalities of the extremists because they subscribe to the same standard for action—that of faith. The terrorists who attacked America were not cowards or lunatics, but were men of faith.[75] Faith, spirit, ideology, god, and country all coalesce in a dangerous way and have as much or more in common than that which separates them. By paying attention only to the particular narratives, without thinking in abstract and principled ways, it is easy to miss the connections that really exist.

Even narratives that appear to be exact opposites can invoke the same principles, and therefore not be opposites at all, or so different after all. Two stories that appear to be opposites but are the same in significant ways may be that of Benedict Arnold and Robert E. Lee. Were one to visit West Point, there would be no doubt that these two particular narratives are opposites. Robert E. Lee is one of the greatest heroes at West Point, and he is much studied here, and Benedict Arnold is the greatest villain and is the paradigm case for a traitor. But are they really so different? Both were great military commanders. Arnold's bad reputation makes it hard for people at West Point to remember that we might still be British subjects if he had not won the day at the Battle of Saratoga. But nobody here pays attention to the battle savvy of Benedict Arnold. By one important measure, maybe both of them are villains: Both Lee and Arnold are technically traitors, were we to loosen the definition of treason a bit, including acts of disloyalty in general. Lee's treason may even be worse, because he took an oath to the Constitution when Arnold did not. But Lee's popularity does not allow us to think of him as a traitor. Arnold's crime is that he switched over to fight for England, and this made him a villain. Yet others went over to fight for England when we went to war, and they, too, should be traitors if we are interested in consistency. One of these "traitors" is Robert Rogers, the leader of Roger's Rangers. Rogers, during the French and Indian War, made famous the irregular tactics that later became the trademark of American fighting in the Revolutionary War. However, during the Revolution, he never stopped thinking of himself as a British subject, and in that war he fought against the Americans. Nevertheless, he is an American legend: the Army Rangers are named after him, and every Army Ranger School student still memorizes his nineteen maxims of battle tactics. Perhaps being a traitor is all a matter of point of view. From a strict American point of view, all of them would be traitors: Rogers and Arnold switched sides during one war and Lee switched to support a seceding government during another war. Drawing distinctions can help to sort out the nature of treason in the three cases. Arnold is different from both Lee and Rogers in that Arnold was deceitful during the war. But Lee and Rogers differ from one another in that Lee switched sides to fight for independence while Rogers remained loyal to the parent government, albeit different wars. Is loyalty to the cause of independence always justified? From the British perspective, Rogers was loyal. Is deceit a necessary feature of treason? Kenneth Roberts has written some magnificent novels about the early American period, in which Robert Rogers and Benedict Arnold are both heroes. Suffice it to say that raising the analysis to consider treason as a principle may help in sorting out the moral status of these three alleged traitors. But until one does such an analysis, simply following or avoiding the examples they set may not be morally justifiable.

Finally, particularists can be guilty of inconsistency because of the very richness and diversity that narratives give them, a richness that is also a source of their efficacy. Yet while narratives can be a rich source to draw upon, this very richness creates a problem of incoherence due to the sheer number and diversity of narratives available to any individual. Take my case, for example, which would be typical or representative of many Americans now living in the United States. As an American, I have all of the history and folk heritage of America as sources that inform my identity. I can also, however, claim a German heritage from my mother's side of the family. Additionally, my father's side of the family came to the United States from England. At the same time, there is good reason to believe that our family name is of French origin. So now I can add the unique characteristics of at least three European countries to the set of American narratives I can turn to for direction. As a military professional, I have all of the military narratives to draw from, worldwide. According to what particularism entails, I can use as models such incredibly diverse characters from the Indian wars in America (actually from both sides, due to some Cherokee admixture), the Visigoths in early Europe, or even the French Foreign Legion. I can turn to the particulars of any one of these narratives for guidance. When considering the harm done to civilians in a military operation, for example, I can turn to the history of General Sherman's march to the sea and the burning of Atlanta in the American Civil War, and Sherman's "war is hell" doctrine, which includes the notion that it was better to get war over quickly—no matter what it takes and no matter what the cost—rather than let it drag out for a long time, no matter what kind of war crimes one commits along the way. How do I choose which narratives will be my moral models? Based on my likes and dislikes? Wouldn't that simply reduce to the criterion of aesthetic preference? What kind of guide is that? The typical warrior likes Sherman or McCaffrey (especially now that he is retired), so the next thing that happens is that the vast majority of the military is quite sympathetic to the narratives of military realism. This line of thinking, military realism—the notion that *inter arma silent leges*—is quite popular in the military even today, and it shows up in many different, but related, forms.[76] These narratives are certainly rich, but how does one live an ethically coherent, consistent, ethical life based on narratives? How do I pick and choose among the narratives? What justifies the stories? Can it be merely aesthetic taste? This approach embodies the complexity and lack of coherence that is the result of this very richness.

Other examples of particularism exist in the field of law. One particularistic practice is that of common law. Common law is derived from particular cases. Instead of being driven and justified by principled thinking, precedent and tradition weigh heavily in this practice. Practitioners find themselves searching for previous cases that resemble their particular current case. They are searching for features and properties of the cases, whose similarities hopefully will help to decide the case at hand. The common law tradition is a particularist tradition. There are other ways of interpreting law that would also be particularist. For example, Supreme Court Justice Antonin Scalia interprets laws in a particularist fashion. His preferred method of interpretation calls for looking only at the expressed laws, found in the statutes themselves, which will not include any principles. He admits that he does not place any stock in principles in law, but looks only for expressed meaning using a method he calls textualism, a way of interpreting texts so that a text—a law—is "construed reasonably, to contain all that it fairly means."[77] When it comes to issues of separation of church and state, for example, he has said that he is not interested in what the Lemon Test may have to offer by way of principle. He is not interested in the principles of secular rationale and secular motivation. He has said that what matters is the weight and inertia of history, precedent, and tradition. Scalia has cited the facts that George Washington was a religious man and spoke of God and prayed in public as good reasons for him to be skeptical of the notion of separation of church and state. This is a particularist approach, one devoid of acknowledging the existence and importance of principles. But while Scalia decries principles, he does invoke them at times, so he is being inconsistent. At the heart of the matter is the paradox that particularists employ principle even when they are trying to avoid principle. Ronald Dworkin criticizes Scalia regarding this inconsistency when he says that Scalia "begins with a general theory that entails a style of constitutional adjudication which he ends by denouncing."[78] Scalia wants to avoid intention, but he cannot escape the semantic intention that exists in the texts of the laws. Principle is hard to avoid. Even in common law, principle is hard to avoid. If a judge distinguishes a current case to be different from previous cases and articulates the difference of the new case based on foreseeability or on privity, then the judge is invoking the principles of foreseeability and privity. I will explore this difficulty in avoiding principle in the next section.

One final reason that narratives can lead us astray is that they are works of art and if not twice removed from reality, as Plato claimed, they are at least once removed from reality. Since narratives are works of art, they may be straightforward representations to be taken at face value. On the other hand, though, they may be ironic or satirical and are not to be taken on face value. If Stephen Crane had every intention to undermine then current notions of courage and cowardice when he wrote *The Red Badge of Courage*, then we may be making a mistake if we take his novel literally, encouraging our soldiers to seek and look forward to similar experiences of initiation and transformation. The use of irony and satire, as well as other rhetorical devices, are appreciated by those who can recognize them for what they are. Many people may not detect such nuance in the narratives they read, hence their collective misreading of such novels as *The Red Badge of Courage*. In any event, narratives can have multiple interpretations, thus making the moral instruction drawn from them even more unreliable. The reading of narratives offers no guarantee against war crimes. And so many warriors remain semiconscious in their battle sleep.

THE VICES OF VIRTUE

Alasdair MacIntyre argues in *After Virtue* (1984) that once Nietzsche had dismantled modern moral philosophy—but not ancient moral philosophy— we were left with the only option of accepting the ancient offering: virtue ethics.[79] Alternatively, many philosophers would argue that Nietzsche did not dismantle modern moral philosophy but that modern moral philosophy did demonstrate the inadequacies of the ancient theory of virtue. Virtue theory lacks any robust theory of right action. Right action is underdetermined in virtue theory. This shortcoming should not be too surprising given that virtues are focused on what we should *be* rather than what we should *do*. Modern moral theory, on the other hand, does focus more on what we should do. Virtue theory is a form of particularism because of the employment of particular values or particular virtues. While engaging in the study, exploration, or exposition of virtue theory would not necessarily be a form of particularism because it would be invoking theory, the mere practice of opaquely transmitting virtues would be a form of particularism. But narratives are popular everywhere for transmitting ethical ideas, and they are extremely popular for transmitting the ethical norms of an organization. The military today draws upon such narratives to transmit these ethical norms. Teaching values or virtues through narratives can be valuable. Augmenting this approach with philosophical principle can enhance an understanding of values. I take up a principled, philosophical critique of values in chapter 3. Just as particularists would expect people to rely on mere insight when seeing moral truths in narrative, virtue advocates expect people to rely on insight when seeing moral truths in particular situations. Aristotle emphasizes the importance of being able to discern particulars and says that "intelligence is about the last thing, an object of perception, not of scientific knowledge."[80] Moral knowledge for Aristotle featured discerning the particulars, being able to look at a situation and being able to see or perceive the moral judgment through insight. Julia Annas claims that Aristotle's focus on perceiving the particulars in a situation entails that when faced with a problem, "what is stressed is not the problem-solving but the direct insight into what is needed to solve it."[81]

Terence Irwin takes Aristotle, at least at times, to be referring to virtues when he is talking about particular objects of knowledge, as in when Irwin claims "the particulars here are not particular action-tokens at definite times and places, but the specific virtues."[82] This interpretation should not be so surprising, since Aristotle differed from Plato, who thought contrarily that moral truths were embodied in universals, forms, and were never embodied in particulars. Aristotle's methodology sought moral truth and understanding in a very different manner from that of Plato, focusing more on the particulars than on the universals. So when some particularists and virtue theorists have us look at particular cases, in narratives or otherwise, we will simply through trained insight see the morally relevant particulars of these situations, and these particulars sometimes will be the virtues themselves. Of course, one does not acquire virtues just by reading about them or perceiving them. The *phronimos*, the virtuous person of practical reasoning, does not need rules to make moral decisions or judgments. The virtuous person simply perceives through trained intuition what she needs to understand about the situation and therefore knows how to act. Experience is the key, yet we can gain vicarious experience through narrative. Communicating the virtues through narratives is one easy way to transmit the virtues as well as being an easy way of being exposed to the virtues because of accessibility, namely by experiencing the virtues vicariously through narratives.

Particularists have been motivated to steer clear of theory by what they believe to be difficulties in the principles and theories of ethics. They feel the pendulum has swung too far for too long in the direction of principles. The pendulum has now swung perhaps too far in the opposite direction, away from principle and toward particulars. Some have placed Aristotle more on the particularist side, but perhaps this is not completely fair to Aristotle. While the practitioners, teachers, chroniclers, and transmitters of virtues are particularists, the virtue theorist is engaged in theory. Aristotle's method does not disallow principles altogether, but the principles would be rules of thumb derived from the particular situations. Aristotle would even have that practical judgment could choose the right narratives. While Plato would have us begin with universals and think to particulars, Aristotle would not. Aristotle would not have us begin with principles and then see insights into our actions based on those principles.[83] Martha Nussbaum talks of Aristotle's skepticism about our ability to achieve moral insight through the Platonic project of universals, from an "external 'god's eye' standpoint." She maintains that Aristotle endorses achieving moral insight through the "method of appearances," a method that allows us to "view the internal truth, truth in the appearances," and she goes further to claim that this method "is all we have to deal with."[84] Annas "talks of Aristotle insisting on the priority of the concrete particular."[85]

Principle becomes inevitable for the particularist for several reasons. Particularists, as we examined before, may employ the approach and be fully aware of the deeper logic and principles that are embedded in their approach. Or they may not be aware of the logic of their methods. They may pretend that principles are not operative when they are. Another way theory is inevitable is that when philosophical particularists do theorize about particularism, they are engaged in a principled inquiry, unavoidably. In other words, when they talk about ethical norms or moral properties—the moral of the story—they are invoking the very principles and theories that they are hoping to avoid by turning away from philosophical inquiry and principled morality in the first place. And the ensuing theories involving the identification, sorting, correlating, and evaluating of particulars is every bit as complicated as the theoretical fly-bottles they are attempting to keep from entering. A further problem is that particularists have mischaracterized ethical theory, and they have mischaracterized ethical principles in particular. Upon reexamination, they should come to understand that theorists who pursue ethical principles could accomplish the same goals as those who pursue ethical particularism.

Particularism, in ethics as in other endeavors, includes the view that there are no principles, no universals. Several philosophers would love to do away with principles, especially when it comes to ethics. However, principles, or principled thinking—philosophical inquiry—is unavoidable in the particularist quest. Richard Rorty argues strongly, "It would be nice if philosophers could give us assurance that the principles which we approve of, like Mill's and Kant's, are 'rational' in a way that the principles of the blood-revengers and the gaybashers are not."[86] He thinks principles get us nowhere and they cannot make fine distinctions within rich contexts. Rorty does not think that we should be philosophizing to find universal moral principles, but supports an approach that focuses on particulars, and Rorty supports Dewey when Dewey "insisted that universal moral principles were useful only insofar as they were the outgrowth of the historical development of a particular society—a society whose institutions gave content to the otherwise empty shell of the principle."[87] Joseph Margolis does not believe we should be looking for invariant principles for our moral thinking, either. He believes that "the self is an artifact of constructive social processes (enculturation), historicized in accord with the variable practices of this society and that."[88] Particularism often takes some literary form, and these literary forms invoke narratives, and narratives can be thought of as a general set of stories that can come in the shape of histories, fables, novels, poems, plays, mythologies, anecdotes, unrelated maxims, or perhaps even case studies. "One of the more interesting claims that emerges from this literature is the suggestion that narratives are a richer resource for moral reflection than theory."[89] An influential philosopher who has embraced the narrative tradition, in addition to Richard Rorty, is Martha Nussbaum. She has written extensively on the subject, and her motivation is at least in part due to Aristotle's claim that practical moral choice revolves not around general principle, but around the features of "mutability, indeterminacy, and particularity."[90] "Aristotle suggests that the concrete ethical case may simply contain some ultimately particular and non-repeatable elements ... [and] rules, seen as normative according to the second conception, fail in their very nature to measure up to the challenge of practical choice."[91] Jonathan Dancy is a leading exponent of particularism and argues for "the nonexistence of moral principles."[92] Instead of relying on moral principles, Dancy claims that "[p]articularist epistemology tells us that moral knowledge comes from our knowledge of cases."[93]

However, I argue that principle is unavoidable. Richard Rorty defends a particularist mode of doing ethics that amounts simply, in his conception, to a recounting of our stories. He speaks of the particular choices that Huck Finn would have to make in relation to his friend, Jim, and Rorty claims that one does not have to resort to ethical theory or identify nonexistent ethical principles in understanding Huck's choice. It is enough to pay attention to the richness of the details as well as the context of the situation: a particularist, pragmatic approach. However, at the time he spoke these words, he was also invoking principles, perhaps principles of friendship and other societal norms. The principled apparatus is there should one want to think about it, and even if the particularists want to claim that the principles do not in actuality exist, we can still employ them as we would employ categories to help think about particulars. Interestingly, Martha Nussbaum has recently embraced Kantian ideas of cosmopolitanism. She now also defends a principled viewpoint of the idea that is much less particularist than much of her previous work.[94]

The particularist approach can sustain a hypertraditional society or institution, one that remains unreflective and potentially susceptible to moral error. Tradition often carries with it the feature that people do not systematically or critically think about the ethical ideas and norms that are transmitted with the tradition. Cultural norms are transmitted through memetic replication at a very deep level. There is no adequate way to critically assess any moral traditions by employing only particularism. So, not only could we unwittingly transmit ethical norms, ideas, and principles unreflectively if we are particularists, but we also cannot judge traditions adequately without invoking principled inquiry. There are two other problems with this approach. One problem has to do with what I will call the normative fallacy. We commit this fallacy any time we mistake or conflate what happens to be the case with what ought to be the case, when we derive an ought from an is. In other words, the word "normative" actually changes its sense from what we take to *be* an empirical norm (what actually happens) to what we think *should be* a norm (what should happen). We commit the fallacy when we unjustifiably turn a descriptive statement into a prescriptive one.[95] I call it the *normative fallacy* because to call it the *is/ought fallacy* is too cumbersome and to call it the *naturalistic fallacy* is technically inaccurate. We potentially commit this fallacy any time we derive a prescriptive claim from a descriptive one, potentially from any historical or fictional claim without a normative (prescriptive) analysis.[96] For example, histories of the French occupation of Spain, as well as Goya's artwork, describe the barbaric nature of guerrilla warfare. Warriors commit the normative fallacy when they turn these descriptions into prescriptions, if they conclude that guerrilla warfare *should* be barbaric. So the descriptions in narratives become moral prescriptions, thus making the particularist approach a well-spring from which normative fallacies pour freely. This means that reading literature and history can do great harm by malforming moral understanding particularly through this normative fallacy.

Another problem with using the particularist approach is that it is backward-looking, and problem-solving is forward-looking, because the narratives are complete and our stories and our moral problems are not yet finished. In the real world, we do not know how our moral problems will turn out. Narratives cannot be action-guiding because our stories, as they unfold, are incomplete. This does not mean that we do not learn from history or learn from other forms of narrative. We do, but there are certain limitations to what we can apply from these narratives to our moral lives. We know how the stories we read ended. We do not know how our own stories are going to turn out. The narratives can never give us enough particulars, no matter how exhaustive the collection of particulars may happen to be, to be able to give us action-guiding insights for our own situations, which will always differ in some ways from the narratives themselves. The narratives can train our sensibilities through the particular circumstances and actions within the narrative, but our original circumstances may call for some guidance that goes beyond that sensibility. Life will often turn out to be more complicated and less inevitable than narratives would have it. Narratives give us a sense of closure and a sense of cause and effect that we may not hope to achieve in our own life stories. We make decisions along the way, and our own story unfolds at every turn in unexpected ways that a narrative would be hard pressed to capture. The true nature of cause and effect is difficult for the particularist to capture. Alan Donagan, in an argument against consequentialism, uses an example of a science fiction novel by Isaac Asimov, *The End of Eternity*. In the novel, scientific time-travelers "look for 'minimum necessary changes' by which great calamities can be eliminated from history."[97] Since we can never predict with certainty how our actions will actually affect the future (and hence one of Donagan's arguments against consequentialism), we never know when, for example, our innocent actions may have bad consequences. "It is a great coup for a technician in the story to point out that, in order to eliminate a major evil (mass drug addiction at a certain period) without compensating ill-effects, the minimum change necessary is that a container be displaced from one shelf to another, and not, as a rival had calculated, that a space vessel be caused to malfunction, killing a dozen men."[98] Strategists in the current war looked back to the example of de-Nazification and copied it with a policy of de-Ba'athification in Iraq. This particularist method resulted in disaster. Particularists think about consequences, but by doing so at the level of particulars they miss the true nature of cause and effect, which may be more accurately explained in terms of chaos and complexity, contingencies and emergences, rather than in terms of Newtonian linearity. Perhaps the true nature of cause and effect can be better understood when raised to the level of system and principle. I am merely suggesting here that principled thinking in new ways may enhance moral understanding.

To believe that our real-world lives will turn out the same way as the stories do is perhaps to engage in a fiction of a different sort. If we add a principled analysis to a particularist one, we can enhance our understanding of unintended consequences, consequences that might be due to a whole host of possibilities difficult to foresee. Yet many people expect similar outcomes in their own lives that they experience vicariously in histories, fables, or other forms of narratives. No amount of analysis of the relevant features or causal connections would ever be enough to make this a perfect enterprise, to be sure. We can learn about making decisions from narratives, but since we cannot amass enough particulars to guide us in all cases, principled thinking can go a long way to augment a sensibility trained through narrative.

Particularists do not evade the abstract philosophical problems of moral theory when they engage in theory themselves. Jonathan Dancy develops a theory of particularism where he draws out the notion that the morally relevant features of a particular case happen to be moral properties. "The epistemological particularist will feel that if a property is morally relevant in a particular case, this can only be because it is generally relevant."[99] As he develops his theory of moral properties, what becomes evident is that moral properties take on the characteristics of other types of properties. And, as a result, every kind of theoretical problem that exists for properties in general also exists for moral properties. Are moral properties primary or secondary? Do they exist in the objects themselves such as properties of substance, position, and extension, or are they phenomena that are equally dependent upon our own perception, such as properties of color, taste, sound, smell, and texture? If moral properties do not exist in the objects themselves, then do we see different properties based on different understanding, background beliefs, and ability to reason? Do the properties inhere only in the individual cases, or in the individual people? Can moral properties also inhere in the relations among people? How about background conditions? Walter Sinnott-Armstrong criticizes Dancy's theory of particularism because moral properties may not be the only relevant features in a moral situation. He gives, for an example, the argument that background conditions are also relevant features.[100] The point here is that he is theorizing in the grand style, and any theory of particulars would possess the same difficult features of any theory of principles, and these theoretical difficulties are precisely what particularists are, at least in part, trying to avoid.

Let's look at the particular virtue of courage. Do moral properties exist only in particular people, or perhaps in particular actions? In *The Red Badge of Courage*, "Henry runs on the first day of battle because of two psychic compulsions—an animal instinct of self-preservation and a social instinct to act as he believes his comrades are acting. On the next day—in a far more fully described series of combat experiences—Henry responds to battle precisely as he had on the first day, except that he now behaves 'heroically' rather than 'cowardly.'"[101] On the first day of battle Henry is still uninitiated; he has not yet been bloodied and feels shamed by his actions. On the second day, because of the symbolic red badge, he has been transformed and feels good about his performance. A particularist view of moral properties, where the moral properties would be features of particular people or actions, could only produce the judgment that he has been transformed. At the particularist level, he was a coward one day but courageous the next. But at another level, a principled level, the motives for the two actions were the same: "Again an animal compulsion (that of the cornered animal made vicious and powerful by anger and fear at being trapped) is joined with a social one (irritation at unjust blame attached to the regiment) to produce a similar 'battle sleep' of unconsciousness in action."[102] At the level of principle, he had the same *battle sleep*, and therefore the moral properties were the same—he is no more courageous on the second day than the first. The moral judgments are enhanced or even corrected when raised to the level of principle. What does this mean? It may mean that a canonical novel that people read for insights into the transformation of the warrior (in the sense that it is archetypal) may be misread if the so-called transformation from cowardice to courage is actually a myth (in the sense that it is not real). Even for Aristotle, there is no exercise of the virtue of courage if the act is motivated by anger or frenzy.

One final problem with particularist theory is that it rejects a principled approach due to the difficulties seen with moral generalizations. The particularists' major argument for particularism focuses on the defects of their competitors—those in favor of moral principle and theory. Dancy claims that his competitors may seek some kind of monism, and in that case a principled approach is flawed:

> But monism, of the utilitarian variety or otherwise, suffers from one great disadvantage, which here I assert without argument. It is false. It just is not the case that there is only one morally relevant property, nor is there only one Great Principle in ethics.[103]

Dancy continues to argue that when a principled approach is not monistic, it will be pluralistic. "If monism is false, whether in the utilitarian version or otherwise, pluralism must, it seems, be the answer."[104] For the particularist, principles will not work, whether principles are monistic or pluralistic. A monistic principled approach is false and a pluralistic principled approach has an indefinite list of principles that will in some way be incommensurable. What he is not considering here is that in a moral system based on principles, there can be a coherent plurality of principles. James D.

Wallace, another philosopher who argues for particularism, makes the claim that the opponents of particularism are all pursuing a theory of "exceptionless moral rules."[105] Again, a principled approach does not have to pursue exceptionless moral rules. There may be ways of sorting out the priority of principles, such as having principles to sort out conflicting principles. For example, Kant gives a principled approach to resolving an apparent conflict of obligations. He explains that the grounds, not the obligations, would conflict. "When two such grounds conflict with each other, practical philosophy says, not that the stronger obligation takes precedence, but that the stronger ground of obligation prevails."[106] Onora O'Neill carries out an example of Kant's principled approach of resolving conflicting principles.[107] A principled approach does not have to be rejected because the principles may at times differ. Chapter 5 will explore a principled approach to ethics. We have seen the shortcomings of virtue ethics, why character is just not enough if we want real moral reform in the military. In chapter 3 we will see why values are inadequate as well. Even character and values together cannot get the job done.

IS MORAL PROGRESS WITHOUT REFLECTION POSSIBLE?

The critique of particularism here does not entail the claim that narratives serve no purpose in ethical reflection; they do serve a purpose. They provide the examples upon which to reflect in a principled way. And I would not want to appear to be hostile to the intellectual or aesthetic pursuit of literature, poetry, art, or film. They are extremely important pursuits, even for philosophers. My objection to particularism is its claim that principles and reflection serve no purpose. Narratives by themselves, however, without our reflecting about them, may not get the job done, and we may potentially commit moral error without a principled analysis or synthesis. People might take the wrong lesson from these narratives if they do not theorize about them and consider the ideas and principles involved available only through theoretical inquiry. If the military succumbs to the temptation engendered by all the realist narratives, why should it not serve up to the enemy their children in a pie as Titus did to Tamora? And they should also think about exactly what inspires them about Henry's speech. When people hear the speech, are they moved intellectually by just war principles, by the ideals and principles of camaraderie and patriotism, or are they moved emotionally through the rhetorical devices of William Shakespeare, or through the rhetorical renditions of Sir Lawrence Olivier or Kenneth Branaugh? It's quite possible that those we normally think of as bad guys are actually good, as when Kenneth Roberts portrays Benedict Arnold as a good guy in his novels about the American Revolution. It's also possible that those we normally think of as good guys are actually bad, as when Gore Vidal portrays Abraham Lincoln as a bad guy in his novel about the Civil War.

The antitheorists would argue that the theorists are lost in the abstractions, but if they are, then the particularists are even more *lost in the particulars.* If there are problems in approaches that employ theories, then there are even greater problems, or at least as many, in approaches that focus on the particulars. Despite what many people want to believe, including many people who embrace particularism, philosophy can help our understanding, philosophical ethics can aid us in our moral lives, and philosophy can help us in our lives in general. If we do not reflect philosophically, we may not be able to see, for example, that embargoes during *peacetime,* by hurting civilians, are every bit as violative of morality as hurting the same civilians during wartime. And both are cases of not honoring the principle of protecting noncombatants. Neglecting this principle is what enabled us to justify embargoes because of precedent or traditional inertia. We've always done it that way. Why should we change? A theory based on principles, one that I have been defending throughout this chapter, could be as rich and as pluralistic as a theory of particularism. I will pursue some of the features of such a morality based on principles, a philosophical theory, in chapter 5. Philosophy can help us understand features of a moral situation that we may not be able to see otherwise.

The military has not escaped philosophy and theoretical inquiry altogether, however. The Air Force Academy, the Naval Academy, and the Military Academy all teach philosophical ethics to their students when they take philosophy as a required academic course.[108] Some mid-level and senior service colleges employ at most one philosopher. The Army's school for majors, the Command and General Staff College, has chaplains in charge of ethics instruction (as in most Army schools), which is inadequate. As an institution, the military does not employ philosophical ethics, but instead relies heavily on moral doctrines featuring particularism as a means of imparting ethical instruction. Professional reading lists always include military histories and stories, readings that not only can inform and educate, but also can socialize, acculturate, motivate, romanticize, and familiarize the military professional with the ethical norms of the profession. The military tactics course for cadets at West Point had at one time been converted into a course on professionalism, and the course employed many narratives designed to didactically socialize cadets to accept the ethical norms of the profession. They read many narratives, but also some dubious expository pieces, such as the one that suggests that commanders are *moral arbiters.* This particular article is largely about the example that a commander needs to set, and it has been widely read within the military profession. If Plato demonstrated the problems associated with gods being the moral arbiters, then those problems multiply exponentially should every commander become a moral arbiter.[109]

The military remains an institution that strongly relies on doctrine and authority. Both must be justifiable through reason, not by edict, not by decree, not by faith. The military and related political institutions should remove all religious influence from its moral and political concerns. We should not be choosing our wars based on apocalyptic prophesies from a millennial mindset or going to war because the commander-in-chief gets orders from above and beyond to attack a country. War is too serious a matter to be left to the mystagogueries of faith. Matters of right and wrong, good and bad, should also be based on rationale that everyone can assent to, which means such matters cannot depend upon moral articles of faith. Chaplains and religious zealots and proselytizers should stay out of the moral and political affairs of the military. And they should not employ religion or spirituality in an instrumental way to recruit for crusades or to inspire courage on the battlefield—such instrumental use of religion diminishes both religion as well as moral courage.[110] While historians and Middle East regional specialists (for the most part particularists) spend their time pointing out the differences— through analysis—between Islam (mostly bad) and Christianity (mostly good) or Judaism (mostly good), philosophers see—through synthesis—more similarity than difference. All three of these religions are Abrahamic, and all Abrahamic religions are Oriental (Middle-Eastern). All Abrahamic religions share the same moral limitations: they are all dependent upon authority and sacred texts that can direct humans to inflict grave moral error upon other humans. For example, in *The Torture Debate*, edited by Karen J. Greenberg, who also edited *The Torture Papers*, there is a chapter that explains how "religious canons—Christian, Jewish, Islamic, and others—have condoned torture."[111] Some are now worried that religion and its influence in politics and war is growing so much that it may actually be rolling back the Enlightenment. The self-destructive irrationalities of faith act as viruses in the mind, plunging societies affected by Abrahamic viruses into epochs of darkness, dark ages that last a millennia or more. The Renaissance and the Enlightenment helped pull the West out of the Dark Ages, but the United States could unilaterally lead the West backwards with its religiosity. Both of the most influential theologians—Augustine and Aquinas—condone the killing or torture of heretics, respectively. Islam is several centuries behind the West and is still in its Dark Age having not yet experienced a Renaissance or an Enlightenment. I wonder how much better the world would be if the Abrahamic religions had never shown up on the scene. The once thriving ancient civilizations would have progressed unfettered without a Yahweh, Christ, or Mohammed.

Unfortunately, edicts from those in authority as well as Army doctrine must be written so that they can be immediately apprehended, without reflection. Reflection requires a suspension of judgment, and the hesitation required to think things through runs counter to the military premise that warriors must at all times be decisive. Doctrine must also be written so that people can immediately put the information to practical use. Doctrine is not a vehicle for reflection, nor can it simply stimulate thought or be written so that it requires comprehension, which requires reflection.[112] Perhaps the military at large is not yet ready to spend time thinking, reflecting, upon the subject.[113]

The military cannot afford to allow its warriors to continue to defer their reflection about moral matters, relegating the moral domain of the institution to moral authority, particularism, and virtue. Philosophy can help us to critique our practices in an edifying way. We do not have to perpetuate our own traditions unreflectively. We do not have to personally experience a particular situation before we can make moral judgments about a moral problem. When we are faced with a particular problem, we do not have to find someone with the same particular story in order to solve the problem at hand. We are not bound by our own histories or our own literature, our own stories. Heroes are the bearers of cultures, the bearers of traditions. If the traditions become faulty, if the institutions engage in moral error, then those heroes become faulty because of that moral error. Perhaps Homer had embodied in Achilles the tragic flaws of Greek warrior culture. Perhaps it is not the heroes that warriors should be looking to for an example. Perhaps they should consider the anti-heroes in the narratives and films of Joseph Heller, Tom Wolfe, James Jones, Stanley Kubrick, and Terence Malick, learning what the anti-heroes may have to teach us. Heroes are cultural insiders, signifying that culture. Anti-heroes are outsiders, challenging the culture. It's possible that what we attribute to a hero as a tragic flaw is actually a tragic flaw of that culture. So anyone who becomes heroic within a culture shares and symbolizes a cultural tragic flaw. Heroic narratives endorse and celebrate cultural norms, without genuinely challenging these norms. Anti-heroic narratives challenge cultural norms and ideals. Heroic narratives glorify war and anti-heroic narratives deny any glory in war. For example, Greek warrior society had an Achilles Heel. Anger does not simply undo the individual, Achilles. It is the Achilles Heel of all warrior cultures: anger or any of its family—hatred or revenge. We do not have to accept the hopeless view that war must always be as cruel as it has been or even that war is inevitable.

This chapter has looked closely at the major methods and sources of moral instruction. What they all have in common is a lack of reflection, the absence or avoidance of theoretical or philosophical inquiry. Moral authority lacks reasoned justification, particularly that of religious moral authority. We defer reflection if we act from moral authority. Yet, God and Country remain highly influential in the warrior's understanding of morality. Particularist narratives are also highly influential, and I have argued extensively why these are unreflective modes of thought, modes of battle sleep. We can look to philosophy to help us not only critique our past practices and stories, but we can also employ philosophy to help us to construct ways of thinking about living together that would be better, to live how we should live rather than simply to perpetuate how we have lived.

3

The Semi-Reflective Life

Instrumental Means

Instrumental means are, most simply, methods that help us achieve some end. "Deliberation, it might be held, is essentially the selection of means to some end. Here, the best known classical tag for the view is Aristotle's statement that 'we deliberate not about ends but about what contributes to ends.'"[1] In one sense, the previous chapter is about instrumental methods, if one could think of these broad approaches—authority, indoctrination, and particularism—as methods used to achieve some end. The methods discussed in chapter 2 are general approaches used by professions to achieve the end of teaching people ethics, even though teaching ethics may not be the final end. My critique of professional ethics up to this point revolves around these approaches that are unreflective, or pseudo-reflective. While the previous chapter explores topics that are instrumental in a wide sense, this chapter explores instrumental methods in a more narrow sense. Instead of the general approaches of authority, indoctrination, and particularism that are instrumental in that they are unreflective means to achieving ethics training and instruction in general, I am focusing on instrumental methods in a more narrow sense in this chapter, for the end of these narrow methods is some measure of reflection in ethics instruction. But they fall short of being fully reflective. Instrumental methods in this narrower sense are deliberate methods employed to get warriors to solve ethical problems.

Instrumental moral methods can lead to the misunderstanding of ethics as well as to the occasion of moral error. To make moral decisions using these instrumental methods is to live a semi-reflective life. Misguided moral methods and their ensuing practices litter the terrain of professional ethics, specifically the narrow field of military ethics or the more global concerns in the ethics of warfare. This critique will offer suggestions to help clear away some of this clutter. After looking at some examples of moral error due to the inadequate methods currently employed, I will offer some suggestions to improve these methods simply by taking advantage of a few philosophical distinctions. Finally, I will show in this chapter how means are inadequately connected to the ends that they serve. The military should refine its application of instrumental means, for they have led to moral error and as such are unjustified, because these moral methods currently employ inadequate decision procedures instead of philosophically conscious critical methods, and at times these instrumental means can become ends-in-themselves.

INSTRUMENTAL MEANS AND MORAL ERROR

Instrumental methods are not in themselves bad; on the contrary, many instrumental methods are quite useful, appropriate, and justifiable. They come in the form of decision-procedures and problem-solving techniques. These methods often feature considerations of optimizing value or maximizing efficiency or husbanding resources. They help engineers build bridges, doctors prescribe medicines, logisticians move armies, or even governments balance budgets and manage scarce resources. But they can also be employed to make the trains run more efficiently, regardless of cargo, destination, or purpose. Many professions currently emphasize ethical decision making[2] and are now employing moral methods that are in some way instrumental, employing means-ends reasoning. Even though professionals often employ these methods with the best of intentions, when people employ instrumental methods to solve moral problems, moral error can ensue. These instrumental moral methods are often quick and dirty procedures that simplify the moral problems too much in the name of expediency. Further, these methods replace the difficult task of transparent moral reasoning with simple yet inadequate decision procedures that are opaque. These decision procedures are opaque, hard to see through, because while they may tell us what to do, they do not tell us why we should do it. Additionally, even if the instrumental moral methods were adequate and transparent, these methods are often aimed at ends that are unreflective or unwarranted.

The ends that warriors work to achieve through their instrumental means are fixtures in the warrior consciousness: victory, mission accomplishment, survival, and force protection. These ends are rarely, if ever, questioned: They exist in the warrior psyche as articles of faith. These ends, firmly fixed, become the goals that warriors are willing to go to great lengths, sometimes any lengths, to achieve. The moral mode is set to a consequentialist default, with the fixed ends justifying any means necessary to bring them about. Ethical decision making procedures become tools to rationalize any method as long as the method can bring about the desired end. Because the procedure is actually couched as one that brings about a decision, the reasoning itself becomes secondary to the decision. Since decision is the focus, given that warriors are already trained in the generic process to make decisions by choosing between options, then it is natural for the ethical decision making process to be about choosing among options. The form of this procedure actually aborts the more important reasoning process in favor of generating options. So the form actually facilitates the construction of "ethical dilemmas," which is an inadequate description of a moral problem, as I will argue below.

Torture has done more harm than good. For those who object to the term "torture," the same is true of harsh interrogations. Political and military leaders have relaxed standards regarding the Constitutional requirement for the humane treatment and due process of all persons, whether they are U.S. citizens or not. It will take some time for the law to catch up with those leaders who set aside the law, but in principle those who are part of the executive branch of the government (the White House and the Department of Defense) cannot set aside statutory law with impunity. I keep hearing from our leaders in the executive branch that the detainees are not prisoners of war and therefore do not have the protections that prisoners should have. First, they should be treated as prisoners with a protected status until an appropriate legal procedure determines otherwise, by law. Additionally, even if a trial determines they are not prisoners, they would still have protections that have been violated. In any event, there is unquestionable, widespread, and manifest legal harm and moral error here. An Iraqi detainee drowned within LTC Nate Sassaman's battalion as a result of the systemic disregard for the relevant laws. The case of LTC Allen West, an artillery battalion commander in Operation Iraqi Freedom, provides another instructive example. Both of these battalion commanders were part of the 4th Infantry Division. West personally used heavy-handed interrogation techniques on a prisoner to gain information. Specifically, he fired his pistol next to the head of the prisoner. The prisoner provided information, which West claims in turn saved his soldier's lives. Recent investigations question the truth, content and value of the coerced information. Information gained this way is highly unreliable and it has the double penalty of being inadmissable later in a trial. Unfortunately, the duress caused by intimidating a prisoner with warning shots to the point in which they think they are in danger, even if successful in extracting information, amounts to assault. His commanding general chose to give West administrative punishment instead of convening a court-martial, and West was relieved of command and fined $5,000. West was allowed to retire from the Army and has done so due to the incident. The Army, the 4th Infantry Division Commander, and West admit to wrongdoing, but West claims it was worth it and that he would do it again to protect his troops. The language used in West's case is couched as a moral dilemma. He could either 1) follow the law or 2) protect his troops. In actuality, among many of his choices were these two: He could either follow the law or break the law; his first choice would allegedly lead to further harm to his troops, and his second choice would allegedly protect them. A complex ethical problem, because of the form of a dilemma, gets reduced to only two choices. One choice leads to a "good" consequence, and the other leads to a bad one. Since only one of the generated choices produces the "good" outcome, that choice usually trumps the other one. This form of problem solving, and the way the dilemma is formed, leads one to believe that there is only one choice to bring about the good consequence, when there may in fact be more than one. This consequential approach will favor bringing about the good consequence at the expense of disregarding the need to use appropriate means—it favors outcome over method. Going back to the types of errors discussed in the introduction, the procedure favors bringing about a good end over preventing harm. It favors Type I errors over Type II errors, even though the first type of error is worse than the first. There are some awakening warriors who see the systemic scope of moral failure that produces examples such as Sassaman and West. However, I'm afraid that these two have far more supporters than critics within the war machine. While each of these cases involved personal responsibility on the part of the commanders, the systemic problem is a much more difficult problem to address.

West may not understand why the first type of error is worse than the first. One reason is that our pre-theoretic intuitions are naturally programmed to think in terms of direct cause and effect, to think locally instead of systemically, to think narrowly instead of globally. The commission of Type I errors may appear to bring about some good locally. But they cause much greater harm on a systemic basis. West's single act of assault no doubt changed the perceptions regarding operating methods used by American warriors for the worse. If this breach of law protecting captives had been more widespread, the very fragile arrangement of protections based on the concept of *benevolent quarantine* could quickly break down, escalating violence and making the entire situation much more dangerous for everybody. A nonmoral example of this more complex notion of causation may help illustrate how seemingly productive local actions can have a negative wider effect. The summer of 1993 produced weather conditions that caused major flooding of both the Mississippi and Missouri Rivers. To protect themselves, people living along the rivers built up their levies to the best of their abilities, only to experience even worse flood damage than expected. But the seemingly productive actions taken locally actually exacerbated the problem. On a wider scale, the collection of levies actually channeled the water with much more speed and force, causing much greater damage overall than if they had done nothing. Wider, unintended consequences occur often during war as long as warriors do not think about ethical problems in more complex terms. Seemingly sensible local actions are often the cause of worse consequences on a wider scale. To use a military example, consider unrestrictive submarine warfare during World War II. At first, German submarines followed maritime law by attacking only military vessels and by rescuing people stranded by sinking ships. In order to protect military cargo, American and British shipping would fly "false flag" by using merchant ships. In turn, German submarines would attack merchant vessels and military vessels alike. After attacking the *Laconia*, German submarines spent hours, even days, rescuing British soldiers, civilians, and Italian prisoners. When an American bomber attacked the submarines, they broke off the rescue. Admiral Dönitz issued the famous Laconia Order, which meant the long-standing convention of sea rescue could no longer be honored. Now merchant ships would routinely be armed to protect themselves and had orders to attack or ram into submarines. In each case, the local measures taken to bring about the good consequence created a systemic and unintended effect that only brought about a more dangerous and worse consequence. Escalation continued until unrestricted submarine warfare became the norm. Interestingly, when Dönitz received his jail sentence at Nuremberg, charges involving unrestricted submarine warfare were dropped not because America was engaged in the same activity in the Pacific (which it was), but because the applicable maritime law was voided once noncombatant vessels acted as combatants. Either we arm our merchant vessels or they will remain vulnerable; either we attack them or they will attack us. President Bush argues that either Congress will change the laws so that harsh interrogations are no longer considered torture, or he will lose one of his major weapons for him to fight his war on terrorism. He is committing the Type I error (harming an innocent person) for fear of making a Type II error (enabling terrorists to harm us). In his efforts to go after Osama and those like him, however, he has significantly contributed to the creation of a thousand potential Osamas. The problem formation into a *dilemma* helps to create the problem. This type of problem resolution of "moral dilemmas" goes awry because it is a misguided moral method. Philosophical ethics can aid us in understanding and even help us in more adequately solving this type of problem. I will compare this less adequate solution with a more adequate solution later in this chapter. This next section will detail some of the specific weaknesses of these misguided methods, followed by suggestions for a more adequate approach.

INADEQUATE DECISION PROCEDURES

LTC West's moral dilemma is in need of revision. His own misunderstanding of the complex nature of his actions could stand for some revision. And warriors who only semi-reflectively judge his actions to be "right" and "justified" could use a more robust understanding of the real ethical nature of West's problem. The ethical decision-making process that employs the concept of a dilemma imposes a false reality, a naïve reality. There are many such processes that invoke some form of false reality. One quite prevalent invocation of naïve realism (meaning that the moral choice we construct is exactly as it appears, or, more exactly, one specific description of the appearance) occurs whenever people speak of a moral problem as a moral dilemma and use the dilemma as a problem-solving tool. A dilemma can mean—among other things—that one has only two alternatives in deciding what to do. Discussions in applied ethics are rife with this type of thinking. A moral dilemma is one that presents only two alternatives—the positing of a false metaphysical reality. There may be cases in which only two alternatives are possible for a moral choice, but these would be extremely rare, if they existed at all—logically or practically. People versed in formal logic would recognize the "ethical dilemma" immediately as a false dilemma; people versed in informal logic would recognize it as *black or white* thinking.[3]

The dilemma is often couched as a choice between two values. There is no necessity to think that values have to stand in tension, or be contradictory. Within professional ethics, the most misunderstood—and perhaps most talked about—concept is that of loyalty. Professional ethicists virtually always want to have loyalty competing with some other notion, often that of honesty. This is imposing a false duality on the issue, when bringing these two values in conflict, again invoking naïve realism. There is no reason to think that honesty and loyalty have to be at odds all the time, or any time for that matter: That is a false assumption with which to begin the process of deliberation. Again, there may possibly be instances of true dilemmas (in the ontological sense), but in moral choices there are almost always additional choices that would be compromises, compensations, or integrations.[4] Ethicists conflate the two senses of dilemma, and they treat their *epistemological* dilemma (not knowing what to do) as an *ontological*, or *metaphysical*, dilemma (having only two choices). The failure is that rarely do applied ethicists describe the ethical situation adequately.[5] What happens here is that they take what happens to be a *dilemma*, meaning they simply don't know what is right in a situation, and they turn it into a *dilemma* in a different sense, meaning that they are positing a moral reality that admits of having only two choices, falling prey to the ambiguity of the term by conflating its usage, turning an *epistemological* dilemma (not knowing what to do) into a *metaphysical* dilemma (having only two choices).

Rushworth Kidder, a popular ethicist and founder of the Institute for Global Ethics, uses this misguided method, or lack of method.[6] Throughout his books and his published material he uses the language of dilemmas as value pairs: truth versus loyalty, individual versus community, short term versus long term, justice versus mercy. In all these cases, he posits a false reality. Moral problems often do not exist with only two morally relevant features. And, naturally, a moral problem could have an indefinite and indeterminate number of moral features. In reality, these pairs—if they were ever really operative and relevant—need not even be in tension. Alan Donagan argues that consistency is an important feature of legitimate systems of morality. It would not make sense to set up a moral system in which we would be in a state of constant inconsistency. He says he knows "of no specific case of *perplexity simpliciter* that has plausibly been alleged to arise in any competently formulated traditional moral system."[7] And yet this unsatisfactory feature of perplexity simpliciter (a built-in problem, perplexity, of the system, even before the system is applied to solve a problem) is the presumption that is present in any ethical decision-making process that employs the language of dilemmas.

Values simply do not have to exist as dualities. We do not necessarily live in a moral universe in which people have to choose between these pairs of features. Principles, maxims, and acts actually exist in a many-many relationship; they do not have to relate in pairs.[8] Values, or goods, or principles do not exist in a one-to-one relationship with actions, either. A more plausible way to think about the relationship of values with actions, or maybe principles with actions, is that there is a many-many relationship among values and actions. This means that there would be several operative values in LTC West's problem. Not only is loyalty to his soldiers operative, but most likely values such as honor, integrity, wisdom, duty, chivalry, justice, law-abidingness, and courage are also operative. Operative values or principles would relate to the actions that agents perform in a many-many relationship. Ethicists who operate based on a false moral reality are not unlike medieval physicians who diagnosed illnesses and treated patients based on the four humors or alchemists who practiced their craft based on the four elements.

But just because values or principles may be more numerous does not mean that we can simply add steps to the decision-making process in order to acknowledge the complexity of moral problem solving. The Army now uses an ethical decision-making process that includes seven steps: 1) clearly define the ethical problem, 2) employ applicable laws and regulations, 3) reflect on the ethical values and their ramifications, 4) consider other applicable moral principles, 5) reflect upon appropriate ethical theories, 6) commit to and implement the best ethical solution, and 7) assess results and modify plan as required. The federal government also has a *ten-step ethical decision-making plan* for government officers and employees. The ten-step plan includes: "1) define the problem, 2) identify the goals, 3) list applicable laws and regulations, 4) list the ethical values at stake, 5) name all the stakeholders, 6) gather additional information, 7) state all feasible solutions, 8) eliminate

unethical options, 9) rank remaining solutions, and 10) commit to and implement the best ethical solution."[9] While the plan leaves it up to the individual
to rank the solutions in step nine, even relying sometimes on intuition and
"gut feeling," it does have the positive addition of eliminating unethical
options in step eight. As trivial and obvious as this step may sound, it is an
important addition to have a step that rules out unethical options. If the
Army process had included this step, or if warriors were even aware of the
values contained in the joint ethical decision-making model, would warriors
still think that LTC West was right? Or with greater awareness, would they
think that West should have acted differently, by following step eight, which
says to "eliminate unethical options," given that his actual choice was unethical (based on the step requiring him to consider applicable laws and regulations)? While these multiple-step decision procedures may be better than the
simplistic dualistic dilemma construct, they are still inadequate.

The ten-step plan does attempt to set forth logical, systematic dissec-
tion of the problem, in the same spirit as Descartes' twenty-one *Rules for the
Direction of the Mind*.[10] Yet even so, the ten-step plan, apart from thinking of
it as having the appearance of a systematic method, offers no real direction in
actually solving the ethical problem. By mixing together goals, laws, values,
and stakeholders, one would be navigating through overly variegated, incommensurable criteria, and no method would be adequate as a guide through
such a maze. The goals may conflict, the laws will be underdetermined, and
the values themselves would provide a bewildering array of overlapping or
inconsistent concepts. More is not necessarily better, when it comes to the
complexity of the structure of a decision-procedure—especially when the
method itself is incoherent and inconsistent. In other words, the ten-step
ethical decision-making plan may not help LTC West any more than the
seven-step ethical decision-making process did.

The Joint Ethics Regulation also lists ten ethical values: honesty,
integrity, loyalty, accountability, fairness, caring, respect, promise keeping,
responsible citizenship, and the pursuit of excellence.[11] An airman would also
have to consider the Air Force values, which are integrity, service before self,
and excellence. A sailor or marine would have to consider the three Navy
values: honor, courage, and commitment. And a soldier would have to add
the Army's seven values—loyalty, duty, respect, selfless service, honor,
integrity, and "personal" courage—to the ten joint values, three of which are
in common with the joint values. Then throw in duty, honor, and country, if
one had gone to West Point. Adding them together, the soldier has fifteen
doctrinal values, the marine thirteen, and the airman eleven.

In the military, there is no discussion that adequately defines what
"value" means, or establishes what criteria would make up a value, or
describes how values function. Since most service members have no con-

scious notion of what a value might be or how it is to function, there is no coherent conception of how they are to apply values. For example, consider describing a value and how it functions through the use of a metaphor. I mention thinking of them in this way only to illustrate how differently people may think about values. Some may view a value metaphorically as establishing an ethical "floor" (a minimal conception—meaning we have to be in accord with the value) and some view a value as being a "ceiling" (a maximal conception—meaning that it is an idealized goal that we can never quite achieve).[12] Others may view values as "gates," "funnels," "markers," "guideposts," or even "compass points." Each of these metaphors poses challenges in portraying what values may be and how they function. Metaphors, while being useful in bringing out some analogous features, always run the risk of being overextended.[13]

As for values-based organizations, most people who talk about them speak as if organizations will change drastically for the better if they become values-based. Weren't the Nazis a values-based organization? Himmler declared that the SS values were loyalty, obedience, bravery, and truthfulness.[14] They sound strikingly familiar. Having values or being values-based will not guarantee morality. The problem is that there is never enough thought going into what these values might be, how they might relate to one another, how they fit into a larger ethical context, how they function in character development, or how limited they are when it comes to guiding action. For practical ethicists, values are often those beliefs that they grew up with, that their parents gave them, or that they learned in church. They are also values that serve and protect the institution. Again, the values are reified into entities that presume a type of moral realism. Most discussions about values remain utterly vacuous because people do not reflect upon them enough to figure out what they really are and what metaphysical assumptions they are positing. Individual values can refer to very different categories of things: goods, moral virtues, obligations, principles, and so on. For example, while courage may be a moral virtue in that it is a state of character or a disposition, duty is not a moral virtue because it is not a state of character or a disposition. The history of axiology is variegated; there is no single systematic development or taxonomy of values. Interestingly, Nietzsche is the philosopher most responsible for introducing the word "value" into our moral vocabulary, when he discusses the revaluation or the transvaluation of values.[15] I say "interestingly" because most of the people who make much ado about values in all likelihood have a tremendous bias against Nietzsche. Dewey notes the problems of understanding values since they range from being emotional ejaculations to transcendent revelations.[16]

With so many possibilities of incoherent and inconsistent conceptual schemes operating in the background of these decision-procedures, I argue that the current decision-procedures are inadequate. Once the deep background features of these decision-procedures are disclosed, one can see why they are unsound and can lead to immoral actions and bad consequences. Instead of thinking of these instrumental methods as decision-procedures, procedures that can lead to "the best ethical answer," perhaps we should be thinking of them as critical methods. While decision procedures are finite and closed, critical methods are indefinite and open. Decision-procedures provide answers in which we invest heavily; critical methods can modestly show us that some answers are perhaps better than other answers, or are less worse than others. But critical methods also show us that these answers are always open to revision. Decision-procedures are often applied unself-consciously, without having their deep structures disclosed. In contrast, critical methods are employed fully self-consciously, with the deep structures exposed. Critical methods employ great care, analysis, and accuracy, since the usage of "critical" here is derivative of the Continental usage of "critique," which means essentially "analysis." We would be seeking too much precision if we thought that ethical decision-procedures could give us answers with any degree of certainty. We should not seek the precision that decision-procedures pretend to guarantee, "since the educated person seeks exactness in each area to the extent that the nature of the subject allows."[17] In the next section, I will offer an improved conception of developing and employing values. The section does not pretend to present any decision-procedure with definite answers, but does show how a more careful, analytical critical method can provide some answers that are better than others. Philosophically self-conscious critical methods will enhance moral understanding and reduce moral error over unself-conscious decision-procedures. Philosophy can help to expose the function and utility of values and their relatively low status within the broad scheme of moral understanding. For example, the Schlesinger Report on the detainee abuse scandal, contained in *The Torture Papers*, concludes that values did very little in helping to deliberate between right and wrong in this sad development. "Major service programs such as the Army's 'core values,' however, fail to adequately prepare soldiers working in detention operations."[18]

A PHILOSOPHICAL CRITICAL METHOD

One inadequate possibility, then, would be for the military to pay close attention to categorization and to develop a self-consciously constructed framework of values that function from vastly different categories, knowing up front that these values may overlap each other or leave huge spaces in between, or may even be completely inconsistent, incompatible, or incommensurable. Another more adequate option is to construct a set of values that are more or less consistent and may even work in concert because they do belong in the same category. This second option is possible if we were to construct a set of values that are moral virtues, in the philosophical, not ordinary, sense. A set of moral virtues as values would offer certain advantages that other conceptions would not have.

A set of values made up of moral virtues, while not being perfect, would at least better meet the demands of the criteria set forth for the formation of categories. I am not arguing here that virtue ethics is not without its challenges, and I am not arguing that it is necessarily better than other competing schemes. I am demonstrating, though, certain advantages that viewing values as virtues would have, as long as we are faced with the inevitability of using values. It happens to be a sociological phenomenon right now that institutions are stuck in the ethical paradigm of thinking of ethics in terms of values. Until that changes, it might be a good moral strategy to develop a more coherent and workable set of values, given the requirement to work within that framework. I could just as easily have developed a set of values that were deontic in nature, or even consequentialist in nature, but I have chosen to put forth and examine a set of values that are moral virtues. We have a rich tradition of virtues and we can draw upon the robust ethical theory that virtues are embedded within. The theory has elements that are cognizant of means as well as ends, and it pays particular attention to the important notions of moral agency. The Greek word *ethos*, closely associated with its primary meaning, "character," illustrates the importance of the relationship between ethics and agency, in ancient Greece as well as today.[19] Much of the emphasis on values comes from this interest in developing and possessing good character. Virtue theory also has prominent notions that relate to proper ends, which are also important in an ethical scheme. *Arete* is Greek for "excellence," and when we are speaking of Aristotelian virtue ethics, we are not only speaking of excellence as something we aim for, but we are also talking about excellence of character. Since the theory surrounding virtues and excellence pays attention to the agent, the end, and the act as well, I will speak of a set of values based on virtues as an aretaic model or approach.

While virtue theory is a particularly active pursuit today among moral philosophers, with richly laden distinctions and concepts, the practice of it developed naturally. Natural language can handle many of the concepts with relative ease, when compared to some other moral schemes. Aretaic ethical language, whether it is used for making decisions about how to act or for making judgments about the self or others, uses terms such as "admirable" for virtuous acts or people and "deplorable" for nonvirtuous acts or people. There are many synonyms for either the positive (excellent, honorable, esteemed, respectable, masterful) or negative (reprehensible, dishonorable, shameful, disgraceful, lamentable, contemptible) judgments. An act, an agent, or an end could be honorable based on the degree of conformity to the virtue of honor, or it could be dishonorable. And moral schemes use their own language of judgments. Other moral schemes employ natural language in their judgments. Deontic schemes employ the language of *right* and *wrong*, language that is normally evaluative of means. Consequentialist schemes employ the language of *good* and *bad*, language that is normally evaluative of ends. Aretaic language is at least as versatile as language from the other traditions because it can often—but not always—relate to at least one or more of the three modes: the act, the end, or the agent.

A powerful critique of virtue ethics centers upon the idea that it does not pay enough attention to the complexities of right action. It is possible to think about issues of right action, even within a virtue theory, if we think of actions being in a way derivative of the virtues.[20] We can subsume actions under virtues. We can pick virtually any virtue and derive an ethical prescription from it: "act courageously," or "be honest." Naturally, this becomes a problem unless we develop a good understanding of what courage and honesty are. I have argued in chapter 2, the chapter discussing particularism, that we cannot be satisfied simply by unreflectively following examples, for, as Kant instructs us, example can be "fatal to morality."[21] We should not simplemindedly just ask ourselves how one of our heroes may act. When it comes to private matters, George W. Bush may very well consult his favorite philosopher and ask, "What would Jesus do?" But what kind of insights could Bush get by asking, "Who would Jesus bomb?" Virtue theory does, however, somewhat rely on this very notion that I am challenging, the notion that moral judgments, in a virtue ethical scheme, become a matter of perception, rather than a matter of tedious mental ratiocination.[22] Martha Nussbaum says,

> in all these ways, general principles, if seen as normative for correct practical judgment, prove insufficient. Nor, for related reasons, is there any general algorithm that will suffice to generate, in each case, the virtuous choice. For one thing, such algorithms have a marked tendency to reduce the many intrinsically valuable things recognized in an Aristotelian account to one thing, varying in quantity only; for another, they simply seem to impose too much on judges in advance. Situations must be grasped with an "eye" for all their complexities: in short, as Aristotle twice remarks, "the discrimination lies in the perception."[23]

Even so, if we did spend enough time to understand the virtues and to philosophically examine and justify the examples, then these virtues could, if even in a minimal way, help us to guide action. If these "perceptions" could over time through deliberation be justified, then it may be justifiable to rely somewhat on these virtues as guides to action.

Several thinkers have pointed out that values differ for different groups. While societal values are ideals for members of society at large, we know that many members of society do not live up to those values. For Aristotle, of course, the rarity of a virtue was a quality that helped to identify it as a virtue. For people in professions, operating in specific capacities, fulfilling specific functions, these values may be more important. While all of us are not courageous, it is important for a fireman, policeman, or soldier to be courageous, for example. Many of these values, while ideals for most people, are very important for members of the military profession. The military would not function as well as it could if it did not highly value courage and honor. Perhaps the most important value, or virtue, of all for the military profession would be that of practical wisdom. Practical wisdom (*phronesis* for Aristotle) embodied the full maturity of well-developed character from the integration of perceptual, deliberative, affective, and practical faculties.[24]

West Point's Honor Code enumerates proscriptions against lying, cheating, and stealing: "A cadet will not lie, cheat, or steal, nor tolerate those who do." These proscriptions are each related to a virtue: not lying is connected to *honesty*, not cheating to *fairness*, and not stealing to *respect*. These virtues are the positive correlates to the negatively stated rules that exist in the form of proscriptions. Honesty is more than merely not lying; fairness is more than merely not cheating; respect is more than merely not stealing. These proscriptions are necessary but not sufficient parts of the aretaic wholes. The aretaic wholes in this way can be more primary and more encompassing notions than their associated, derived proscriptions. Since these aretaic virtues entail at least these rules, the virtues can, at least in even a modest way, provide some guidance toward right action. We might get more mileage out of an honor code that enumerates a few virtues rather than one that enumerates several proscriptions.

In an aretaic ethical scheme, the agent becomes virtuous by actually doing virtuous acts. He becomes virtuous by making virtuous attitudes, actions, and emotions part of himself; in other words, he habituates himself into being virtuous. Habit is an important part of Aristotle's ethical scheme, "but the virtues we get by first exercising them, as also happens in the case of the arts as well. For the things we have to learn before we can do them, we learn by doing them, e.g. men become builders by building and lyre-players by playing the lyre; so too we become just by doing just acts, temperate by doing temperate acts, brave by doing brave acts."[25] We should not confuse the Greek word *hexis* with one of the common connotations of "habit." Habit, in an aretaic scheme, does not mean that something is performed involuntarily; "for Aristotle moral virtues are paragons of voluntariness, and thus the very opposite of habits."[26] "Habit" in an Aristotelian sense carries with it the idea that we are doing it by choice. Yves Simon has recommended that we use the Latin word *habitus* instead of "habit," since "habit" does not carry with it the same notion of voluntariness.

One very useful distinction out there in virtue theory is that between self-regarding and other-regarding virtues. This distinction is useful because it helps to separate virtues so chosen into different categories. Since they are in different categories, the distinction helps us to pick virtues that are more than less mutually exclusive, more than less exhaustive of the "moral space," and are separated by the differentia distinguishing between self- and other-regarding. By having virtues that are in different categories, we avoid redundancy and help to cover more ground. Self-regarding virtues match up very nicely with our present-day notion of character traits. They exemplify "ethos" in a primary sense, that of character. Other-regarding virtues are not character traits of the agent, but we can say they exemplify "ethos" in its secondary sense, that of an ethical atmosphere or spirit.

Self-regarding virtues are key to a virtue-ethical scheme. They are primary to and necessary for the other-regarding virtues. In fact, self-regarding virtues are enabling virtues, in that only when the agent possesses the self-regarding virtues can he be capable of adequately possessing and displaying the other-regarding virtues. For example, it takes fortitude, consistency, and self-control (all self-regarding virtues) to be able to engage in the virtue of loyalty (an other-regarding virtue). It takes at least one of the self-regarding virtues, and normally some combination of them, to be able to exercise any of the other-regarding virtues. These self-regarding virtues being closely akin to character traits enable their possessors to act for themselves as well as for others. By enabling the agent, the aretaic notion of a virtue gives fundamental evaluative significance to the well-being and moral agency of the self as well as significance to others.[27] Self-regarding virtues would include, but not be limited to, prudence, fortitude, circumspection, judiciousness, sagacity, equanimity, providence, farsightedness, policy, probity, patience, consistency, self-control, self-mastery, moderation, rationality, wisdom, integrity, candor, courage, and honor. Other-regarding virtues would include justice, kindness, generosity, benevolence, compassion, commitment, and loyalty.[28] Significantly, there are many more self-regarding than other-regarding virtues. Contemporary critics may view this as one of the weaknesses of virtue ethics, since contemporary commonsense morality holds that ethics is largely about helping others. In defense of the ancient conception, however, it could be argued that there is much work to be done to improve the self. And not only is there much work to do to improve the self, but being able to help others depends upon this self-improvement.

Then what about the Army's value of selfless service? If self-regarding virtues are important, then the concept of selfless service is an awkward idea, because it denotes an annihilation of, or at least an indifference to, the self. The military may want to subordinate some aspects of individuality in order to function as an organization, but it is not appropriate or even linguistically accurate to say that people should be "selfless." This language has caused at a minimum great confusion and quite possibly even great harm. It resonates with religious warriors, because of the idea of self sacrifice at the heart of the Abrahamic faiths. Selflessness in the sense of self-sacrifice is a very frightful idea, since the men who sacrificed themselves by flying planes into buildings six years ago were selfless. As a governmental institution, warriors should avoid selflessness because of its coded linkage with religion, given the potential for religious extremism. The virtuous mean may very well lie closer to selflessness than to selfishness, but it would not be at either of these two extremes. The Air Force has a more reasonable and less confusing way of talking about this idea by phrasing it as "service before self."

Aristotle had a name for this legitimate sense of self-regard, *philautia*, which would include the idea of having a healthy self-regard as opposed to selflessness. Included in having a healthy regard would be self-respect and self-esteem. Self-respect and self-esteem are important in being able to hold esteem for and respect others. To be truly selfless would require that people would utterly lack these qualities. Rather than telling soldiers that they should be selfless, the Army should be outlining and delimiting the boundaries for self-regard, recognizing the role that self-regard plays in establishing positive moral agency. In this way, the military could help to establish a soldiery that possessed a healthy and appropriate self-respect and self-esteem, rather than paternalistically creating a schizophrenic soldiery, one that is expected to do something that is impossible—to become selfless.

What would it mean to be selfless? What would it mean to the soldier to be told to be selfless? Should not the military mean what it says? If the Army does nothing other than tell people they have to be selfless, then the soldier will very likely be living a contradiction. On the one hand they are being told to be selfless, and on the other hand they probably know this is impossible, even if these conflicting ideas remain undisclosed and unarticulated. In logic, anything follows from a contradiction. Likewise, in this case anything can and does follow from this contradiction. It would be very hard to be in charge of people or to lead units in combat without some kind of ego. If the soldier thinks that he both should and should not be selfless, knowing that this does not make any sense, then being told to be selfless may not mean anything to the soldier. Any kind of action follows from this contradiction. For example, there are many megalomaniacs in the military. There are also many who work constantly, never take their vacations, and drive their people the same way. In many cases the megalomaniac is also the workaholic. So, the egoistic and narcissistic actions in the military profession may follow if only indirectly from the lack of guidance people get in acknowledging the need for and development of a healthy self-regard. The Army would be better off defining the boundaries rather than letting people act in a variety of ways since they cannot live up to the expectation. They should not include "self-less service" as a value, primarily because it is not a virtue but part of a formula for deep neuroses.

The value of selfless service is there in large part due to the recent trend in military ethics to create a military that is made up of *moral saints*. Selflessness is derivative of our religious heritage. There is much language that includes the rhetoric of "selflessness" and "sacrifice." It is no accident that the language of selflessness and sacrifice burgeoned while the chaplains had influence over the domain of ethics in the military. Susan Wolf discusses the weaknesses in character that would exist in a person who happened to be a moral saint.[29] The same defects would exist in moral saints who happened to be military, maybe even more so. The soldiers who were truly selfless would work themselves and their people too hard, and the soldiers who were too sacrificial would needlessly sacrifice themselves and their people too much. A truly selfless person would by definition lack important qualities.

Another useful distinction will help to relieve some redundancy. There is a distinction to be made between honor and integrity. Honor is irrevocably tied to public codes, where integrity is based on personal codes. Integrity comes from the same root as the word "integer" and denotes wholeness (*integritas*), but this wholeness is relative and self-defined. I can act dishonorably by failing to live up to a public code, but I will act with a lack of integrity only if I violate my own private code. If this were not the case, then it would make no sense to talk about one's personal integrity. Based on this distinction, some people may be critical of honor because it would be relative to each public group that defined its public code. But if this critique did hold, while honor would be relative to each group, integrity would be relative to each person. An institution such as the military should have more reason perhaps to favor the virtue of honor to the virtue of integrity.[30]

There is another reason to pick just one of these two virtues. Both function as higher-order virtues, meaning that they encompass or comprise other virtues. All other operative virtues can be thought of as species, or subsets, or instantiations of either honor or integrity. For example, if we lack any of the other virtues—say, courage—then we also lack honor if courage is part of our public code. Similarly, we would lack integrity if courage were part of our private code. Since each of these virtues—honor and integrity—encompasses all of the other virtues, any scheme that included both of them would be redundant, unless the two sets of virtues differed. If they are redundant, then we should not use both of them. If they are different, then we may have an additional problem of having members of a group who do not share the values of the organization.

Integrity and honor are identical in a shame culture because there the personal code and the private code merge.[31] Anthropologists, historians, and philosophers talk about shame cultures, which have existed in ancient Greece and Rome as well as in the Far East. Shame cultures do not need to rely on guilt as part of their moral psychology. In our moral psychology, we feel guilt when we violate a public code, and we feel shame when we violate our private code. Their prime moral motivation is to avoid shame, and this shame avoidance can motivate significant demands and constraints. When the private and public codes merge then it is enough to avoid only shame to ensure both integrity and honor. Many martial organizations have been shame cultures in that they have tied their own personal codes of integrity to their public codes of honor, and they have placed a high price on the concept of honor. If soldiers are persuaded by arguments for taking honor seriously, then that is also a good argument for thinking that honor is indispensable, further reason for keeping honor and abandoning integrity (since honor would accomplish exactly the same results). Many military theorists and ethicists have made arguments for honor codes. Some argue against such codes because of the difficulty in enforcing them. But despite the difficulties, they may still serve a valuable function in an ethical understanding within an organization—if the honor code could be well-formed and articulated.

If the military profession, or any part of it—say, the Army—were to adopt an honor code, the code should be constructed using positive forms of the character traits or virtues, rather than listing them in the form of legalistic proscriptions, as in West Point's honor code. For example, instead of telling people not to lie, cheat, or steal, the code should tell people that they should work to possess the virtues of honesty, fairness, and respect. These three virtues do not make up an exhaustive list, but we should be able to see that the negative legalistic formulation of proscriptions is a more minimal account than the positive correlative formulation made up of virtues. In other words, "fairness" is a much more encompassing notion than the avoidance of stealing.

So, if I were to offer a recommendation for an honor code, it would begin, naturally, with the virtue of honor. Since honor is a second-order virtue that comprises the other virtues, the next step is to select the relevant constituent virtues that would compose the virtue of honor. It would also make sense to select some virtues that are self-regarding and some that are other-regarding. With such a mix of virtues, we would cover more of the ethical space.

Three self-regarding virtues would be important in a military organization. Honesty is important and is the first to consider. Practically speaking, honesty helps people to carry out morally justified means and achieve ends, although it becomes a scarce commodity during conflict. It is also important logically, because a lack of honesty would make it impossible to achieve being honorable due to the inconsistencies dishonesty would cause. This reasoning also applies to integrity. Some people consider integrity to be chiefly honesty. The only reason honesty is important to integrity is that it would be impossible to maintain integrity while being dishonest. The second essential self-regarding virtue to consider is courage. Courage is an easy one for which to argue. It was one of the cardinal virtues and the virtue most discussed by Aristotle, in a military context. Both honesty and courage are important enabling virtues. Yet perhaps the most important enabling self-regarding virtue is that of practical wisdom, which is the third to consider in this ethical scheme. Wisdom is the intellectual virtue that probably more than any others allows us to exercise and develop the other moral virtues.

Three other-regarding virtues are important in a military honor code that features virtues as its constituents. The first I will recommend is that of justice, since it is a bit more encompassing than fairness. The exercise of fairness is a key element in ensuring justice. Fairness is the positive virtue correlate to the proscription against cheating. So, practically, it works to ensure that all the members in a military organization train, learn, and develop into competent soldiers. It also goes a long way in ensuring that justice is achieved on the battlefield, since fairness is an important idea that undergirds any conception of chivalry. The second other-regarding virtue in this scheme would be respect, which is important for the members of the same organization. But it is equally if not more important when considering the enemy. Respecting the moral equality of the enemy is vital to moral action on the battlefield.[32] Had LTC West understood philosophically the value of respect, he would not have assaulted his prisoner. Had the military understood the value of respect, even for the enemy, we would not have engaged in widescale abuse at Abu Ghraib or Guantanamo, nor would we have turned captives over to secret torture facilities in other countries. A philosophical understanding of respect would be extremely helpful, especially Kantian theory that deals with respecting persons. The third virtue to consider is loyalty. Loyalty is a vital military virtue, as long as it is properly understood as entailing only legitimate obligations. No one should be able to exact an illegitimate obligation from someone in the name of the virtue of loyalty. In other words, a senior should not be able to judge a junior as being disloyal if the senior imposes an illegitimate obligation.

I have argued not to include the "value" of duty in this list, primarily because it is not an aretaic value. The concept of duties in ethics belongs to a completely different tradition in the history of ethics. Basing ethics on virtues largely directs people toward developing themselves and performing positive actions. In contrast, basing ethics on duties can at times, but does not necessarily, direct people toward restricting themselves and avoiding proscribed actions. The other reason not to include duty as a "value" is that it comprises the different sets of obligations that one has. These various obligations are the sources of potential moral conflict, especially if one does not have the tools to think through the various conflicts toward satisfactory solutions. One of the major strengths of having a system of values that are virtues is the idea that virtues exist in a unity. Within virtue theory, this idea is captured by the doctrine of the unity of the virtues. The virtues work together, not in conflict with one another. In fact, they are not supposed to work at all unless all of them work together since the exercise of one virtue is not even supposed to be possible without the presence of the other virtues.

We can see that the virtues are interdependent, but what happens if they come into apparent conflict? Principles can come into conflict. This is now a possibility, since I have included loyalty as a virtue, and I've also stipulatively defined loyalty as entailing legitimate obligations. Since obligations involve potential conflict, people who value loyalty may potentially come into conflict when trying to live up to the obligations entailed by their loyalties. It is possible to arrange the varying loyalties lexically, which means that they exist in a nonbranching hierarchy of importance (not technically a taxonomy), from most important to least important. The Navy has adopted such a hierarchy because "the Naval Academy now teaches a hierarchy of loyalties: to the Constitution, the country, the Navy, the ship, the shipmate, and lastly, the self."[33] The Navy does not prescribe loyalty to the boss, which is important because it avoids the difficulties that the Army is facing with its rhetoric of loyalty to superiors—loyalty to the boss harkens back to the loyalty oaths to commanders that rogue armies require. Another important addition to the Naval model is that the self is not extinguished, but is part of the set of obligations one has. A person with such a model would understand that her loyalty to herself or her unit has maximum freedom from constraint, unless those loyalties conflicted with any of the lexically superior loyalties.

If we are going to have an honor code or if we are going to have to work with a set of values, then I would propose the following virtues as values. The honor code would consist of seven virtues, beginning with honor. Under *honor*, it would include the three self-regarding virtues of *honesty*, *courage*, and *wisdom*. It would also include the other-regarding virtues of *justice*, *respect*, and *loyalty*. The virtues would act in harmony, as long as they were properly understood and practiced. Character would be the focus of the ethical scheme, which reinforces its aretaic nature, and is both the subject and the object of acting virtuously. Excellence is the aretaic term that describes the person who has mastered not only herself, but also all the virtues. This conception covers all the ethical requirements in any of the competing schemes of values. For example, a person with character, with fully developed virtue, would do her duty. The converse relationship may not necessarily hold. We have all kinds of people who do their duty (for any number of reasons) who may not have fully developed character. As a Chinese proverb reminds us, "when the wrong person does the right thing, it usually turns out wrong."[34] A virtuous person would perform the right action for the right reason and would also have the right emotions. Emotions, against the background of this theory, could provide deep insights into that aspect of ourselves we call character. The virtuous person would be "integrated," acting for the right reason, reasoning based on critical philosophical deliberation, deliberating in accord with previous virtuous action, and acting with a consistent pattern of appropriate attendant emotions.

When talking of emotions here, the notion includes the sense of long-standing, consistent, dispositional emotions. These features are characterized not only by the emotion itself, but also by the accompanying desire to have that emotion. For Aristotle, the *phronemos*, or the person who manifests phronesis, or practical wisdom, is a person with well-developed character, one who has well-habituated virtues accompanied by the correct emotions. This person perceives the proper ethical judgments, with the appropriate attendant emotions. This kind of person, with fully developed character based on practical wisdom, would be the person who had the potential to become virtuous and could serve as a good example.

People have different emotions associated with some of the different virtues, differing roughly over this same self-other distinction. People experience shame when they violate a self-regarding virtue and experience guilt when they violate an other-regarding virtue, or, at least according to the distinction, they should.[35] For example, I should experience shame if I am cowardly instead of courageous, and I should experience guilt if I am disrespectful instead of respectful. These attendant emotions are important. It is significant that people who commit crimes and do not feel guilt or remorse are considered unstable or psychopathic in our court system. Currently, warriors will trade guilt for shame, going along with the group to prevent any guilt by violating group norms, which leaves them with only shame by violating personal norms. It's an easy step from there to remove the shame: adopt a stance of shamelessness through a simple act of self-deception. Interestingly, Jonathan Shay's work on post-traumatic stress disorder indicates that concern over moral wrongdoing is one of the primary sources of the disorder. Additionally, there are very few officers who have suffered from the syndrome. One explanation is that officers are much more effectively professionalized and socialized, and this professionalization through self-deceptive narratives and instrumental reasoning can shield the socialized officer from experiencing the guilt or shame that he should be feeling.

This discussion sets out a way to employ philosophical ethics to derive a set of virtues as values, within a well-established ethical theory, which provides a framework to explore ethical problems using a philosophical critical method. This is just one of many critical methods. Critical methods could employ one theory or a combination of theories. They feature the conscious employment of normative ethical theories because deliberation occurs carefully and with full cognizance of important distinctions and concepts that make up those theories. For example, the resolution of LTC West's ethical problem would look different should a philosophical critical method be employed. West may have acted differently with a more philosophical understanding of values, and, perhaps even more importantly, warriors with a more philosophical understanding would judge him differently. People who employ critical methods are typically also careful of their use of language, which also helps to facilitate the proper resolution of more precisely articulated ethical problems. Sassaman's case is even more difficult because it is a systemic problem, perhaps a morally corrupt culture within the battalion itself, the 4th Infantry Division, the entire Army in theater, or perhaps the entire military institution.

DISREGARDING ENDS: WHEN MEANS BECOME ENDS

Many of the methods—means—employed to reach some end can be inadequate, as I've discussed already. There is a different problem with these means, apart from the inadequacy of the method employed as a means, a different problem that is at least as important. This other problem is that means and ends are usually not adequately coordinated. Generally put, an adequate relationship between means and ends is rarely understood or achieved. Means and ends are for the most part not fully and properly integrated, but they should be. While this may be true of many institutions, it is especially true of the military. To be fully and properly integrated, legitimate ends would drive means, but at the same time only proper means would be employed to achieve those ends, and proper means may also then guide us to alter or revise our ends. Without this full integration and reciprocity, with ends influencing means and means influencing ends, we will not have an adequate conception of ends-means reasoning. This lack of integration between ends and means fractures them apart, causing us to lose sight of either ends or means, or at least to lose sight of how they should work in concert. I discussed the inadequate relationship of ends to means in the section of this chapter on instrumental means. I will discuss in turn the inadequate relationship of means to ends in the chapter on ends. And finally, I will argue for an adequate integration of means and ends in chapter 4 as well.

John Dewey's discussion of means and ends in his *Theory of Valuation* (1939) provides a framework from which to expand and articulate a critique of the ends-means reasoning that is prevalent in military ethical thinking. I will employ some of Dewey's ideas and distinctions to facilitate my analysis. In the normal course of ends-means reasoning, we have an idea of a particular consequence we would want to bring about, this idea of an end being an *end-in-view*. We employ some means to achieve this end-in-view, only to bring out some actual consequence (which may or most likely may not be the end-in-view originally envisioned). The new "consequences achieved [would] be valued in turn as means of further consequences."[36] In other words, new ends achieved become means to further ends that we want to achieve, and this is one of the basic concepts of Dewey's *continuum of ends-means*. For example, the military may hold victory as an end-in-view. The consequence of victory, once achieved, now becomes the means to another end, that of reestablishing peace. The first end, the end of victory, we may call a first-order end. The further end of peace we would then call a second-order end. So, the first-order end becomes the means for a second-order end. In this example, the first-order end of victory becomes the means for the second-order end of peace. The continuum works in this direction, where intermediate ends actually become means to achieve further ends.

It would also be natural for the continuum to work the other way, where means become ends. Means can become ends just as ends can become means. Once someone had an end-in-view, then they would adopt some means to attain that end. To focus only on the means in order to reach an end would also amount to viewing the means as an intermediary end. In this way means become ends, working backwards, because one has to work toward a more immediate means in order to enact the original means. The first-order means, the means that most directly bring about the original end, would have a second-order means in order to enact the first-order means (again, thinking in a backward direction). In my simplified example here, the end of victory would be the first-order end, to be brought about by the first-order means of, say, some kind of military operation. In order to successfully complete the mission of the military operation, which is a first-order means, we would have to work toward a second-order means—say, training for the successful completion of the operation. In this way a first-order means is an end for the second-order means, and a second-order means is an end for a third-order means. In this example, the first-order means of the military operation becomes the end for the second-order means of training for the operation. The continuum moves in both directions, from lower- to higher-order.

While it is natural in the process of the ends-means continuum to have ends become means to further ends as well as to have means become ends, it would be an aberration and would be quite unnatural or undesirable to cut or truncate the continuum, thus cutting through the chain of events or sets of conditions. I do not want to use the language of cause and effect; that language is too linear, too simple, when considering human action in an open system. For example, it would destroy the continuum to truncate it, not realizing that it stretches in both directions. One way this can happen is if we allow means to become ends-in-themselves, losing sight of the continuum of ends. However, this unintended conversion of means into ends-in-themselves is exactly one major problem that contributes to the inadequate relationship of ends-to-means reasoning within the military profession. It happens because people in the military can lose sight of some of the further ends they set out to achieve. The military loses sight of the purpose for the end, or the end of the end, that it works to achieve. The military should always be employed to achieve some political purpose, called to action through the legitimate political process by the legitimate political authorities. The military is subordinate to the political leaders and is supposed to be employed constitutionally to "provide for the common defense." As a general principle, when the military is employed to fight, it is more practical and traditionally held than not that the military should win, for winning enables the political leaders to help achieve their objectives.

For example, when the coalition of forces went to war with Iraq in 1991, the coalition had the political goal of liberating Kuwait. It would be much easier to achieve that political goal through the military means of a coalition victory. In principle, to reach that goal, it was much more practical to achieve that end if the coalition forces actually won. A military victory gives the political leaders the leverage they are looking for in order to bring about their political objectives. The liberation of Kuwait, which was the political goal and the end of the military campaign, now becomes the means to a further political end, which is the restoration of peace, the *status quo ante*. Should we reach the end of reestablishing the peace through the liberation of Kuwait, then that peace, which was an end before, becomes a means to another political end—the restored ability to function unencumbered in all of the cooperative arrangements as a member of the international community. Following the transformation of an achieved end into a means toward another end, ends become a means to further ends. In the case of the Gulf War, the liberation of Kuwait (which was an end) becomes the means to reach the further political goal of reestablishing peace, and the peace once established (which was an end) becomes the means to achieve the end of normal relations of that state within the international community—so goes the continuum of ends-means. Even Clausewitz has this ends-means relationship in mind. "The original means of strategy is victory—that is, tactical success; its ends, in the final analysis, are those objects which will lead directly to peace. The application of these means for these ends will also be attended by factors that will influence it to a greater or lesser degree."[37]

However, the military often confuses the means for the end. The military should never be fighting just to be fighting, even though warriors are happy to do just that, nor should it be winning just to be winning. Victory should only be a means to achieve the political goals. And it is important for the military to keep sight of the fact that victory is the means to achieve this end. What happens, though, is that the military loses sight of the political goals and focuses so hard on the means to achieve the end—victory—that the military actually transforms the means of victory into the end of victory, the final end. It is easy for the military to lose sight of the idea that victory is a means toward an end. "The complex problem of reasoning a [military service] at all is liable to occupy his mind and skill so completely that it is easy to forget what it is being run for."[38] Victories become ends-in-themselves, completely divorced from any further purpose that they may serve. Victory has innate value now, because it is thought of as an end, and ends have innate value. Now that the military's means has become its end, victory, it turns to other means, instrumental means, to achieve that end. Any value that the means may have in working to achieve victory would be of merely instrumental value.[39] Many people intuitively give innate value more weight than instrumental value. If innate value is of greater importance than merely instrumental value, then the end of victory takes on much greater importance than the means employed to reach the end of victory. And so is born the very strong idea that the military has to win at all costs—they must keep their "eyes on the prize," as the saying goes. The crux of the problem in the current Long War is that we are losing sight of further ends while exercising the military instrument of power.

We prize ends and we appraise means.[40] So, if the end of victory is more important than the means employed to achieve victory, then the *prizing of victory* will overshadow the *appraisal of means* employed. The appraising of the means employed, whether the means are moral or immoral, will not be as important as the prizing of victory as the end. This is how immoral means can be dismissed if they can bring about victory, and how the military favors making Type I errors (the more egregious type) over Type II errors. Even acts that are manifestly illegal or manifestly immoral can be dismissed or forgotten if these acts helped to bring about victory. Many people in the military still applaud the bombing of Japan, for example—the fire-bombing as well as the nuclear bombing—because they believe these actions were decisive in an American victory. We have to ask why the warriors are so persuaded to dismiss the manifest immorality of the Japanese bombings. Why are they so willing to morally justify America's actions? Their conclusions can very strongly be attributed to the inadequate ends-means reasoning that the military institution employs. Those who argue to justify the manifestly criminal actions over the past several years in the name of secutiry are avoiding the appraisal of means employed.

The problem with this phenomenon of ends-means reasoning is that further goals are compromised in this very attempt to forgo all other considerations in the pursuit of victory as an end. Very often, if victory is obtained through immoral means, then the goal that victory was supposed to bring about will be much harder to achieve. John Rawls echoes the same sentiment when he says, "The way a war is fought and the actions ending it endure in the historical memory of peoples and may set the stage for future war."[41] By the way, while fighting in the Pacific, Rawls refused a military commission as a result of the nuclear bombing of Japan, because he believed that officers were responsible for the actions of the military. If the restoration of peace is the goal of victory, then that very peace may be jeopardized if victory is brought about through illegal or immoral means. Just before the United States dropped the atomic bombs on Japan, the Japanese Navy had been defeated; their army was incapable of continuing to fight since the U.S. Army had captured the outer islands and the Marines had captured the inner islands, not to mention "there had been discussions in Japan for some time about finding a way to end the war, and on June 26 the government had been instructed by the Emperor to do so."[42] We did not need to employ such drastic means to end that war, and the excessive means employed jeopardized future relations. Some even argue that the "bomb was dropped to impress the Russians with American power and make them more agreeable with our demands."[43] Just as the local construction of levies caused the Missouri to flood more violently along its entire length, the local destruction of Japan ushered in the much more dangerous global conflict known as the Cold War.

It will be a long time before the Japanese people and the rest of the world find a way to forget what America did to them to end the war, if ever. From the Japanese point of view, the beginning and the ending of the war stand in ironic contrast. Militarily, the Japanese started the war by attacking only military targets at Pearl Harbor, years before Hawaii became a state, and the Americans ended the war by indiscriminately attacking noncombatants in more than sixty Japanese cities with weapons of destruction on a scale never before seen. Japan was the first to strike militarily, yet it did so roughly a year after America unilaterally placed economic sanctions on Japan (involving military presence) with the intention of eliminating the Japanese influence throughout much of the Pacific region. Today, it would be possible to argue that the Japanese are still carrying on the war, through economic means. It is noteworthy that Japan, making up so little of the world geographically may again rival American economic strength as a partner in a future Asian co-prosperity sphere.

The military does not pay attention to moral considerations at all when it considers means. A bold claim many will reject, but let me explain. When the military is making tactical decisions, according to the military decision-making process (MDMP), and especially according to the deliberate process (DMDMP), there are separate evaluations of *ends*, *ways*, and *means*. The referents in the language of *ends*, *ways*, and *means* differ from those in the more generic language of means and ends. "*Means*" refers to cost; "*ways*" refers to means. Means and *means* refer to different ideas. The military stipulates the nature of the evaluation concerning each of these considerations. When considering *ways*, it is an evaluation of *feasibility*. When considering *means*, it is an evaluation of *acceptability*, or cost. When considering *ends*, it is an evaluation of *suitability*. The test of feasibility, acceptability, and suitability is affectionately known as the FAS test. I will go through each of these considerations to demonstrate that nowhere in these three evaluations is there any moral consideration of the means employed in a military operation.[44] Without a moral check built into this system, it is possible—and even likely—that a course of action could be adopted that would pass all the elements of the FAS test and still be an immoral action. The destruction of Fallujah serves as an illustrative example.

Feasibility is a measure only of possibility. *Ways*—evaluated by feasibility—are essentially courses of action. Courses of action are developed unconstrained, meaning that as long as the course of action exists as a possibility then it is feasible. Courses of action are considered if they are possible, without constraining them yet by any other considerations. Destroying the city of Fallujah to eradicate particularly dangerous insurgents was indeed a possibility. There is no evaluation as to the rightness or wrongness of the action to be taken. It was possible to attack the city, and the attack occurred. It was possible to prevent males of fighting age to leave the city, and so it happened. And it was possible to change the Rules of Engagement so that anything that moved could be killed or destroyed as the Marines moved in. All three possibilities listed are legally and morally problematic. Moral considerations do not in any way act as constraints when developing courses of action according to their feasibility. The feasibility test involves no moral test of the *ways* employed, which would be the means in the context of a means-end continuum.

The second evaluation involves the *means* involved, and in this stipulative sense of means, it involves an evaluation of cost only. How much would it cost (in terms of people, materiel, or money) to execute each of the courses of action? The cost equation rarely if ever includes the cost to the enemy. There was acceptable cost from the point of view of the American forces in the takedown of the city of Fallujah. The Iraqi losses were not part of the equation. However, by any measure the destruction of a major city has created more insurgents than it destroyed and did much to fuel the insurgent cause for generations to come. Such neglect in the calculation will usually come around to wind up costing the American effort, but usually at a higher, systemic level. But again, significantly, there are no moral considerations in the acceptability evaluation, except insofar as pure utility calculations may be considered to have moral content. The acceptability test involves no moral test of the *means* (cost), which would contribute to evaluating the means of a means-end continuum.

The evaluation of the final consideration, of *ends*, is a check for suitability—or rather it is a check for what is stipulated to be suitability. Is the course of action suitable? Does it accomplish the end that is set out to be achieved? The end for the military is victory—to kill insurgents, bad guys. So the suitability check for each of the courses of action is simply that of checking to see if each course of action will lead to victory, as if killing enough bad guys will lead to victory. "If the concept meets the higher commander's intent and will accomplish the unit mission, the concept is deemed suitable."[45] The suitability evaluation has no moral considerations; it is merely a check to ensure mission accomplishment. The suitability test involves no moral test of the *end* and offers no evaluation of the means in the context of a means-end continuum.

So, throughout the evaluation of ends, ways, and means—suitability, feasibility, and acceptability—there is no check built into this decision-making system to ensure that the means employed are moral means. The government's use of the term *means* has a completely different sense than the one employed in this book. Feasibility (focused on ways) is about possibility; acceptability (focused on "means" in a different sense) is about cost; and suitability (focused on ends) is about completing the mission. Consider Desert Storm, a comparitively clean conflict. The first course of action, the air campaign, could not have continued indefinitely; eventually the coalition would have run out of ordnance. But it did exceed every measure of proportionality and necessity, even military expediency. The public saw a lot of media coverage of the precision-guided bombs. However, precision munitions made up about 7 percent of the bombs that were dropped on Iraq. The coalition dropped 88,000 tons of ordnance on Iraq over the period of several weeks before the ground campaign, about 10,000 tons each week, equivalent to one nuclear bomb each week. Some of this ordnance was directed at military targets in Iraq. But a lot of it was directed at targets that produced questionable military advantage.[46] Much of the country's infrastructure—which had no military connection—was destroyed. Just how many military targets are there in a city?

Given that the military objective was far away in Kuwait, many of these targets were destroyed needlessly. For example, the Navy had accidentally discovered, off the San Diego coast, that chaff blown out the back of an aircraft to confuse incoming missiles would knock out power grids if the chaff landed on the grids. The coalition forces, capitalizing on this discovery, knocked out many power grids in Iraq by blowing chaff out of passing aircraft. Many of these power stations had nothing to do with military targets and provided power to the noncombatant citizens of the cities—not to mention hospitals and schools.[47] Sometimes military lawyers will recommend against destroying certain targets, but there is no moral check built into the military decision-making process when it is employed in a tactical operation.

When the coalition forces carried out their frontal attack course of action, they held nothing back. To help prepare for the attack of the Iraqi defensive positions, they used every kind of ordnance possible on the defenders. The close air attack on these defensive positions included fuel-air explosives (FAEs), which are known as near-nukes because they produce a blast overpressure of over 1000 psi. FAEs are one type of weapon banned by recent protocols. They also dropped cluster-bomb units (CBUs) on the defenders, bombs that have an overwhelmingly devastating effect. The coalition forces, particularly the United States, used depleted uranium rounds, which are also banned by recent protocols because of the radioactive effects that they have on the enemy personnel as well as on the environment. The coalition forces were known to bury the Iraqi defenders alive in the sand. Again, nowhere in course of action development and execution is there any consideration for moral deliberation. Although little known or acknowledged, it is vitally important that independent satellite surveillance indicated a far different picture than that painted by the American military. There was nowhere near the build-up of Iraqi forces on the Saudi border that American intelligence portrayed. There was not enough of a force built up along the border to conduct offensive operations into Saudi Arabia. There was also nowhere near the size force that Iraqis ostensibly took into Kuwait. The huge troop build-up and the size and character of the Kuwaiti invasion were propagandistic exaggerations. The film footage of Iraqi soldiers allegedly shooting Kuwaitis turned out to be incidents of Iraqis shooting Iraqi soldiers for crimes. The report of Iraqi soldiers taking babies out of incubators had been fabricated, reported by the daughter of a Kuwaiti representative living in the United States at the time with no direct knowledge of the alleged incidents. Significantly, that false testimony had been key in persuading Congress to pass the very narrow vote that authorized the American invasion of Iraq in the early 1990s. The Pentagon's propaganda ministry has been doing its job well. Operation Iraqi Freedom is a continuation of Desert Storm, in terms of the abandonment of morality. The main moral failing was the belief that victory was the final end. America is in the situation it is now in because the military viewed victory as the final end. The American Army has always worshipped at the altar of the offensive, and *blitzkrieg* has been one of the chief gods of war. Shimon Naveh gives a critique of *blitzkrieg* in *Pursuit of Military Excellence*. While tactically successful, *blitzkrieg* suffers from operational or strategic unsustainability. The U.S. military essentially conducted a *blitzkrieg* to capture Baghdad. It was tactically successful but operationaly and strategically unsustainable. The American occupation of Baghdad is even less popular than was the German occupation of Paris. All indications are that conditions will worsen the longer the American military is in Iraq. Unless the strategic conditions improve, the military cannot solve the problems there. They could not see beyond the victory; the means as end can have devastating consequences. This one long war is an agglomeration of Type I errors committed to achieve quasi-reflective means that were mistaken for the end. The most likely outcome given continued strategic failure will be the eventual ejection of American forces. The worst case scenario is that American forces would have to fight their way out, as in Xenophon's *Anabasis*.

The closest that the military comes to taking into account moral considerations is the fact that military lawyers, Judge Advocates General (JAGs for short), are placed within the tactical units to sit in on the targeting cell meetings. They can make staff recommendations to the commanders regarding the illegality of targets and types of targets, but the commanders have the prerogative to ignore their recommendations. But giving a legal imprimatur to a military action is no guarantee that the action is moral. One way to look at lawyers on the battlefield is that "they provide harried decision-makers with a critical guarantee of legal coverage, turning complex issues of morality into technical issues of legality, so that whatever moral or operational doubts a commander may have, he can at least be sure that he will not face legal consequences. The Geneva Conventions have become a casuist's bible, and close readings of their fine print are supposed to eliminate the moral and political risks associated with military violence."[48] Even so, the lawyers are among morality's best friends in the military.

As long as the military remains so intent on achieving victory at any cost, oblivious to the "tyranny of the mission," without paying attention to the fact that victory is a means rather than an end, then the military will continue to commit moral error. Warriors should not lose sight of what should follow after the victory is achieved. And they should not lose sight of the fact that victory is only a means for a further end—peace. Instead of the military employing the rhetoric pronouncing its purpose being that of "fighting to win the nation's wars," the military should consider its purpose as being that of "fighting for a better peace."

ARE MORAL MEANS POSSIBLE?

Given the level of moral complexity on the battlefield, we should not oversimplify the methods we use to gain moral understanding and to sort through moral problems. We should turn away from closed, inadequate decision-procedures and toward open-ended philosophical inquiry in the form of critical methods. I compared the Army's inadequate moral decision-making procedure with a more adequate philosophical critical method, all in the context of dealing with values. The military has not yet in this regard moved from the inadequate decision procedure to the more adequate critical method. The following describes the difficulty of overcoming inertia in an organization and details what happened to the proposal of Army values that would have been made up of a set of virtues. Within the past few decades, after the advent of the values-based organization, so prevalent in corporate America, the U.S. Army decided to espouse its values. For a while, they were listed as the 4 Cs: courage, competence, candor, and commitment. Then there were five: compassion was added.

The set of virtues as values was an actual proposal for the Army in 1996.[49] The paper became the think-piece upon which the Army values were formed. The process was a political process, though—much more a process of *manufacturing consent* concerning likes and dislikes rather than *rationally deliberating* over issues of substance. The set of virtues as values was transformed into the set the Army now has through the following process. A set of virtues had the advantage of at least being commensurate and could exist in harmony, consistent with the ancient vision of there being a "unity of the virtues." The original set of virtues had three self-regarding and three other-regarding virtues with one virtue supervening over and containing the other virtues. The three self-regarding virtues were *honesty*, *courage*, and *wisdom*, and the three other-regarding virtues were *loyalty*, *respect*, and *fairness*. The encompassing, supervening virtue was that of *honor*. It supervened because it would exist when all the others were present, and it would not be present when any of the others were not there.[50]

The Army employs numerous mnemonic devices in its instructional methods to aid in memorization. Mnemonic devices are employed to aid in the indoctrination of values too, but should not be so employed. The Army Chief of Staff in 1995 had decided that the Army was going to be a "values-based" organization, with values that would be easy to remember. So the Pentagon was interested in forming an acronym so that the resulting mnemonic device would aid in the learning of the values. The proposed values seemed to defy the formation of an acronym. Completely independent of the motivation to form an acronym, a special staffing process forced the substitution of three of the proposed values. Army leaders did not think that young people were capable of being wise, so wisdom dropped out. At the same time, Army leaders insisted that the Army could not do without duty and integrity (even though none of the other services need these values articulated). The Army also could not do without selfless service (while the Air Force also has service before self as a value, the Naval Forces seem to be getting along fine without espousing it). As a result of this process of *manufacturing consent*, integrity replaced honesty, selfless service replaced wisdom, and duty replaced fairness.[51] Even with the substitutions, the seven values did not lend themselves to the creation of an acronym. The values were published in some forms in 1997, including the new officer evaluation report, without an acronym. Sometime after that somebody or some group had figured out how to arrange the values into an acronym by replacing *courage* with *personal courage*. The Army values took their current form, forever emblazoned in soldiers' minds with the acronym LDRSHIP, which comprises loyalty, duty, respect, selfless service, honor, integrity, and personal courage.[52] The new acronym, while making the values easy to remember, completely destroyed the conceptual relationships that the values had with each other. For example, honor could no longer include the notion of being an overarching, supervening value, not without being an instantiation of *Russell's Paradox*, because with honor also being the fifth member of the set, the set of all values now contained itself. But it was now just as easy to train soldiers to remember the acronym LDRSHIP as it was to remember the 4 or 5 Cs.

One way to categorize ethical problems is by making the distinction between *problems of the will* and *problems of the understanding*.[53] Many who engage in applied ethics think that we have no problem in understanding what we ought to do; the problem is in having the will to do what we already know we should. Recall step ten in the ethical decision-making plan, which is the step to actually commit to and implement a solution. Step ten is in the plan precisely to remind people that they have to move from understanding to action. But it could be that attaining understanding is more difficult than common sense would have it. This may especially be true for professional ethics when considering, for example, the political profession and the practice of statecraft.[54]

There is nothing ordinary or common about the ethical situations that statesmen, doctors, police officers, politicians, and members of the military routinely face. It is not adequate to turn to precepts or maxims such as the Golden Rule. George Bernard Shaw stated it elegantly and succinctly when he said, "Do not do unto others as you would have them do unto you; they may have different tastes."[55] Common sense and sacred scripture are both underdetermined when it comes to difficult issues, such as the saving or taking of lives. Only logical and philosophical inquiry can inform these difficult problems. If methods can be difficult for ordinary problems, they can be very hard for professional ethics, especially military ethics.

Many people unwittingly employ theory, or theory fragments, that might not be justified upon adequate reflection. Keeping in mind that I am focusing on an institution and its institutional or corporate ethics, the cost of invoking unexamined ethical theory can be high. One of the specific problems that needs scrutiny is the imposition of some kind of value system based on moral foundations. Any *foundation* would require the presumption of some kind of moral realism. There is no type of moral realism that would be appropriate for a governmental institution in a democratic society. Some may ask about the foundational documents of the Declaration and Constitution: What about the truths our forefathers found to be self-evident? I agree that these documents provide normative force. But they are not foundational in the sense that a moral realist would view them, as ontological realities that exist in some metaphysical way. As self-evident as those truths must have seemed back then, they were not self-evident enough to apply to all men—or to women at all. These documents are not sacred texts, and even if they were they would not posit metaphysical truths that we should consider foundational. The normative force comes not from a foundational account, but from a constructivist account, which I will explore in chapter 5. Unreflective practice happens in many ways because there are many ways either to avoid or misuse theory. Moral philosophy perhaps should become the first philosophy, instead of metaphysics or epistemology, where we could use overlapping consensus as starting points rather than metaphysical positions and their indefinite interpretations over which we could never begin to agree. Morality should not be about foundations, but about what we can justify.

Much of the critique that centers upon the problems associated with applied, or professional, ethics is caused when theory is either ignored or badly exercised. Ethical practices and methods that either shun ethical theory or misuse it will pose a problem. The methods I have critiqued in this chapter are not justifiable at the level of theory. So the systemic moral failure comes from the methods themselves: the methods related to solving moral problems based on values and the methods the military uses to make decisions. The theoretical frameworks and conceptual relationships are ignored when applying values. And since the military decision procedures are about decisions, they have more to do with the intuitive preferences of those in charge than with reasoning all involved can share. We are left with only a record of decisions when what we need is a record of the rationale for decisions. The nature of the instrumentality of these methods is morally problematic. They are instrumental in that they serve some end, relegating any means secondary to consideration of its end. The end can justify any means. Deitrich Dörner explores the vagaries of instrumental methodism in his important book, *The Logic of Failure* (Perseus Books, 1996). Since these misguided methods are devoid of any conceptual coherence or normative justification at the meta-ethical level, they are bound to lead to failure. In the end, moral practitioners, especially within professions, will be better off understanding and looking to philosophy and philosophical ethics in their practices than not doing so. I now turn to a closer examination of the inadequate ends that the military has come to embrace.

4

The Quasi-Reflective Life
Inadequate Ends

Inadequate ends are ends that are in need of revision in order for them to be legitimate or moral ends. Unless we are fully conscious of what our ends are and how they fit into a larger moral context, they could be inadequate. As long as we do not deliberately challenge, discuss, debate, and deliberate over ends, they could be inadequate. We have to carry on a moral dialolgue about these ends. Dialogue is a philosophical conversation that differs from all others. Dialogue is an exchange of ideas among those who consider themselves to be colleagues. Needless to say, given the military's rank structure, dialogue is a difficult form of communication to achieve within the war machine. As long as we are not fully aware of the relationship that ends should have with the means employed to reach those ends, they could be inadequate. In chapter 3 I argued that ends are not sufficiently coordinated with means. In this chapter I will argue that means are only dubiously connected to ends; in fact the moral nature of the means are often overshadowed or even ignored in the pursuit of the end. Operation Iraqi Freedom exemplifies both errors when it comes to means and ends: means becomes ends and ends eclipse means.

I will bring up several real-world examples. I use these examples in part because they are more interesting than imaginary examples. I find that using real examples in the classroom is much more stimulating than trying to come to grips with a hypothetical example such as Bernard Williams' case of Jim and the Indians.[1] I want to remind the reader that I am not generalizing from those examples. The examples are logical and practical consequences of an inadequate theoretical understanding. In addition, I am not merely making a descriptive account of the state of moral awareness, understanding, and action of the military. In addition to the description, I am making normative judgments not only about what we are actually doing, but also in many cases about what we should do. After looking at some examples of moral error brought about by inadequate ends, I will continue the critique of the inadequate relationship between ends and means followed by an examination of the presumed nature of these ends and the need to deliberate over new ends. The military should refine its pursuit of these inadequate ends, for they have led to moral error and are in need of revision because the value of these ends eclipses the value of the means; the ends are presumed and are either dubious or unjustified; and there is no adequate deliberation over new ends.

INADEQUATE ENDS AND MORAL ERROR

So, what is wrong with the military thinking that its end should be victory? Douglas MacArthur reminded the cadets at West Point that their "mission remains fixed, determined, inviolable—it is to win our wars."[2] Within a few years after hearing MacArthur's words at West Point in 1962, these cadets found themselves embroiled in a conflict in Vietnam, and they did their best to do what they had been told. They did the best they could to win, at least militarily. The military actually did win, at the tactical level, in the skirmishes, engagements, and battles. Colonel (Ret.) Harry Summers recounts his anguish at coming to realize a great irony about hollow victories: "'You know you never beat us on the battlefield,' I told my NVA counterpart in Hanoi five days before the fall of Saigon. 'That may be so,' he replied, 'but it is also irrelevant.'"[3] The great irony is that "winning all of the battles, as General Charles Cornwallis' experiences in an earlier revolution should have alerted, does not guarantee winning the war."[4] Summers argues for strategic victory in addition to tactical victory. A further irony beyond the fact that tactical military victory may not win the war is that winning the war strategically may not be enough, either. Military victory has been neither a sufficient nor even a necessary condition for success at the political level in the history of conflict since the Age of Battles.

The officers who were young during Vietnam were in charge of the military during Desert Storm. They were determined not to have any more hollow victories. Indeed, Desert Storm was supposed to be the model for getting this victory business right.[5] This time the conflict would have a clear military objective—defeating the Iraqi Army in order to liberate Kuwait. This time there would be popular backing. In addition to overwhelming American support, in the words of General (Ret.) Norman Schwarzkopf, "we had no less than nine United Nations resolutions authorizing our actions, and we had the support of virtually the entire world."[6] The coalition air campaign against Iraqi forces commenced on January 12, 1991, followed by a ground campaign beginning on February 24. By February 27, the coalition forces essentially destroyed the Iraqi Army, which triggered the cease-fire. The new generals had achieved the decisive victory that they so craved but couldn't quite achieve in Vietnam—tactical, operational, and strategic victory. It became known as the 100-Hour War. America had finally solved the problems of achieving decisive victory on the battlefields—replacing the policy of limited response with overwhelming force according to the "Powell Doctrine." The American and coalition forces had achieved victory; they had lived up to General MacArthur's fiat. But how much did we really achieve with this "victory"? What we did was replace the "Vietnam Syndrome" with the "Victory Syndrome."

After a decade of sanctions and another war, victory is still nowhere in sight. What began as United Nations embargoes sanctioned by the Security Council in August 1991 immediately after the Iraqi invasion of Kuwait turned into embargoes sanctioned only by the United States. Embargoes are implemented and enforced through a variety of means, including military blockades. The UN Security Council passed Resolution 661 on August 6, 1991, which reaffirmed the military goals of the war set out in Resolution 660, but also laid out the parameters of the economic sanctions.[7]

The war had succeeded—as everyone had predicted—in expelling Iraqi forces from Kuwait, and so the main requirement set out in Security Council Resolution 661 had been achieved. Now, it seemed, there was no longer a requirement for economic sanctions. Perhaps they had failed, though they weren't given long to achieve all their objectives, but Kuwait had been liberated. In fact, the winning of the war gave Washington the chance to impose a fresh sanctions resolution. But the goalposts would be changed—at the time of the ceasefire and repeatedly thereafter—with the express intent of maintaining sanctions on Iraq for the indefinite future.[8] Over the ten-plus years of U.S.-led economic sanctions that were imposed on Iraq, there have been studies to show that by 1995 "more than one million Iraqis have died—576,000 of them children—as a direct consequence of economic sanctions."[9] Current estimates double these figures.

For years there was no United Nations resolution to authorize the economic sanctions. So why did the sanctions continue? The last relevant Security Council Resolution was SCR 687 of April 3, 1991, which included measures outlining not only the cease-fire, but also spelled out provisions that would require Iraq to destroy its weaponry and submit to inspections ensuring that they did not develop weapons of mass destruction (WMD).[10] Neither the United Nations General Assembly nor the Security Council favored punitive sanctions in the event that Iraq did not comply with weapons inspections. Granted, Iraq had not been fully cooperative with the demands of the weapons inspectors. But other than showing good faith, the most thorough inspections would not be adequate to ensure that Iraq complied completely with the resolution. While it would be fairly easy to find evidence of nuclear weapons, biological weapons could be stored or even built just about anywhere, without much chance of detection. The resolution implied a requirement that is unverifiable. Further, it provided no measures should Iraq not follow the provisions. Neither Resolution 687 nor any subsequent resolution set out authorized responses either to enforce compliance or to punish Iraq for noncompliance. Nevertheless, the sanctions continued, followed by a second war, ostensibly because of Iraq's noncompliance.

So, the strategic goal was not achieved as a result of Gulf I. Former National Security Advisor Anthony Lake articulated the post-Cold War doctrine of containment: "As the sole superpower, the United States has a special responsibility for developing a strategy to neutralize, contain, and through selective pressure, perhaps even transform these backlash states into constructive members of the international community."[11] Economic sanctions provide the primary means to exert this "pressure." Bombing shored up any gaps that the economic sanctions missed. The U.S. and Great Britain imposed illegal no-fly zones over Iraq (ironically condemned by the UN), and commenced bombing Iraq almost every day between Gulf I and Gulf II. In the run-up to the second Gulf war, The UN passed UNSCR 1441, which outlined an inspections regime. The United States rhetorically altered the terms of the resolution, claiming that it required Iraq to prove it had no weapons and that lack of such proof in turn authorized any means necessary, including a preemptive military invasion, to disarm Iraq. The resolution did neither. While Iraq had a responsibility of full disclosure, it did not have the burden of proof. If it did, there would have been a logical and practical problem. The resolution did not have a provision requiring Iraq to *prove* it had no such weapons. Disclosure is not proof. Proving one's innocence is a logical and a practical impossibility. The most that can be done is to falsify one's innocence, otherwise known as proving guilt, which the inspections regime was intended to do. Lack of proof is not proof. Discrepancies between disclosure claims and inspection results cannot serve as proof since other explanations exist. Significantly, the resolution did not authorize an invasion. The second article in the UN Charter protects sovereign nations from aggression. And, very, very importantly, articles trump resolutions in the legal world. Even if the resolution contained language that could be interpreted as having authorized an invasion and regime change, which it did not, the articles and clauses of the UN Charter have more legal and moral force than the UN's declarations and resolutions.

Unfortunately, this pressure that comes in the form of sanctions was harming the population at large in Iraq. Furthermore, after ten years of pressure, Iraq's leaders seemed not to have felt pressured. We have to consider the fact that America is, or at least the possibility that America may be, committing moral error here through these conflicts and sanctions. These economic sanctions target people indiscriminately. Economic sanctions usually involve military blockades, so they would at least in a nominal way involve the military. As a general principle, whole populations should never be the targets of any kind of attack. Unfortunately, the whole population of Iraq was the target of the economic sanctions; otherwise, the sanctions would not work. "Those opponents of the Gulf War who advocated a prolonged blockade of Iraq seem not to have realized that what they were advocating was a radically indiscriminate act of war with predictably harsh consequences.... Just-war theory as I understand it would require that food and medical supplies be let through—but then it is unlikely that the blockade would serve its purpose."[12] If we are contributing to the suffering and death of hundreds of thousands of people, are we not committing moral error? Most people in the military as well as the public at large do not want to admit that this is moral error. Others will recognize the immorality yet believe it is nevertheless justified. They may ask, "ethics aside, shouldn't we do this anyway?"[13] The military institution, and the individuals who make up the military institution can come to hold such beliefs because of the final end they presume that the military is supposed to achieve—the final end being victory.

The greatest source of moral error is the emerging doctrine that focuses on effects, known as the Effects Based Approach (EBA), with its derivative Effects Based Operations (EBO). The doctrine is an elaborate pseudo-science that attempts to analyze the labyrinth of reasoning backward from *effect* back to *cause* (Kant, as well as Aristotle referred to such reasoning—inferring a cause from an effect—as a paralogism, or a fallacy of logic). The doctrine then calls for moving forward in the imagined chain of events, bringing about the desired effects from the requisite causes. The doctrine calls for the management of effects, by imposing a teleological basis to operations, teleological because Aristotle's final causes become part of the causal framework. The teleological orientation in Scholastic scientific thought was expunged in modern science, beginning with Descartes, and was replaced with a mechanistic view that orients on efficient causes. Military planning in EBA is a reverse-engineering project that begins with a teleological goal called an end-state. Once telos becomes part of this pseudo-scientific method, then it no longer resembles science as scientists and philosophers understand it. Falsification becomes an impossibility within such a process. Once the goal is identified, then there is no amount of contrary evidence available to falsify the pursuit of the goal. And so a goal of transforming Iraq into a democratic friend of the United States can suffer massive moral error, year after year, with no end currently in sight. In other words, since teleology has disappeared from scientific thinking in the modern age, the Effects Based Approach is the flat-earth doctrine of military operations.

DISREGARDING MEANS: WHEN ENDS ECLIPSE MEANS

In the previous chapter on means, I approached the problem associated with means and ends not being fully integrated. There I discussed one side of the problem of means being cut off from the relevant ends. This is one type of fracture between means and ends, the issue of losing sight of the ends, particularly further or higher-order ends, when carrying out the means. When we lose sight of our ends, then it is possible to view mere means as final ends or ends-in-themselves. People in the military often transform the means of victory into the final end of victory, and this confusion can lead to moral error. The current fiasco in the Gulf suffers from this type of moral error. In this chapter, I will talk about the other side of this problem, the problem of losing sight of the moral aspects of the means when pursuing the ends. This other side of the problem exists when ends overshadow means, causing us to lose sight of the morality of the relevant means. The current debacle suffers from this type of moral error as well.

I have already mentioned that many people view ends to be more important than means. They view ends to have innate worth or value, and they view means to have only instrumental value in reaching those ends. People simply view innate value as having more worth than instrumental value. After all, actions that have instrumental value help us to reach our ends that have innate value. When means have only instrumental value, they are valuable only insofar as they help us to achieve our ends, ends that have innate value or are valuable in themselves. When people assign to means only instrumental value, these means lack innate value by virtue of having only instrumental value. Since they lack innate value, they are not valuable in themselves. Anything that is valuable in itself is going to be more valuable than anything that is otherwise valuable, and here means are less valuable because they help instrumentally to bring about an end that is valuable in itself. In this way, ends become more important than means, as long as people make a distinction between ends and means over the notion of ends having innate value and means having instrumental value.

The distinction between innate value and instrumental value is not necessarily a helpful distinction. It has even caused much harm because of the tendency to give innate value more importance than instrumental value. In a continuum where achieved ends become means to further ends, an end that had innate value while viewed as an end would then have only instrumental value while viewed as a means. Since the same pursuit viewed in one

way can be an end and viewed in another way can be a means, this same pursuit would have both innate and instrumental value. So, the distinction is not
completely helpful here if it assigns more value to the same pursuit as an end.
In a properly arranged continuum, any particular pursuit is perhaps important
both as an end and as a means. So it is just as important to consider how we
achieve an end via the means as it is to actually reach the end. I will give an
example to help illustrate the generalization.

It is easier to make the mistake of assigning more weight to the end than
the means used to reach the end if we think of ends as final ends when in fact
they are not final—hence the error. In viewing victory as a final end, the military will be making this mistake. If the military views victory as a final end, it
will be making this mistake. In viewing victory as a final end, the military will
be assigning innate value only to the achievement of victory. Victories, by
being final ends, will be ends-in-themselves. If there is a continuum of ends
and means that goes in each direction indefinitely, then it makes no sense to
talk about ends-in-themselves or about final ends. Any end reached will
potentially become a means to a further end. And the way we reach that
end—through the means—becomes important if that new end achieved is to
play a role in the pursuit of a further end. To speak of ends-in-themselves
introduces a conflicted concept against the background of a continuum of
ends and means. We may achieve an end at great cost. For example, the military can achieve a victory at great cost, particularly at great moral cost, squan-
dering America's moral capital. Since the military values what it loses in order
to achieve the victory, then a victory is not the only end sought or valued.

> But there are also many occasions in which persons find that,
> when they have attained something as an end, they have paid too
> high a price in effort and in sacrifice of other ends. In such situa-
> tions enjoyment of the end attained is itself valued, for it is not
> taken in its immediacy but in terms of its cost—a fact fatal to its
> being regarded as "an end-in-itself," a self-contradictory term in
> any case.[14]

Even in a military context, Pyrrhic victories are hardly worth the cost.[15] The
"tyranny of the mission" can drive the military to pursue victory at the
expense of every other consideration. To destroy one's own military while
winning would be Pyrrhic, because it would value its continued existence,
and the cost of losing what is valuable can equal or surpass the value of the
end achieved.

To win by destroying the ability to make further peace would also be a
morally Pyrrhic victory, even if that cost were not recognized, because the
further end of peace is compromised. The notion that ends become means to
subsequent ends also destroys the concept of ends-in-themselves. If victory is

an end-in-itself, and the means are less important than the victory to be achieved, then the end could justify the means. "The conception involved in the maxim that 'the end justifies the means' is basically the same as that in the notion of 'ends-in-themselves.'"[16] Dewey begins his discussion of the ends-means continuum by recounting an imaginary story about the origin of roast pork. After an accident in which a house is burned down with pigs inside of it, and upon touching the burned pigs inside with their fingers, the owners of the house tried to cool their fingers in their mouths. "Enjoying the taste, they henceforth set themselves to building houses, inclosing pigs in them, and then burning the houses down."[17] In this example, the end of producing roast pork was worth the extraordinarily excessive means of burning down houses in order to achieve the end. As ridiculous as the story sounds, the military applies the same principle whenever it employs extraordinarily excessive means to achieve a victory. Many warriors today do not like Francis Ford Coppola's classic movie on Vietnam, *Apocalypse Now*; they judge the characters as being factitious and surreal. If they do like it, they like it for the wrong reasons. Coppola has perhaps accurately *represented* the type of psychosis that many warriors actually possess. Many of my seniors, peers, juniors, and students are drawn, for example, to the character of LTC Kilgore, played by Robert Duvall, especially when he says, "I love the smell of napalm in the morning...it smells like...victory." I suggest that the pursuit of the aesthetic pleasure of LTC Kilgore is not completely dissimilar to Dewey's example of people burning down houses with pigs in them to pursue the aesthetic pleasure of tasting roast pork. Many warriors have developed a taste for victory. And in both examples the means employed to enjoy the acquired taste are excessive. The taste for victory is unlike Dewey's example of those with a taste for roast pork because this taste for victory is untoward and psychotic since the excess is part of the enjoyment. For some, the more excessive the measures are in acquiring the victory, the better the taste. The warrior ethos is all about fostering a psychology that develops in the warriors a taste for victory. There are many other names for this taste for victory. It has come to be referred to as part of the *battle culture of forbearance*. It is the dreamlike mentation of Henry Fleming's *battle sleep*. Simone Weil describes this phenomenon of heightening one to a dangerous emotional state and the resulting possibility of transformation in even the kindest of souls: "The blood that flows all around him only incites him to spill his own and that of others. By degrees he grows inflamed and will come to experience the *enthusiasm of carnage*."[18] Anyone who has sampled any of these flavors, experiencing their seductive and intoxicating power, understands how such a taste can be acquired.

A continuum suggests that in principle there could be no final end. Every time a final end would be reached, that end could serve as a means to some further end. If an end is an effect that is brought about by means that are causes, then "nothing happens which is final in the sense that it is not part of an ongoing stream of events."[19] Dewey argues that we should abandon the idea of ethics being guided by final ends. As a pragmatist in this regard, he is opposing many of the starting positions of some of the major conceptions of morality, the search for the final end, the highest truth, or the greatest good.[20] Of course, the idea of placing too much emphasis on a final end, or even considering a final end, is rooted in teleological ethical systems and worldviews. Happiness, for example, was the final end in Aristotle's teleological ethical system. We can pursue ends because they are valuable—health, education, virtue—yet these ends we also pursue for the sake of something else. Happiness in the ancient scheme is the final end because it is the only pursuit that is not sought for the sake of anything else. "On Aristotle's view, for example, virtue and pleasure are also sought for the sake of happiness."[21] Henry Richardson describes Dewey's argument against Aristotle's view here as *antiteleological holism*. "This traditional notion of an ultimate end Dewey sees as combining four flaws: fixity, 'finality,' single-mindedness, and noninstrumentality."[22] His views on finality as a flaw when considering ends push Dewey in the direction of also maintaining that ends will not be choiceworthy for their own sake, but only choiceworthy when considered alongside the means employed to attain them. The current pursuit of permanent war along with the installment of the warrior ethos are fatally flawed. To what end are we executing this unwinnable war against terror? We keep hearing that we must stay the course until we achieve victory. Were we victorious in the war against piracy? The war against drugs? The war on crime? No. Will we be victorious in the war on terror? No. All of these are crimes and it only takes a modicum of reasoning to understand we can't win a war against crime.

Dewey is not against ends for their own sake, as in the case of consummatory values. Dewey's stance against ends-in-themselves hinges on the notion that ends should not be sought solely for their own sake, without considering further ends, since ends are effects that become causes for further effects. For example, victory can be enjoyed for its own sake, but it is not the only end. Dewey's position on the impossibility of the finality of ends influences his reluctance to allow ends to have value apart from means. "It thus discloses in a striking manner the fallacy involved in the position that ends have value independent of appraisal of means involved and independent of their own further causal efficacy."[23] The main danger of maintaining the idea that any of our goals are final ends, ends-in-themselves, lies in the entailment of the value of the end *eclipsing* the value of the means employed to attain that end. If the ends eclipse the means, then it is possible for people to justify inappropriate means to obtain these ends.

Dewey outlines a further problem that arises if we accept ends passed down to us through tradition because the pursuit of unreflective and potentially illegitimate ends can lead us to more readily accept illegitimate means. "In one group money-making would be such an end; in another group, possession of political power; in another group, advancement of scientific knowledge; in still another group, military prowess, etc."[24] There are legitimate means of attaining money, political power, scientific knowledge, and military prowess. However, there are also illegitimate means of attaining these ends as well. Since we prize ends but appraise means, the focus on defining success as measures of effectiveness or even measures of performance says a lot about the effect we prize yet nothing about the appraisal or evaluation of the means.

In the case of the sanction regime, invasion, and occupation of Iraq, America's leaders were able to sustain such an unjust punishment upon the population of Iraq because of their focus on achieving the end they wanted to bring about. Before Operation Iraqi Freedom, the United States wanted to achieve the end of Iraq's embargo: compliance with weapons inspections. The leaders did whatever it took to force this compliance. The focus on the end of compliance eclipses the focus on the means of sanctions and their consequences. The end is more important than the means; the end justifies the means. The end of regime change eclipsed the means as well. Many are not aware of the moral gravity of the sanctions or of the invasion. Some are aware of the great harm the wars and sanctions have caused, but dismiss this harm because they think the end is important enough to forgive harm imposed by the means. After all, so the argument goes, isn't it a good thing that a madman is now out of power? And yet others are fully aware of the effect of this strategy and are still not apologetic. Currently, American leaders are not accepting moral blame for the harm caused by the sanctions, even though they acknowledge the effects. Rather, they say that Iraq is to blame for the sanctions because it would not comply with the weapons inspections demands. In like manner, offensive defense, carried out by preventive war at the strategic end by warriors imbued with the warrior spirit, will ultimately be counterproductive.

So who is causing the harm? It may be true that Iraq's action—noncompliance—in this matter poses a necessary but not a sufficient condition for the suffering. It is also true that America's actions—wars and sanctions—create the necessary and sufficient conditions to bring about this current state of affairs. And, further, it may be less the case that Iraq is creating a necessary condition than is America. America's actions are more proximate to the suffering. Even more telling is the fact that sanctions continued even during the period of time when Iraq *was* cooperating. So, America would be imposing the sanctions no matter what Iraq was doing. In one conceptual scheme regarding causation, a *sufficient* condition for an event can be said to be a maximally causal condition. Correspondingly, a *necessary* condition can be said to be a minimally causal condition, the *sine qua non*, the *not without which*. Since America is creating necessary and perhaps sufficient conditions for the sanctions, and Iraq is at most creating only a necessary condition, under this scheme it could be argued that America is perhaps more responsible for causing the suffering to a much greater degree than is Iraq, or at least is more responsible than many may want to admit.[25] At a minimum, American leaders cannot pretend that we play no role in causing the harm. American leaders should accept their share of the responsibility for the harm brought to the Iraqi people.

Disregarding the moral consequences of means can certainly lead to great harm. Apart from the consequential considerations, though, there is another casualty when deliberating in the normal way by allowing ends to eclipse means. Ends are naturally associated with consequentialist considerations. When the end becomes the object of action, then consequentialist considerations can eclipse other moral considerations and schemes. So, in this preference of ends over means there is also a preference of consequentialist schemes over other, competing ethical schemes. Consider a moral scheme based on principles. Such a scheme could sometimes be at odds with a scheme oriented toward bringing about a certain outcome. In the example of Iraq, there is a well-established legal principle that disallows one nation from targeting an entire population. This principle is operative whether or not the nations are at war. Since the end eclipses the means here, ethics by consequence also eclipses ethics by principle, again leading the war-making machine to make the graver form of moral error, a Type I error. Given that laws and legal principles are an extremely important feature in international ethics, this preference of ends over means—consequence over principle— puts us in a very precarious position indeed. This practice entails the notion that the laws of war and international laws that govern means are always going to be subject to being overridden by the desired consequences that constitute ends, namely victory or national security.

Principles associated with the laws of war and international law will also be subjugated by this drive to reach our ends, if we allow ends to eclipse means. The principle of discriminating between combatant and noncombatant or between responsible leaders and civilians will be in danger of being set aside if the principle comes into conflict with the end being sought. American leaders have violated this principle by making civilians the target of the sanctions, thus abandoning even an instrumental proportionality calculation of inflicting an exceedingly high rate of collateral damage during the war. The principle of restraint—restraint from excessive force and unnecessary harm—has also been violated in the process of imposing these practices. Whenever we carry out some means to bring about some end, we can potentially be subject to moral considerations in the form of principles. If ends completely obscure means when we act, then we will be in a position in which we may be foregoing principles. The military can come to disregard law and principle because it sees no innate value in the means employed to bring about an end; it values only ends innately. "The case is so clear that, instead of arguing it directly, it will prove more profitable to consider how it is that there has grown up the belief that there are such things as ends having value apart from valuation of the means by which they are reached."[26]

The current conception of reasoning with means and ends is unsatisfactory because of this fracturing between means and ends. When means overshadow ends and we lose sight of the further ends—as covered in chapter 3—then this type of fracture creates an unsatisfactory situation by truncating the continuum in one direction. Likewise, when ends eclipse means and we lose sight of the moral gravity of the means—as discussed just above—then this second type of fracture correspondingly creates an unsatisfactory situation by truncating the continuum in the other direction. The conception is unsatisfactory because it represents a mode of reasoning with ends and means, a mode that is not fully integrated. So far, in this chapter as in the previous one, I have established the unsatisfactory nature of being quasi-reflective when reasoning with means and ends. In the next section, I continue my critique on ends. In the section after next, in contrast to the negative project of critiquing the defects of the current reasoning about means and ends, I will engage in a positive project and discuss a relationship between means and ends that will be more adequate, a conception of reasoning with means and ends that is integrated and morally justifiable. The great paradox is that America goes to war against forces that it plays a large role in creating, and each war spawns new threats of largely its own creation.

PRESUMED ENDS

Values predominate in military ethics. Are values really valuable, in themselves? In other words, do values have innate value? Or are they only instrumentally valuable? Every branch of U.S. military service has within the last decade proclaimed the importance of being "values-based organizations," and they have each fashioned a set of values.

Values predominate because they are the central feature of ethics instruction now in the military. The Army even added one week to basic training so that new recruits could "inculcate" the Army values. Every soldier carries a plastic card in his wallet and a tag (along with his dog tags) around his neck with the Army values on them. At West Point, every cadet endures something on the order of eighty hours of instruction through the Center for the Professional Military Ethic—in addition to the academic curriculum—instruction that is entitled "values education training," VET for short. Much of the instruction revolves around the use of values to aid in moral understanding and judgment. The new Army Chief of Staff, General Peter Schoomaker, is championing the warrior ethos project for the military. He has developed a new Soldier's Creed, which is one of his initiatives to spread the new gospel, the new creed. The new creed introduces the new values surrounding the warrior ethos. Historically, ever since soldiers became professionals in the early modern period (indeed, the word "soldier" derives from the Latin word for pay, *sold*), it was enough for them to be soldiers. Now it is not enough to be a soldier; the new requirement is to be a warrior. Soldiers used to protect the nation by providing for its defense. Now warriors are, according the new creed, to "deploy, engage, and destroy the enemies of the United States." The new creed provides the ominous acronym from *deploy, engage, and destroy*: DEAD.

The fact of the matter is that for all the emphasis put on values as being evidence that the military is ethical, these values as employed are only instrumental to the military's explicitly stated purpose and final end—that of victory. If these values did not aid in achieving victory for the military, they never would have been chosen as values in the first place. This claim may sound extremely cynical. A darker view of values is that they are not there primarily to promote ethics. Institutional values primarily serve the institution. That's why institutions choose them, and if a value does not serve the institution, then the institution would not keep it. "Individual values of loyalty, duty, and discipline derive from the technical needs of the hierarchy. They are experienced as highly personal moral imperatives by the individual, but at the organizational level they are simply the technical preconditions for the maintenance of the larger system."[27] And these values serve the military's stated purpose, which is explicitly stated: to fight and win the nation's wars.

The senior-most leaders in the Army continually tout the rhetoric that the purpose of the U.S. Army is to "fight and win the nation's wars." The last several Army chiefs of staff have explicitly articulated this purpose,[28] and subordinate leaders at every level echo the same. So the official final end of the Army, at least descriptively—in the eyes of those who run the Army—is victory. Every other end the Army works to achieve is instrumental to the final end of victory. Victory is the end, the background requirement, the commonplace; in other words in it is the presumption upon which everything else rests and the end at which the entire military aims. Even ethics in the military is bounded by this constraint, and this is perhaps one of its greatest ethical challenges. Some readers may be asking at this point: What should the purpose be if it isn't victory, winning the nation's wars? Let me bring some ideas together here. In the previous chapter I set out to establish that victory is a means to further end. We lose sight of this relationship when we call victory the purpose. The preamble to the United States Constitution establishes the purpose of the military is to "provide for the common defense." The constitutional purpose is much more amenable to morality than the purpose of victory. "Defense" entails fighting defensive wars, which are the only kind of wars that are moral. The currently stated purpose of victory does not rule out offensive wars, be they preemptive or preventive. The current purpose sustains the Long War's program of endless preventive wars.

The worst case of this constraint—that everything the Army does must somehow lead to victory—entails the notion that ethics should be abandoned altogether. One of the command manuals for senior leaders essentially abandons ethics when it says, "Ethical decisions also sometimes involve tough choices rather than mechanical application of academic principles."[29] It may sound as if the statement is simply resisting the temptation to resort to academic philosophy in order to make a decision, which, of course is one of the themes in the military: avoiding philosophy. But the use of the phrase "tough choices" often works as linguistic code to signify that leaders are choosing to do something that would be wrong by some measure. Use of this linguistic code often helps to soften the blow of doing something wrong, to attempt to justify doing something bad; it is a euphemism. While serving a euphemistic function, having to make tough choices does not proffer real justification. In this case, making "tough choices" or "tough decisions" at the expense of moral principle could be an indication that the decision would be wrong ethically. Interestingly, the cadet prayer contains the phrase that encourages people to "choose the harder right instead of the easier wrong."[30] Sometimes the right thing to do is the harder thing to do, but often people in the military confuse this with the idea that something is right because it is harder to do. This confusion is related to the problem of tough choices discussed above and can lead to unfortunate consequences. A similar confusion exists in the senior leadership and command manual when it talks about moral toughness, which "will motivate soldiers collectively to gain moral ascendancy over their enemy."[31] The term "moral ascendancy" in any of its senses is a concept that the military should not embrace. The military often conflates moral ascendancy to refer to ethical superiority in one sense and psychological superiority in the other. In the first case it would be contrary to any kind of ethical understanding based on the universality of morality. The military's inability to recognize the moral equality of the enemy is actually a great ethical challenge. In the second case, the military should avoid using the term "moral" if it is referring to the psychological. This language of moral toughness and superiority is more evidence that the military is more interested in using professional ethics to serve the practical needs of the institution rather than to serve morality itself. All of this language of moral

toughness and the harder right has more to do with Victorian ideals of priva-
tion and discipline than with morality. Many times people talk of *the military
professional ethic* more as a type of *work ethic* than as a subject dealing with
moral matters.

Yet while morality itself may not be important to national decision
makers, the appearance of moral behavior is of the utmost importance. When
they do address immoral actions, military and political leaders use the language of national security, expediency, or force protection. These constants
and variables all are part of the equation of victory. The mere appearance of
acting ethically should not be enough, however. American military and political leaders recognize the moral gravity in certain cases yet act immorally
because the final end motivates them to work to reach it, even when that
end overrides moral considerations.

Acting morally is not a *primary* concern for the military. I find it hard
to imagine how some people take issue with this claim, even considering
America's recent experiences. Moral error is a consequence of the lack of
substantive moral concern and a poor understanding of the subject matter. I
have argued that these problems at the level of theory have always been present, and that moral error has always been the logical and practical consequence. Bad theory leads to bad practice. We did not get better at this after
Vietnam. Our bad understanding led to moral error throughout the 1980s
and 1990s. For example, in the Bosnian campaign Admiral Leighton Smith's
forces had bombed as wide a selection and range of targets as possible while
remaining within the legal constraints of targeting. After servicing these targets with little effect, the American military leader wanted to do more bombing. The American political leaders told him that he could bomb the same
targets again. Unsatisfied with the idea of bombing the same legitimate targets again, Smith insisted that he wanted to bomb new targets, a wider range
and selection of targets.[32] Was morality the primary concern of Admiral
Smith as he sought a wider selection of targets, given that he initially was
given the widest range of legal and moral targets to begin with? Was morality
the primary concern when pilots less than discriminately bombed military targets later on in Kosovo from 30,000 feet? The same could be asked of the
excessive collateral damage in Afghanistan or the decade-long devastation of
Iraq—was morality the *primary* concern? With victory in war being the final
end that the military keeps aiming at, the military has often lost sight of
moral concerns, even those of great consequence. For example, America is
one of the last countries in the world yet to sign the land mine ban treaty,
joined only by members of the so-called axis of evil. Land mines kill indiscriminately, even when used with utmost care and usually for decades after
conflict ends, and military and political leaders from around the world recognize the gravity of the indiscriminate killing. Indiscriminate killing means

that noncombatants die or suffer injury, and so the continued use of land mines violates this primary moral and legal principle. Military leaders argue that land mines are essential to protect American forces that may be in harm's way. But in reality, land mines are not essential even though they may sometimes enhance a defensive position. Military leaders, backed by their political bosses, argue that protecting the American forces through the use of land mines is more important than the possibilities of mishaps due to the mines, preferring the Type I over the Type II error. The military is also afraid that the banning of one type of weapon will lead the world down a slippery slope, as evidenced when Army Chief of Staff Dennis J. Reimer was among those who voiced concern "that banning land mines would lead to the out-lawing of other weapons."[33] They do not want to give up their ability to use land mines because land mines will increase their chances of achieving their final end, even at the expense of acting ethically. How can America tout moral ascendency while standing with rogue nations when it comes to issues such as the proliferation of land mines, or nuclear weapons for that matter? Should America continue to say one thing and do another? One way of set-ting conditions to achieve a better moral understanding and practice is to become more reflective concerning the way we think about means and ends.

How can we ensure that our continuum is integrated? I'll lay out four principles of integration: connectivity, transitivity, fungibility, and reciproc-ity. First, and minimally, to visualize a continuum, one has to recognize that ends and means should be connected; an end should be connected to a means and a means should be connected to an end. Thinking of means and ends along a continuum helps to see how ends and means should work in concert. Second, the principle of transitivity would involve keeping higher-order ends in mind as well as higher-order means in mind, which helps to integrate ends and means along this continuum. Third, and following from the second principle, it also helps to view ends and means as being fungible when we view any particular end as being a means also and any particular means as being an end also. Ends become means once we reach them, and means become ends when we work backwards to enact the means. The con-tinuum demands that we view ends as means and means as ends, as long as we do not lose sight of further means and further ends. And the fourth prin-ciple is that of reciprocity in the form of regulation. Justified ends should reg-ulate means, and the employment of only moral means should regulate ends.

Speaking generally in a military context then, first, when warriors engage in an operation, they should keep in mind that the means they employ should work toward some end. At the same time, they should also keep the means in mind when they strive to reach an end. In other words, the means and the ends are both relevant and each is connected to the other. People generally have this idea when means and ends are involved.

This view is essentially the standard view, but by itself it does not ensure a justified view of the way ends and means should work together. Further, and second, to think of the continuum adequately, warriors should look in both directions along the continuum and keep higher-order ends and higher-order means in mind. Third, they should realize that any point along the continuum should function as both a means and an end. Fourth and last, warriors should apply the principle of reciprocity, working only toward justified ends with moral means. Consider the following example to illustrate these principles.

I'll start with the typical warrior viewpoint, which holds that our bombing of Japan was morally justified. In the current model of ends-means reasoning, warriors have come to believe in the morality of the bombing because the bombings brought about the end of the war—and thus brought about a victory. The sole focus is victory; it is the main relevant factor here. This standard view of means and ends shows the manner in which the pursuit of ends can become more important than considerations of means. It also helps to explain how people can come to embrace the idea that *the end justifies the means*. As long as the relationship between means and ends remains binary, one can always apply a consequentialist override to justify any means used. The warrior viewpoint on this matter will not likely change, but an application of the first principle would at least get them to recognize that means and ends are both relevant factors. Once they start thinking in terms of means and ends, we can work to apply the other principles, possibly even influencing their point of view.

The next step is to apply the second principle, which demands that the continuum be more than a binary system involving one end and one means. The second principle requires that we think of higher-order ends and higher-order means as well. So far, the warrior view illustrates the defect discussed in chapter 4 because it shows how one point along the continuum can overshadow every other point—victory is viewed only as an end without any consideration of further ends. Consideration of further ends can be powerful when one is trying to demonstrate that ends do not necessarily justify means. It usually is revelatory for warriors to realize that the purpose of victory is to establish peace, at least a peace that is as good as the one that existed before the hostilities. If peace is not obtained, and it rarely is, then at a minimum they should have improved rather than worsened conditions on the ground. To lose sight of the further end of peace by focusing on victory truncates the continuum so that they cannot see any further ends. The standard viewpoint also illustrates how the moral quality of the means is disregarded. A full exploration of the effect that means have on higher-order ends normally weakens considerably the view that the end justifies the means. Applying immoral means—dropping bombs on noncombatants, causing unnecessary harm and excessive damage—while bringing about victory may at the same time hamper further ends, higher-order ends, particularly if that further end is peace or improved conditions. The warrior assessment may begin to change should they recognize this second principle.

The third principle establishes an idea that lies dormant in the second principle. If an achieved end, as, say, a point along the continuum, becomes a means for a further end, then that point on the continuum is both an end and a means. The same point can be the end for a prior means and also a means for a further end. In the standard warrior view, to continue this example, victory is the end that the military seeks. When applying the third principle, warriors should be able to see that victory also functions as a means to the further end of peace. Carrying out the logic of the continuum, then, peace when viewed in one way would be the end of victory, yet would also be a means when viewed in another way: Peace would be the means to reestablish normal and healthy national and international relations, including having people engaged in meaningful work, education, research, commerce, and travel. The continuum works in the other direction as well. If victory over Japan were the end sought, then America had to consider the means to bring about this end. Let's say that the means of bringing about this victory would be engaging enemy military forces with superior military forces (superior in quality), with superior strategy, and superior operational campaigns. While this engagement of superior forces would be a means when viewed from one point of view, from another point of view it would also be an end. One of the means of bringing about the end of engaging the Japanese military with superior military forces would be to have a superior Navy. Having a superior Navy would be a means, but it would also become an end. Moving backward to find higher-order means, in order to realize the end of having a superior Navy, we would have to employ the means of training and equipping a superior Naval Force. We did this part right, for we did have a superior Navy. By the time America dropped the nuclear bombs on Japan, the Japanese Navy had already been defeated. Understanding that each point along the continuum can function both as a means and as an end paves the way toward the idea that each point along the continuum should be evaluated as being both a means and an end. Recognizing that the continuum goes indefinitely in each direction helps to set the stage for the fourth principle. Each end must be morally legitimate, and each means must be so, also.

Reciprocity is the fourth principle, and it helps to complete the model of the continuum so that people can think about means and ends in an adequate and morally justified way. Once people can see that each point along the continuum is a nexus or link that we can view as either a means or an end, based on the point of view, then the next step is to evaluate each nexus or link as a means and an end. In order for us to set goals and perform actions that are legitimate and morally justified, the moral considerations of both ends and means become very important. In general, we would be erring any time we pursued an end that was not morally legitimate or any time we employed means that were not morally justified. One way to check the ends the military works toward is to qualify the ends. The military will be pursuing legitimate ends if it pursues an honorable victory, an enduring peace, and good social relations, each in turn. To carry through with our example, if the military pursues an honorable victory by employing means that are consistent with moral principles, then they are employing moral means. Let's say that the American Navy defeated the Japanese Navy to bring about an honorable victory (perhaps apart from the unrestricted American submarine warfare in the Pacific). Let's say, for the sake of argument, that the rest of the military had followed suit and had defeated the Japanese military, gaining an honorable victory. Then the end of achieving this honorable victory would have been the means to achieve an enduring peace. The end of this enduring peace would in turn have become the means to achieve normal, healthy international relations. This is how the continuum should work. But it did not work this way. The way American ended the war with Japan helped to start the Cold War. Remember, Walzer called it an act of terrorism that left America vulnerable for reprisals. And the 1993 bomber of the World Trade Center, Ramzi Yousef, testified that his motivation was to avenge the deaths that America inflicted by the bombing of Japan. So the way we ended World War II helped to motivate not only the Cold War but also the acts of terrorism against us today. The pursuit of victory in World War II ran counter to the constitutional purpose of "providing for the common defense," when considering the long view and the global system.

Let's take a closer look at the code of the warrior. Victory loses its meaning if nation-states are unwilling to lose. The same warrior code that Westerners admire as part of Japanese culture—a code that encourages victory at any price while forbidding defeat—paradoxically escalated the brutality of World War II until it ended in a horrific cataclysm. The warrior code appears to be admirable at first glance: never give up, death before dishonor, and so on. But should it be so admirable? The Japanese soldiers were fanatics, even becoming suicidal (from a Western viewpoint—the Japanese did not consider it to be suicide). The suicidal fanaticism displayed by the Japanese soldiers on the Pacific Islands was met with like determination by the Americans, which led to fighting as barbaric as any in history. The code appears to work fine as long as only one side in a conflict practices it, but barbarism returns as soon as both sides adopt it. As soon as one side has adopted the code, however, it has departed from one of the foundations of conventional warfare. This conventionality has come and gone from the world stage, beginning perhaps in the Westphalian arrangement and lasting scarcely two hundred years. As part of the convention, militaries fought each other to a decision—one side won. But in order for one side to win, the other side had to lose. The side that lost went through certain protocols of defeat. When political, social, and cultural forces began to resist the idea of losing to an enemy with a stronger military, then conventionality began to decline, and the outcome of warfare was no longer in the hands of a military contest. The new American warrior code—never give up, win at any cost, death before dishonor—sounds very noble. The warriors like it a lot. But do we like it because we think we are the only ones who now hold such a code? What happens when everyone follows our lead and adopts the warrior code? A couple of examples may help to illustrate this subtle yet vitally important point.

Robert E. Lee was confounded during the first two years of the American Civil War because he enjoyed stunning military victories over the Army of the Potomac, yet the war did not end but continued for years. Lee eventually surrendered. He could have led his Army through years of guerilla warfare, but it appeared that Grant adopted the warrior ethos to a greater degree than Lee did. Grant and his generals, driven by Lincoln, were prepared to go to any extreme to win. Lee was not; enough of the chivalrous code was left in Lee to surrender in an honorable way. Grant's imposition of the "unchivalrous and ungenerous" edict of unconditional surrender foreshadowed the equally unchivalrous and ungenerous occupation and reconstruction that was to follow. What would have happened if Lee too had adopted the warrior ethos of never giving up? Well, while Lee was chivalrous enough to surrender his Army, the population at large resisted their defeat in numerous ways, refusing to go through the protocols of defeat. While Lee was an honorable soldier, some of his juniors resisted their defeat by being instrumental in the Ku Klux Klan—with the goal of kill or be killed. Lincoln proclaimed emancipation for blacks in the South, but this resistance to defeat prevented full emancipation for another century. Military victory is no longer decisive in warfare. On the European continent, only a few years after the prolonged war experienced by the Americans, the Prussians were intent on winning quickly by defeating the French with even more spectacular victories. Sure enough, the Prussians defeated the French decidedly at Sedan and accepted the surrender of the French Army. But the war continued for years because of the uprising of the people in Paris, who refused to give up, which led to a bloody civil war of their own. The reparations that Prussia demanded caused tensions that took most of the next century to work out. These examples help to illustrate the paradoxes of victory and defeat, which we need to rethink in a vigorous and desperate way.[34] Military victory is indecisive when the people of the nation-state refuse defeat. When a significant part of the population refuses defeat, then warfare is no longer conventional, and the convention of victory and defeat loses its meaning. The effects of military conflict become much more costly, taking not just decades but centuries to work out. History has long taught us this insight. Why are we surprised, then, when an American president can stand ceremoniously on the deck of a carrier and proclaim victory in Iraq, only to find months, and inevitably years, later that military victory did not bring an end to this war? Political and military leaders need to rethink the precepts upon which we are now engaged in perpetual conflict. For starters, we need to rethink the meaning and efficacy of military victory.

However, we know that the ideal continuum of moral means and legitimate ends does not work in actuality. America did exact a victory over Japan, but it was a dishonorable victory. The terms of victory included unconditional surrender, complete disarmament, and a humiliating occupation. Interestingly, Roosevelt's imposition of unconditional surrender was a continuation of the policy first implemented by Grant. This dishonorable victory and the enduring tensions that it created were the means not to bring about an enduring peace, but a hollow peace, with negative consequences to this day and most likely far beyond. This end of hollow peace that we achieved has been the means to bring about not an atmosphere of true trust and cooperation between the two countries, but a clouded relationship that is fraught with tension and circumspection. Japan continues to remain militarily disarmed in a region of the world that is increasingly volatile. At the same time, the American military presence has been unwelcome there for quite some time, from the point of view of the Japanese people, and it took only the 2001 incident of the submarine USS *Greeneville* rising into the Japanese fishing vessel near Hawaii to bring this issue to the surface. This tension between the two countries has had a huge impact on international trust and cooperation, not the least of which is the example that America set, contributing no small part to the nuclear paranoia holding the world hostage during the Cold War. The example has recently been reinforced, leaving little doubt that America will go to any extreme necessary to "defeat" anyone it finds threatening. What happens when others adopt these twin pillars of policy: preventive war and the warrior ethos, perpetual war and unconditional surrender?

For the principle of reciprocity to work, the moral aspects of means and ends have to be considered. The consideration of legitimate ends will regulate means employed, and the consideration of moral means will also reciprocally regulate ends. Ends can regulate means. Henry Richardson argues that ends should regulate our means to achieve those ends. He gives an example of this regulation when he says, "the goal of becoming surgeon general should regulate (and here delimit) her aim of being a person of integrity."[35] He goes on to say that it need not work the other direction.

There is nothing about being a person of integrity that necessitates becoming a surgeon general. Ends become regulatory in that we would adopt those means that would contribute to achieving the end, and we would not adopt any means that would not contribute to the end being sought. I largely agree with Richardson's analysis, and for my purposes, this is a good starting point. Means have to work to achieve ends. However, this is basically the suitability criterion, suitable in that the means adopted work to achieve the end being sought. I want to extend this idea and consider the idea of allowing means to regulate ends as well.

I would propose that we should invoke the principle of reciprocity here. If ends should regulate means, then perhaps means should also regulate ends. "No case of notable achievement can be cited in any field (save as a matter of sheer accident) in which the persons who brought about the end did not give loving care to the instruments and agencies of its production."[36] If there is reciprocity here, then just as ends can regulate means by restricting immoral or undustifiable means, then means can regulate ends by restricting immoral or unjustifiable ends. So, just as regulatory ends can revise means, regulatory means can revise ends. The application of moral means will help to avoid the pursuit of dishonorable victories and help to ensure honorable ones. The application of honorable victories will help to regulate the end of peace that we hope to achieve and will help steer us away from pursuing a hollow peace and toward an enduring peace. Means can regulate ends by making our ends more modest, less ambitious, never allowing for an immoral and unjustifiable policy such as the Project for a New American Century.

Richardson differs from Dewey on this point of being able to value an end in itself by arguing that "a final end can be regarded as choiceworthy in itself while at the same time being employed as a means to further deliberation and being critically evaluated in light of the costs in achieving it."[37] Dewey does not want to separate the value of ends from the value of means in his continuum, while Richardson wants to argue that a mere means that becomes an end can be valued without considering the further end because "what was a mere means is thus transformed into an independent project in the course of his deliberation."[38] I would resolve this tension by adding that our moral evaluation of each point along the continuum—or nexus or link—should be choiceworthy when considered as an end as well as when considered as a means. When warriors see how all of the principles of integration work to illuminate ends and means and the way they should work together, they will be much less inclined to embrace our dropping of the bombs on Japan. When they are less inclined to embrace our past immoral bombings, perhaps they will also be less inclined to contemplate future immoral bombings.

DELIBERATING NEW ENDS

Julia Annas points out that Aristotle used both *telos* and *skopos* when he was talking about ends, and then she claims that the interchangeable usage may be unfortunate because they refer to two different concepts. While people refer to *telos* when they are talking about their aims or goals, *telos* essentially also carries with it the connotation that the person is engaged in activity. This means that *telos* essentially refers not to the target itself, but actually to the hitting of the target. *Skopos* would be the target itself.[39]

This subtle difference between the hitting of the target and the target itself, or between *achieving the end* and *the end itself* is a significant aspect of the problem of instrumental reasoning. And the equivocation that exists between the two senses of "end"—achieving the end and the end itself—makes the ambiguity of the word "end" potentially a problem. The end itself can be presumed, given, and any discussion of its legitimacy can be suppressed. What becomes important is achieving the end. If the military is concerned only with achieving the end—victory—without reflecting upon, deliberating about, and justifying the end itself, then that places the military in danger of achieving a dishonorable and hollow victory, even if they win. Can we justify the end? When the end is just presumed, or passed down from generation to generation without justification and philosophical scrutiny, then all the work that goes into achieving the end itself, the presumed target, can be accompanied by some results that would run counter to other, more appropriate ends. When the target itself is presumed, and in the case of the military that would be victory, then the end in the sense of *skopos* remains subdued, and what becomes important is the end in the sense of *telos*, that of hitting the target, achieving the end. The achievement of the end, victory, is somewhat measurable. The military can gauge whether it is doing its job in terms that are most of the time fairly concrete and tangible. But the problem here lies in the fact that while the military can feel justified in achieving the end, it may not be moving toward a justifiable end. The end in the sense of the target for the military appears to be "a given." There seems to be no possibility, desire, or need to deliberate over new ends. Previous Army chiefs of staff have stated the policy explicitly. The rhetoric and the reality exist at all levels of command, and all leaders accept this end unquestionably. And there does not seem to be any great desire on the part of the military institution to look for new ends. There certainly appears to be no need to deliberate about new ends.

The military can hit what it shoots at—it can hit the target. But is victory really the end, the target that the military should really be shooting at? Has the military arrived at the right end? General Reimer cites MacArthur as helping to validate the end of victory. Reimer believed that the purpose, and

hence the end, of the military is "to win the Nation's wars." Reimer continued to explain that "General Douglas MacArthur, in 1961, summed it up
best when he said: 'Yours is the profession of arms, the will to win, the sure
knowledge that in war there is no substitute for victory—and that if we fail,
the nation will be destroyed.'"[40] So it appears that the reasoning involved
here is that since it is of utmost importance to win, then winning must be the
end of the military. Winning is a necessary feature here, a necessary condition, but it also appears to be a sufficient condition as well. According to
MacArthur, if the military fails, then the nation will be destroyed. This is a
dubious claim, given that there are several counterexamples; many countries
have lost wars without being destroyed. This is not to deny, however, that
the possibility of destruction certainly exists should a country lose in war. In
the new Global War on Terror, things may not be as they now appear. The
basic reason for Gulf II may indeed not be primarily about the resources in
the Middle East. Instead, the basic reason may be a national demonstration
of the warrior spirit, putting the rest of the world on notice that America has
the battle culture of forbearance. But this strategy of taking the war to the
rest of the world so that the war does not come here will be ultimately counterproductive. Military power and economic coercion do nothing to relieve
the tensions that are causing the terrorism to begin with. We can win militarily all day long, but if the motivation of terrorism is not dealt with, then terrorism will persist; wars become permanent, as in Orwell's novel *1984*
(perhaps Orwell was only about twenty years off). War is peace, Freedom is
slavery. Ignorance is strength. Offense is defense.

A different leap in logic makes this claim dubious—to jump from the
claim that winning is necessary to the claim that victory is the end of war.
Quite simply, just because winning is an important feature does not make it
the final end, even if it is not a necessary feature. MacArthur himself uses the
same phrase "there is no substitute for victory" in the completely different
context of his speech to Congress in 1951 after his dismissal as commander of
the forces in Korea. In this context, though, he was comparing victory to
diplomacy, arguing that victory is much more convincing than the diplomatic
process the country would use to seek to appease China.[41] In this case, in this
other context, victory and diplomacy are both means to some other end.
Victory cannot be the final end. Later, when he addressed the Corps of
Cadets on May 12, 1962, and he used the same phrase, "there is no substitute
for victory," it still carries with it the same meaning—victory is more convincing than diplomacy. The fact that he adds the sentiment that the nation
will be destroyed if the military fails still only reinforces the point that military victory is the preferred method to end a war. It does not mean that the
final end in war should be victory. This misreading has led the military's leadership astray on this issue for decades.

At West Point, a former superintendent exhorts the same rhetoric. He had been concerned that the "no substitute for victory" slogan could be having an adverse effect on the cadets. He wrote in a letter that "the mission of the United States Military Academy is to prepare cadets for commissioned service in America's Army, an institution that is morally obligated to 'fight and win the Nation's wars.' There are no trophies given on the battlefield for 'most improved army,' and unlike other endeavors, where it can be easy to rationalize lack of success, there is no justifiable alternative to 'winning' in the profession of arms."[42] His concern was limited to the way that cadets engage in athletic activities, though. Here the two alternatives would be *winning* and *losing*, and this is how he is interpreting the choices. If there is no substitute for victory, then one cannot lose—and this entails the requirement that one must do anything possible to win. He does not want to "win at all costs" on the playing fields at West Point. Yet at the same time he admonishes the military community should they confuse this requirement on the playing fields with the requirement on the killing fields. War is different, or so he claims. He says that war is different because the prize is different. To say "there is no justifiable alternative to winning in the profession of arms" does entail that the military must do what it has to in order to achieve victory.

But he is missing MacArthur's main distinction, and by doing so has suggested a requirement that will greatly challenge any conception or practice of ethics in the profession of arms. When MacArthur talks about there being no substitute for victory, he is not thinking of the alternative choices between *winning* and *losing*. Instead he is talking about the alternative choices between *victory* and *diplomacy*. In this he means that especially once a war is ongoing it is far better to bring the war to an end through victory than through diplomacy, which he fears would not bring a long-lasting peace, based on his interpretation of historical precedent. When considering the choice of victory over diplomacy, there is no reason to do away with winning honorably. Winning honorably would be completely compatible with having to win, if one were merely the choice of victory over diplomacy. One cannot legitimately derive the military's purpose as being *winning the nation's wars* based on a preference of fighting over negotiating. It does not necessarily follow. And because the military's leaders continue to believe that nothing can substitute for victory in the wrong context, the military has been driven toward a morally questionable end—that of not only winning, but also winning at all costs. When the military goes out to win at all costs, it will give up its moral concerns. We lose in the long term when we give up moral concerns. And perhaps MacArthur was wrong, anyway. Our leaders are learning the hard way that *there is no substitute for diplomacy*.

It is safe to say that the issue of harm to others is a moral concern. Victory is of practical concern as well as of moral concern. Practical concerns

would include efficiency, cost, resource husbandry, and victory. These practical concerns are important, and I am not suggesting that the military disregard them or discount them completely. But even the concerns that are
seemingly only practical have a moral dimension. Hurting noncombatants,
using excessive force, inflicting unnecessary harm, and acts of perfidy are
among those activities that would be immoral. Being inefficient, overspend-
ing resources, and even losing have moral considerations. Military necessity
often drives warriors down the road of wrongdoing.

Military necessity is an ambiguous and difficult term. Since the first laws
were codified "in the Lieber rules of 1863, military necessity was defined as
'those measures which are indispensable for securing the ends of war, and
which are lawful according to the modern law and usages of war.'"[43] This historical account is consistent with the current conception of "military necessity, which has been defined as that principle which justifies those measures
not forbidden by international law which are indispensable for securing the
complete submission of the enemy as soon as possible."[44] In this first sense, it is
lawful to commit acts that would ordinarily be proscribed during times of
peace, but it would be unlawful to commit acts that are proscribed by the laws
of war. Over the past several decades, though, military necessity has taken on
new meaning. In this new sense, the acts committed do not have to be in
accordance with the laws of war. The term "military necessity" has often been
invoked in this new sense, in the sense that some action is necessary for the
military mission even if it means the laws of war are overridden. Telford
Taylor, the chief prosecutor during the Nuremberg trials, admitted that
modern warfare has influenced the way that military necessity affects the laws
of war. Two factors have an impact on this phenomenon. The first is that it is
very hard to determine exactly what is militarily exigent in war. The second is
the increasing devastation that better technologies bring to warfare. Taylor
says "other examples of the impact of military necessity on the laws of war
come readily to mind. A signal and terrible example during the Second World
War was the growing acceptance of aerial bombardment of population centers.... I mention it here to underline the lesson of all these examples, which
is that the laws of war do not have a fixed content but are constantly reshaped
by the exigencies of warfare."[45] Sometimes the slippery slope is not a fallacy.

These two factors that influence the transformation of military necessity into a defense of illegal activity—the slippery notions of inevitable and
increasingly devastating technologies—are pragmatic concerns. Reasoning
about these factors has revolved around practical concerns that should not
be in conflict with moral concerns. The idea of necessity is driven by the
need to achieve victory. Technologies built for war are built according to
practical requirements. The military and the scientific community alike are
not considering moral criteria when they work to increase power and accuracy. In the case of increased explosive power, the more power weapons have

the more possible and probable it is to violate principles of discrimination, proportionality, and restraint. And in the case of increased accuracy, the more accurate it is, the better the military can hit what it wants. Neither the military nor the scientific community are pursuing more accurate weapons in the name of these moral principles, but only to help them better and more efficiently hit their targets. The scientist is interested only in the practical aspects of the weapon: the faster bullet, the bigger explosion, or the more concentrated laser. The warrior wants to weaponize any potential technology. And as scientists and engineers develop new generations of dangerous weapons that blind the eyes, disrupt the nervous system, or microwave human tissue, the engineers and the military liaisons are asking only scientific and engineering questions—they are not asking the moral questions.[46] Weapons are becoming more indiscriminate and are causing more unnecessary harm, violating no doubt many important moral principles. Just beyond the horizon are technologies more dangerous than those technologies that produced nuclear, biological, and chemical weapons (NBC)—the traditional culprits making up weapons of mass destruction (WMD). "The 21st century technologies—genetics, nanotechnology, and robotics (GNR)—are so powerful that they can spawn whole new classes of accidents and abuses.... Thus we have the possibility not just of weapons of mass destruction but of knowledge-enabled mass destruction (KMD), this destructiveness hugely amplified by the power of self-replication."[47] The moral principles should be part of the criteria when the scientists and engineers go to make new weapons. The manner in which the military goes about fighting is important. And as long as the means are moral, then the military can pursue victory. But should victory be the final end?

Philosophers, military thinkers, and legal theorists have made a strong case for peace as a more appropriate aim for war than victory. Kant says in his *Metaphysics of Morals* that

> it can be said that establishing universal and lasting peace constitutes not merely a part of the doctrine of right but rather the entire final end of the doctrine of right within the limits of reason alone: for the condition for peace is the only condition in which what is mine and what is yours are secured under laws for a multitude of human beings living in proximity to one another and therefore under a constitution.[48]

Henry Richardson suggests that ends regulate people's choices and activities.[49] Kant speaks of ideas that are regulative, that direct people toward a certain goal.[50] Clausewitz understands that strategy regulates tactics and the idea of peace regulates strategy when he says, "The original means of strategy is victory—that is, tactical success; its ends, in the final analysis, are those objects which will lead directly to peace."[51] Clausewitz attended Kiesewetter's lectures on Kant, and sometimes wrote using Kantian phraseology.[52] When Francis Lieber drafted the first American legal code, *General Orders No. 100*, for Abraham Lincoln, he said in article twenty-nine, "the ultimate object of all modern war is a renewed state of peace."[53] I think Kant is perhaps important in firmly establishing the idea that peace is an end to be pursued, and I think he influenced these other two thinkers. Each of these two thinkers could have thought of peace as an end independent of any Kantian influence; the idea is fairly readily accessible. However, it is also possible that Kant helped to give purchase to the idea of peace as a final end. The 1999 leadership manual does mention, importantly, "The ultimate end of war, at least as America fights it, is to restore peace. For this reason the Army must accomplish its mission honorably. The Army fights to win, but with one eye open on the kind of peace that will follow the war."[54] The sentiment exists nowhere else in military doctrine, though.

The end of military activity should be to achieve a better peace than that which existed before the hostilities. If the moral method is instrumentally aimed at victory (which it often is) instead of attaining a better peace, then we will not be moving toward the proper moral end. The official policy is that the military exists to win the nation's wars. Not only is this concept too narrow, but it misses the further end, which is something beyond victory. If the military achieves victory through immoral means, then it will not achieve its further end, which is a better peace. The military has much work to do to straighten out its thinking about its end, its purpose. Even though the concept has been embedded in doctrine, it will be a long time before that doctrine takes hold, if it does at all. Philosophical deliberation about the proper final end for the military is vital—the end will regulate the military's actions, and the notion of victory as a final end regulates the military in a much different way than the idea of peace as a final end would regulate it. That difference is, significantly, a moral difference and worth a significant amount of time over which to reflect.

What kind of moral error is the pursuit of victory causing today? How much more analysis of Vietnam do we have to be hit over the head with before we start to understand that the pursuit of victory in Vietnam in order to liberate an oppressed people was a hollow pursuit? When will we start to learn from our own history? The terrorism we are facing today was caused largely by our foreign and military policies over the last century, particularly the last several decades. We are experiencing the unintended consequences of our past pursuits, what Chalmers Johnson calls "blowback." Consider again the German development of unrestricted submarine warfare as a clear example of counterproductivity. The Germans knew that this practice would very likely bring America into the war. They pursued the policy anyway. And this very pursuit sealed their fate—their pursuit of victory by any means brought about their defeat. Just as the Germans were defeated by their practices, which amounted to Type I errors, America could be facing the same result should it commit Type I errors. America is prepared to keep fighting fire with fire, or terror with terror, through a policy of illegal and immoral wars of prevention. Counter-terrorism is largely terrorism, as is counter-insurgency. Mohammed Hafez has documented that the counter-insurgency operations in Iraq have resulted only in an increase of violence.[55] The military has worked on nothing harder than its ability to rapidly deploy. What is the good of deploying large forces within days if these military deployments can occur faster than the political processes necessary to legitimate these deployments? Success in the end will depend on legitimacy more than anything else. The Middle East is now doubly occupied by illegitimate military force: The Iraqis experience a military occupation by the Coalition of the Willing, and the Palestinians by the Israelis. In the summer of 2006, Israel chose to defend its homeland by launching an offensive war into Lebanon. Given that we are experiencing terrorism in large part because of Western occupation and influence in the Middle East to begin with, are we relieving the tension causing the terrorism by a double military occupation? The double occupancy creates the very dangerous conditions for even greater violence. Intelligence agencies world-wide agree that American and Israeli belligerancy in the Middle East have increased the threat by several magnitudes of order. There are relevant similarities between our situation today and our situation in Vietnam that we should not be afraid to explore. Teaching can get in front of doctrine at times and practice can lag behind it. In any event, philosophical reflection, particularly methodical thinking, does help us to think about the relationships among doctrine, education, and practice; we should work toward achieving *reflective equilibrium*, as John Rawls would call it, or toward the exercise of *reciprocal illumination*, as Michael Walzer would call it—the healthy exchange between theory and practice.

ARE MORAL ENDS POSSIBLE?

Many warriors today, perhaps even most, lament the American military loss in Vietnam. They do not lament American involvement, even though perhaps they should. What warriors lament is something like the following set of beliefs: We could have won if only the military's hands had not been tied; we could have won if only the commie press hadn't betrayed its military; we could have won if only we had applied what has come to be known as the Powell Doctrine—the application of overwhelming military force for a clear political purpose. Oh, if only Colin Powell had been a general instead of a major back then. I say many if not most warriors think along these lines because I have perennially witnessed this view as the predominant view in the classroom since the early 1990s—the predominant view has not changed among the warriors, despite much excellent scholarship that dismantles this view. The Americans did enjoy tactical military success the vast majority of the time. Military success simply did not translate into strategic success. Overwhelming military power would have made no difference, because the political goal was neither clear nor legitimate. Our political ends that shape military action have to be legitimate in order for military success to amount to political success. At best, the Vietnam-era leaders who were in charge of the military during Desert Storm did not solve the problems they faced in Vietnam. At worst, they introduced new and more dangerous forms of moral error through a lack of moral understanding and a lack of philosophical ethics. The Powell Doctrine, thought to be the solution to the loss in Vietnam, has created the problems we face today, not the least of which was the Victory Syndrome. When there is a lack of systems thinking, today's cures create tomorrow's diseases. For example, the chief of staff of the Army is quoted in a recent *Military Review* article on "Improving Strategic Leadership" as saying that employing proxy forces in Afghanistan is a great idea. It is not a great idea; what good does it do to empower warlords if one of the political goals is to disempower warlords? Afghanistan is still cynically referred to as Warlordistan. This kind of thinking fails logically and morally—it does no good to employ tactical means that will work against strategic goals.[56]

It is sometimes said that if America were to have an official religion, that religion would be anti-communism. During the Cold War, Americans were so affected by their anti-communism that we could not recognize that Ho Chi Minh was favored by a populist movement and would have been the leader of the Vietnamese people through any political process. The South Vietnamese government installed by the United States had no real popular support, and through an objective set of eyes one could see that it was America that had invaded Vietnam. Our interference in that part of the world arguably made things worse for Vietnam, Laos, and particularly Cambodia. American intolerance for communism runs high, even when communist governments are democratically elected. Take, for example, the American-backed coup that installed Pinochet in Chile, supplanting the democratically elected Allende. It was Henry Kissinger and his immoral realist policies that wrote this deplorable episode into our history. The cold hand of Henry Kissinger is still crafting American foreign policy. He has been among the White House's most frequent visitors during the debacle in Iraq. Adept observers recognize his handiwork. Haiti experienced the same fate at American hands. The opposition forces America supported in Haiti were no more legitimate than Oliver North's Contras. Military might will not succeed if the political end is illegitimate. Legitimate ends are a prerequisite for the successful employment of military forces. Have we still not learned this insight from Vietnam and elsewhere? Today we find ourselves back in Iraq, after having won a decisive military victory, even by employing the Powell Doctrine, and our warrior leaders cannot understand why we have not won this war. It could very well be that we have not won the war because the political goal, the end of the military expedition, was not legitimate. America is unlikely to win the unwinnable Global War on Terror, or even any part of it, if our political goals are not legitimate—even when the military is victorious.

Many people, even some philosophers, want to do ethics without philosophy. They think that philosophical ethics is just for professors and their graduate students, and that it cannot give people any sound or practical guidance. One philosopher claims that moral theorists "do not even *purport* to be offering guidance to the morally perplexed, but only reflective thoughts *about* morality to the philosophically inclined."[57] This widely held view is one of the root factors that motivates those involved in professional ethics to eschew philosophical ethics. This view leads professional ethicists to look toward rejecting philosophy as they do when they turn to indoctrination, particularism, and instrumental moral methods in order to achieve presumed ends. General Charles C. Krulak, USMC (Ret.) criticizes the teaching of philosophical ethics at the Naval Academy. He says, "I know about the leadership challenges of war and peace, and I know that what brings success is not an understanding of Kantian ethics. Rather, it is good, old-fashioned leadership that is fostered by great examples (living and dead) and experiences generated by a knowledgeable faculty and an Academy that allows freedom to fail but ensures accountability and, therefore, allows learning to occur."[58]

By rejecting, avoiding, and diluting philosophy these professional ethicists believe they are enhancing the moral understanding and judgment of those people within the professions. The possibility exists that they may be imparting sound doctrine when they indoctrinate, passing on exemplary stories when they tell narratives, and employing justifiable methods when they teach their heuristic devices that make up their instrumental methods. And these approaches may very well improve the moral understanding and ethical judgment of those within the profession who take advantage of this type of ethics instruction. The professional ethicists deride those who emphasize "thinking about" morality over "offering guidance." It is this very "thinking about" morality that we need—that philosophers do—in order to make sure that professions have it right when they are "offering guidance." Philosophers, and others for that matter, should spend time and effort to ensure that any doctrine employed is sound, examples used are justified, and any methods manipulated are defensible.

Despite the fact that many will support the opposite view, philosophers can be good litigators when it comes to defending or prosecuting ideas, their cases dependent on them being able to pass the bar of reason. Paying attention to language, logic, and conceptual consistency is important when imparting doctrine, examples, or methods. If there are mistakes in the reasoning, there will be mistakes in the application. These mistakes lead to moral error. In the professions, these moral errors can amount to a great deal of trouble, especially in the military profession, because of the potential destructive forces they have at their disposal. Better practice requires better theories. I have never been one to think that things can't get any worse. Indeed, my argument here includes the idea that the world continues to get worse and that the United States shares a larger part of the blame than most of us can admit. As bad as things are now, they could get markedly worse. Truman and Eisenhower's policies toward the post-war world created the American security state. The path from a security state to a police state is a short one. Some say that we are only one terrorist attack away from becoming a police state. But we already possess many of the features of a police state. America also has many recidivistic features of a more primitive warfare state, evidenced most by the undeniable fact that our foreign policy is dominated by military considerations.

Essentially, the issue centers on the nature of moral education. Moral education in turn informs us how we should deliberate and solve moral problems. Philosophy can tell us that we should not pursue instrumental moral methods and that we should be cautious about moral decision-procedures. A proper moral method would be a complex critical method that takes into account agency, right action, moral worth, and appropriate ends. It also recognizes the fact that there are no decidable and complete decision-procedures. Philosophy would be helpful as part of an ethical education. The antitheorists will claim that there is no perfect philosophical moral theory. They are probably right, but this claim is really beside the point. They will also claim that moral theory does not help directly with giving us guidance, at least not in every situation. Philosophical ethics is important not because it is perfect, but because it helps us to improve our moral understanding and moral judgment. Even if it gives us nothing in a given situation—no definitive answers, no certainty—it will help us to move away from doctrine, examples, and methods that philosophers can show will lead to moral error—the subjects of the last three chapters. So, at a minimum, moral theory has a negative role, that of falsifying approaches that can demonstrably lead to moral error. But philosophical ethics has a positive role as well. The next chapter will pursue this theme. While it may not be able to give us guidance in every situation, it can help us in many situations. Most importantly, though, by improving our understanding and judgment we will better be able to figure out what we should do and what we should be. In addition, it can help to show us why. The other approaches can possibly give us the right answer, but if we turn to philosophical ethics as well, then we can also know why some answers are better than others and why some errors are worse than others, making an opaque moral understanding more transparent.

5

The Fully Reflective Life

Autonomy for Automatons

Every ethics teacher in the military hears the same perennial questions from the warriors they teach. What was wrong with dropping the bombs on Japan? Wouldn't we have lost a million soldiers, or several hundred thousand? Why didn't they leave the military alone during Vietnam so we could have won an overwhelming victory? Didn't we help win the Cold War by fighting communism? We have some new questions that compete and become perennial questions themselves. Didn't we get rid of an evil dictator by going into Iraq? And didn't we justify our military might by losing only thousands while the Iraqis lost tens of thousands? If America doesn't lead the fight against evil, who will? Don't we have to kill all the terrorists we can? They're just fanatics, anyway. And doesn't all this talk about morality just make it harder to win? The military institution creates, transmits, and sustains a culture that fosters a warrior mindset from which such questions flow easily. The warrior mindset is a web of belief that contains many precepts that are inconsistent with morality. Consider two prolific writers—Robert Kaplan and Ralph Peters—who have done much to create and sustain this cultural milieu by appealing to the political and military warriors. Both are widely read within war-making circles; both are hot ticket items on the military speaking circuit; both are held in high esteem among students and faculty here at the Command and General Staff College and elsewhere. Their writings and talks bolster the mindset that sustains the precepts that belong to the worldview of political and military realism: *realpolitik* and *realmilitare*. For the political and military realist, might is right, and morality is for the weak. Moral concerns at either the political or the military level of conflict are simply naïve to Kaplan and Peters and will only get one killed in this

Hobbesian world that is *solitary, poor, nasty, brutish, and short*. Robert Kaplan in *Warrior Politics* (2001) advises the princes that they should abandon moral concerns because of the geopolitical realities of this violent world. Ralph Peters, in his essay "When Devils Walk the Earth" from the book *Beyond Terror* (2002), advises the warriors not to follow the argument of the campus, that argument being not to be lowered to the level of the terrorist, but instead the warrior should follow the argument of the battlefield, which is to go ahead and lower oneself and engage in this *tough* and *dirty* business. And hence the time-honored maxims and precepts of the warrior are sustained: Kill or be killed; if it stands, level it; if it moves, destroy it; if in doubt, wipe it out; go ugly early; if you hesitate, you're dead; shoot them all and let God sort them out. As a result of this mindset, the warriors retreat back to the barbarity of Homeric warfare as they don the armor of Achilles. Mercy puts one at a disadvantage; morality is for the loser.[1]

The more time they spend in the military, the more warriors adopt these notions as part of their unreflective but deeply rooted beliefs and attitudes toward warfare. If we keep only the model of unreflective heteronomy, soldiers will simply pass on those intuitions they have inherited, perpetuating cultural norms through memetic replication, and then future ethics teachers will continue to be challenged with these questions. There are a few military schools that employ philosophers, who introduce students to philosophical ethics and engage the students in philosophical dialogue, using logic and ethical theory as tools for this dialogue. As a result of engaging the students in an open philosophical dialogue, the students have the opportunity to think these issues through for themselves, a requirement for living a fully reflective, autonomous life. Even over the course of a single semester, many students do begin to question the precepts of their heteronomous ethical precepts listed above. They also come to appreciate the understanding they gain by thinking things through themselves. In this way, the possibility is opened up for a moral model based on autonomy. Students receive an ethics education based on free inquiry from those who teach the subject of ethics philosophically. This benefit is often soon lost, however, as the warriors leave school and reenter the traditional ethically challenged milieu of the military institution. This culture is not improved by the ethics instruction warriors receive outside the academy of free inquiry, because outside of an academically free education they receive ethics training and instruction, not education. Ethics instructors in the military at large are often chaplains or others who will not adequately or systematically engage students with the rigors of philosophical ethics. Chaplains, by virtue of their function, will include notions, or at a minimum a tacit approval, of their faith and other dogmatic beliefs related to the field of ethics, inevitably reducing philosophical ethics and dialogue to fixed notions of moral truths and ethical foundations. And over time without the intellectual self-defense offered by philosophical ethics, the warriors

eventually succumb to the precepts derivative of worldviews that are supportive of *realpolitik* and *realmilitare*. The model of moral authority is the culprit
here. It is no accident that the vast majority of officers in the U.S. military
are both right-wing republicans and Christians. This officer corps is
extremely vulnerable to authority, and authority is a key element in both
right-wing conservative politics and in religion. Those who are skeptical and
philosophical would not be so vulnerable to authority, and such people are
rarely found to be conservatively political or religious. Conservative, religious officers are quite comfortable with the idea of moral authority. As
such, they find it more difficult to question our leaders and our government
about the current Long War. This common denominator of moral authority
explains the fact that the group that supported the illegal and immoral invasion of Iraq was largely both conservative politically and religious. They also
supported Israel's invasion of Lebanon.

Autonomy has its advocates and its critics. I will discuss its friends and
foes in this chapter. Autonomy has many meanings, but I am interested in
the word "autonomy," especially moral autonomy in the Kantian sense.
Likewise, the word "automaton" has more than one meaning. People use the
term pejoratively when they are talking about moving or behaving in a
mechanical way. However, it may also have a more promising connotation
when the relevant concern is that of self-operation. I will argue that moral
autonomy is a goal worth working toward, and I will focus on these positive
and promising aspects of this concept. People are morally autonomous if they
live as morally reflective people, if they live by beliefs based on rationale they
understand, beliefs that are open to correction or abandonment in the presence of good reason. A person who says, "there is no amount of evidence you
could show me to change my mind" cannot be autonomous. The model of
moral autonomy I propose is compatible with good order and discipline. I am
advocating reasoned dialogue when and where it is appropriate and condoned. Fostering dialogue in the military is not now widely practiced, but it is
becoming more widely preached. Good leaders welcome and condone reasoned dialogue.[2]

A Kantian view incorporating moral autonomy makes the best case
against a heteronomous enculturation. My work here is a philosophical
examination of military ethics, an examination of where we are now and
where we need to go. The moral understandings and practices that we have
now are not all bad, despite the extent of my previous critique. In this
chapter I will even show where such indoctrination may serve a purpose,
even under a new model. But we can do this only after the military, as an
institution in an ostensibly free and democratic society, justifies the moral
conception through a process of philosophical inquiry, by engaging in *public
reason* in a Rawlsian sense.[3] I choose to elaborate on Rawls because he is
one of the important philosophers who has demonstrated how to actually

operationalize a Kantian moral philosophy. Kant's moral theory (as well as his aesthetic theory) featured what he called intersubjective validity. Intersubjectivity is *possible* confluence among different people, different *subjects*. In other words, people could construct moral notions that they held to be in common, to be intersubjectively valid. This Kantian constructivism would be an alternative to seeking out objective truths or settling on the moral relativism that resides in subjects or communities of subjects. Rawls is dealing with a similar theoretical notion when he draws out his moral theory that features overlapping consensus. Perhaps many traditions, customs, and doctrines would pass such scrutiny and justification, and these should be embraced and even passed on. But right now, without going through that process, nobody can with any degree of certainty say what these justified traditions, customs, and doctrines may be. Right now they stand as items of policy, and as policy, they stand as givens, justified by fiat only. I have argued that at the same time there are probably several traditions, customs, and doctrines that are not justified, and while I may believe them to be unjustified, they deserve public attention and appropriate scrutiny through the use of public reason. My intent is to explore new avenues so that we can improve what we now have. This improvement requires an honest assessment as well as a willingness to reject what is bad and replace it with something that may be better. A Kantian or Rawlsian moral project would lead to ethical interoperability, a concept worth considering in an increasingly interactive world.

The previous chapters have been a sustained critique of the current paradigm of the ethics of warfare, which is thought of as a type of professional ethics, not too unlike other types of professional ethics such as medical, legal, or business ethics. I have employed critique, or analysis, as a general strategy thus far, thereby engaging in philosophy's negative project (arguing against a position). This last chapter will also contain the positive project (arguing for a position) of outlining a new moral model, one of moral autonomy to replace that of moral ideology. The current ethical paradigm centers on a conception of ethics that amounts to a professional ideology. This professional ideology is transmitted through the approaches I have critiqued in the last four chapters. The ideology has been contained within a "black box" through the years, meaning that the average warrior has not been a part of, or even aware of, the mechanisms that are at work within the black box. I have attempted to disclose the mechanisms that have created the ethics of warfare as it now exists. We can assess these mechanisms once they are disclosed, and we can critique them to see if they are justifiable. I have argued that they are not justifiable, largely. It is time to seriously challenge the current paradigm that rests on authority and tradition. Yet, by disclosing and challenging the paradigm, we are better able to see where we need to go. As we move away from morality that is based largely on authority and tradition, the natural question arises: Where should we go from here?

In this chapter I will examine more contributions that ethical theory can make. I will start by describing an alternative model or paradigm for the ethics of warfare, and by "alternative" I mean that the new model is one that should replace the old one. If it does not replace the old one, and realistically it probably will not, it should at least be used to radically augment the existing model. In the first section of this chapter, the new model will demonstrate how philosophical methods can generate and justify to us moral principles that are important for the military. After describing the new model, in the second section of this chapter I will advance some Kantian ethical principles of warfare. I will also show in the third section *that* moral autonomy and philosophical ethics can reformulate the moral intuitions of the military. The war machine does not simply need to adjust its moral intuitions; the war machine has them largely backwards. It is no accident that the current war machine could scarcely be moving more backwards. In the last section in this chapter, I will demonstrate *how* the new model can reshape our moral intuitions while greatly enhancing the military's moral understanding, motivation, and action. The military should replace its heteronomous ethical paradigm of centralized authority with a model of moral autonomy. The movement can generate superior and more justifiable autonomous modes and methods of philosophical ethics, generating a set of justifiable ethical principles of war. It will reformulate moral intuitions and will create better moral understanding and motivation. Ultimately, the systemic improvements could potentially improve the function and employment of the war machine, reversing its morally backwards movement, so it can start moving in the right direction.

AUTONOMOUS MODES AND METHODS OF PHILOSOPHICAL ETHICS

While relatively few make the case for philosophical ethics to be a necessary feature of a complete moral education, many others are making a case against it. Kant himself believed that a sane person of normal intelligence could be autonomous and live a moral life.[4] The methods I will proceed to outline in this section are methods that anyone could understand and employ. Philosophical ethics functions, however, in three ways. It can clear away modes of morality that are inadequate. It can identify other modes or develop new modes that are more adequate. And it can justify the dismissal of inadequate modes and the adoption of more adequate ones. Justification is a practice philosophers engage in for the benefit of others; we justify something *to* somebody. Much of the contemporary debate at large about morality is about the foundation of morality. The project of justification can avoid issues of foundation. Talk of foundation often entails getting embroiled in metaphysical issues. While philosophical ethics draws upon many philosophical tools—concepts, logic, categories, and distinctions—it does not have to get bogged down in the open-ended controversies in metaphysics, or epistemology, for that matter. Philosophical ethics can empower the average person with the concepts and the vocabulary to ensure that we do not get bogged down in endless metaphysical debate.[5] The call for philosophical ethics here is not inconsistent with Kant's idea. People as individuals, morally autonomous people, will be able to apply morally sound principles. The call for philosophical ethics, however, is for the institution of the military, since the military is attempting to establish institutional ethics. The application of philosophical ethics will aid the institution in developing well-formed modes and methods of ethics while avoiding bad ones.

There is no lack of commentary containing moral prescriptions or judgments in the newspaper, on the television, at the office, from the pulpit, or around the dinner table. The interest in applied ethics may even be increasing in the professional arena. People in the medical, business, and military professions are spending increasing amounts of time discussing values-based organizations and applying ethical decision-making procedures to their ethical problems. Colleges and universities are expanding their curricula to accommodate the fashionable idea of "ethics across the curriculum," and there is an increasing demand for more applied ethics courses: medical ethics, business ethics, military ethics, environmental ethics, to name just a few. Ethics centers are opening on campuses in increasing numbers. The applied ethics business is booming. But while applied ethics has become a growth industry, philosophical ethics has not; the interest in moral philosophy has not grown in like proportion.

There are many reasons for this lack of interest in philosophical ethical theory: many have great difficulty with it; others question its appropriateness; and some think it has limitations. It can be a difficult subject due to the fact that it is largely isolated terrain that philosophers have clearly marked and kept well-protected for themselves. So, while some practitioners are comfortable with ethical theory, the vast majority find ethical theory to be an esoteric and mind-bending enterprise that employs impenetrable language, perplexing logic, and abstract concepts, all of which seem far removed from practice. Many people, including some moral philosophers, think that ethical theory is appropriate only for moral philosophy and that it is inappropriate for the everyday person to use in everyday life. The avoidance of ethical theory due to its difficulty, inappropriateness, and limitations is deeply rooted in a desire to be practical, a penchant for pragmatism. The challenge is to be able to appeal to theory for moral reflection while avoiding any appeals to meta-physical realism.

There is great resistance to and fear of philosophical ethics; many react the same way to the notion of moral autonomy. Any friend of moral authority would at the same time have to be a foe of moral autonomy. Those in favor of moral authority and ideology think they have special access to moral truths and think that ordinary individuals do not have this privileged access. Their resistance to moral autonomy is due to their own misunderstanding: a misun-derstanding of their own conceptions of ethics (which I have argued against up to this point) and a misunderstanding of moral autonomy (which I will argue for now).

The model of moral autonomy would have several features that the model of moral ideology does not have: The accepted ethical conceptions, norms, and principles would be generated and validated through the use of public reason and philosophical ethics, not dictated by fiat with no rationale or justification; the model would be guided by standards of good reasoning and sound argument, not by the political manufacturing of consent; the mode and expectations of the justification would be that of an open-ended critical method, rather than that of a closed, complete, decision-procedure. Perhaps our use of public reason is important here, since this is a Kantian notion, for Kant remarks that enlightenment includes the "freedom to make public use of one's reason in all matters."[6] When officials communicate the dictates of their office, they are employing private reason. "But I hear on all sides the cry: *Don't argue!* The officer says: Don't argue, get on parade! The tax official: Don't argue, pay! The clergyman: Don't argue, believe! Only one ruler in the world says: *Argue* as much as you like and about whatever you like, *but obey!*[7] Onora O'Neill suggests that the difference in Kant's usage between public and private reason is that of the audience. "In speaking of the communications of officials as private he is not suggesting that these acts express the personal or individual opinions of officials, but pointing out that they address not 'the world at large,' but an audience that has been restricted and defined by some authority."[8] Kant provides some examples of these dic-tates in his time. He notes that Frederick the Great encouraged the use of public reason, and Kant sees the Great King's encouragement as representa-tive of the Enlightenment project. Prussian society was quite liberal even if the Prussian military system, which the Great King inherited, had a reputa-tion to the contrary.

I am arguing that military ethics should be explored and expressed through the use of public reason, not private reason. The subject of military ethics should be open to public reason even within the restricted audience of the war machine. It should also be open to public reason for the wider audi-ence—a national, international, and even a global audience. To move in this direction, the ethical domain should be wrested from the control and influence of the chaplains. Since I will employ Rawls' *devices of representation*, I will be using language that is Kantian and Rawlsian. I will now briefly outline an example of the type of moral conceptual scheme that is possible through the use of such a critical method, as opposed to a decision-procedure.[9] The following method demonstrates how adequate moral principles can be derived and justified.

How can we use a philosophical method to derive these principles? What would justify these principles since they were not established anywhere in the legal codes that govern military conflict? I will show how we can derive and justify to ourselves these moral principles of warfare in two different ways, in each case applying the Kantian method of John Rawls to the ethics of warfare. I want to reemphasize the nature of this project. It is not one of establishing some kind of moral foundation; moral foundations are avatars. It is a project of justification. There is not much hope in settling all the otherworldly aspects of a moral foundation. However, it is possible to justify different moral schemes. Justification is a process we engage in to validate certain ideas *to* ourselves. As I have briefly mentioned before, we justify something *to* somebody. In this case, that something will be the core principles for the ethics of warfare and that somebody will be us. By "us," I mean warriors, the war machine, America, the world—everyone. We could never establish moral *foundations for* everyone, but it is possible to provide moral *justifications to* everyone. Moral foundations require *actual choice*, while moral justifications require only *possible choice*. The concept of possible choice will become clearer as we examine Kantian constructivism more closely.

On the Kantian view that I shall present, conditions for *justifying* a conception of justice hold only when a basis is established for political reasoning and understanding within a public culture. "The social role of a conception of justice is to enable all members of society to make mutually acceptable *to one another* their shared institutions and basic arrangements, by citing what are publicly recognized as sufficient reasons, as identified by that conception" [emphasis added].[10]

John Rawls suggests such a critical method to derive principles, and a quick summary of the method would include the following.[11] His method begins with the identification of competent moral judges, judges that "need not be more than normally intelligent."[12] The second step is to enumerate a set of judgments made by the competent moral judges, judgments they would make without disclosing the moral principles, for "if we allowed these judgments to be determined by a conscious and systematic application of these principles, then the method is threatened with circularity."[13] A third step would be to explicate a set of principles based on these judgments made by competent moral judges, for "an explication of these judgments is defined to be a set of principles."[14] While Rawls has more criteria to then test the justifiability of the derived principles, a principle would be justified largely "if the explicit and conscious adoption of a justifiable principle (or set of principles) can be, or could have been, the ground of the judgment."[15] Further justification of the principle would exist if the principles were consistent with our considered judgments. Should there be some judgments that were inconsistent with the principle, this principle would pass a test of justifiability "when a subclass of considered judgments, rather than the principle, is felt to be mistaken when the principle fails to explicate it."[16]

We can consider the actual formation of the laws of war in effect to be an embodiment of the first two steps above. The first step is satisfied when we think about the formation of laws, since people we could consider to be at least competent moral judges perform the process of creating legal statutes. Many of the framers of these legal statutes exceed the criteria for being competent moral judges, since in addition to being of normal intelligence and capable of reasoned argument, they are also subject matter experts, with a specialized legal education as well as experience in legal adjudication and litigation. The different codifications of the laws of war resulted from the numerous conventions and conferences that met over many decades, and the framers deliberated and contracted these laws through a process of drafting, proposing, debating, and ratifying. The nation's first code of law, directed by Abraham Lincoln, and published April 24, 1863, may be somewhat unique in that it was "prepared by Francis Lieber, LL.D., and revised by a board of officers, of which Maj. Gen. E. A. Hitchcock is president, having been approved by the President of the United States."[17] The framers who created the laws that make up the war conventions, from the actual law-making conferences or sessions, drew heavily on this groundbreaking work of Francis Lieber. These actual sessions span virtually an entire century and include conventions from the conferences in Geneva in 1929 and 1949 as well as conventions at The Hague in 1899 and 1907, various treaties, and the *Uniform Code of Military Justice* (UCMJ).[18] There were other conventions, but these are the main conventions from which current military law derives. Other events have also been significant, such as the two key military tribunals to try war criminals from Germany and Japan after World War II. The actual history of these conferences is too complex and varied to summarize, but the relevant feature of these conventions, treaties, and tribunals is that there were many competent *moral judges* present as well as many who exceeded the criteria for being competent moral judges because they had expertise in legal matters.

The laws of war themselves also exemplify the second step of Rawls' method. The laws could be the considered judgments of the competent judges discussed in the first step. They are discrete prescriptions and proscriptions (mostly proscriptions) based on particular experiences and concrete situations.

For example, many of the laws deal with prisoners of war. Prescriptions include that "prisoners of war must at all times be humanely treated [and] are entitled in all circumstances to respect for their persons and their honour."[19] Many of the laws also deal with the "wounded or sick, [who] shall be respected and pro-tected in all circumstances."[20] The law also prescribes the necessity of wearing uniforms, for members of the armed forces "lose their right to be treated as pris-oners of war whenever they deliberately conceal their status."[21] Many such laws are counterintuitive to warriors, particularly those laws that regulate and restrict covert operations, the arming of noncombatants, and the mistreatment of prisoners. These laws are representative of considered moral judgments by competent moral judges, and the framers of the laws of war came to these par-ticular judgments by thinking about the particular cases and experiences over years, decades, and perhaps even centuries of fighting. Discrete cases of mal-treatment and lack of care and respect for prisoners led the lawmakers to pass protection legislation. The sheer magnitude of the suffering of the sick and wounded—even if motivated by nothing more than Humean pity—also pro-vided motivation to pass laws. And the longstanding practice of operating behind enemy lines with "sterilized" uniforms and equipment, particularly for special operations forces, has motivated lawmakers to require proper marking at the peril of losing prisoner of war status if caught or captured. While the competent moral judges have made these particular judgments, all with reasons based on the particular experiences, many in the military are not so supportive of these judgments. Many in the military would let the specter of military necessity trump these particular laws, and they would be tempted to forego them altogether if sterilizing their uniforms or equipment,[22] mistreating prison-ers, or neglecting the sick and wounded would in their minds facilitate either of the two objectives motivating military necessity: that of achieving a victory or protecting one's own, following the warrior precepts of "mission first, men always." As for those who claim that detainees were not prisoners, the Fourth Amendment of the Constitution—that to which warriors (and political lead-ers) swear (or affirm) an oath—requires humane treatment and due process for *all persons*, not just prisoners. Those who attempted to sidestep the law here are responsible for the abuses at Guantanamo, Abu Ghraib, and many other loca-tions. After being checked by the Supreme Court, this same White House group encouraged Congress to pass new legislation that would not only legalize future abuse, but also provide political cover for abuse that has already occurred. This series of episodes concerning the avoidance or revision of legal judgments on torture starkly illustrates the failed moral understanding of the warriors in the White House and Pentagon.

The third step in Rawls' critical method is to explicate the operative principles that would be consistent with the considered judgments by the competent moral judges. The explicated principles would not be the principles from which the judges made their judgments; otherwise, the derivation would be circular. And while I do not have room for even a modest compendium of the legal history of the laws of war, the varied and unsystematic evolution (or perhaps violent revolutions) of this body of statutes, codes, and treaties would very likely not permit a simple set of principles as the source for informing the framers of the judgments. The principles are simply not in the laws themselves, and they do not exist in any codified fashion. There is disparate mention of some of the principles, but nobody has attempted this kind of derivation of them. The mosaic of disjointed and inconsistent precepts making up the Just War Tradition does not reflect these well-considered judgments. We are in need of some new principles that do reflect the spirit of the laws, these well-considered judgments. Some may ask, why do we need to create principles *de novo* when we have this long and rich history of principles from just war theory and our Just War Tradition? The short answer to this question is that the stated principles from traditional just war theory and our Just War Tradition are no longer adequate, *jus ad bellum* and *jus in bello* principles. The longer answer will become more apparent in the next section.

For principles to be viable, they must satisfy the next step of Rawls' critical method, which is that the principles must serve as a basis for the considered judgments if they were so used by a normally rational, intelligent person. The principles would inform a person so that an application of the principle would be consistent with the considered moral judgment made by the competent moral judge. The unreflective dogmatic application of the master precepts of mission accomplishment and force protection do not meet the Rawlsian criteria. For example, early in 1991 during Desert Shield, before Desert Storm began, the philosophy faculty at West Point received a letter from a Lieutenant Siebert asking for advice.[23] The lieutenant's battalion commander had made the decision to mount the medical vehicles of the unit with machine guns for purposes of force protection. LT Siebert thought that this did not sound quite right, based on what he had learned in philosophy class, not too many years before, but he was not able to articulate exactly what was wrong with it. The battalion commander's rationale to arm the vehicles was based on survival—the apprehension on the part of the coalition forces when it came to the potential nonobservance of the laws of war on the part of the Iraqis once the fighting started. They did not believe the Iraqis would honor the protected status of medical personnel and their equipment, and so the American commander was prepared to protect his medical troops based on this apprehension. The warrior intuition, which is trained by years of reinforcement of the master precepts of mission accomplishment and force protection, was to arm the medical personnel, and it trumped all other considerations.

The question eventually made its way into legal channels within the military in the Gulf, and they determined, made the judgment, that the machine guns would have to come off the medical vehicles, based on legal precedent. The philosophers at West Point said that the machine guns should come off because they violated at least the principle of discrimination between combatants and noncombatants. Medical personnel are noncombatants and are not supposed to be fighting on the battlefield. Mounting machine guns alone on their equipment, as well as the potential for them using the machine guns, made them combatants. The distinction made by the principle of discrimination separates fighters from nonfighters; arming noncombatants blurs the distinction. If they became combatants, their ability to do their jobs would be diminished in at least two ways: First, they would become targets, and second, they would potentially have to fight to defend themselves. If either of these possibilities became a reality, then the medical people would be severely constrained in performing their jobs. Conversely, because of their noncombatant status, the law says they should not become prisoners of war.[24] Many warriors find this legal and philosophical finding against arming noncombatants to be counterintuitive. The same rationale predominated when America and Britain armed their merchant vessels in World War II. In the movie *Courage under Fire* (1996), a medical helicopter clearly marked with a red cross is making a landing with a crewman on board hosing the ground with a Squad Automatic Weapon (SAW), and even destroys a tank by dropping and igniting a fuel bladder on it, the crew thereby becoming combatants. Many warriors who watch this scene see nothing remarkable, when in fact it should strongly register to them a visual non sequitur. LT Siebert, or any other intelligent, rational person, would be able to use the principle of discrimination to arrive at the same judgment as those of the competent moral judges in this case. In Rawls' terminology, the principle of discrimination would have served as the "ground of the judgment."

Consistency is the final check. The principles are largely consistent with the laws of war. One or more of the principles would serve as a ground for the vast majority of the laws. For example, the principle of minimal harm would serve as the ground for the laws that deal with weapons restrictions. Among the weapons considered to be forbidden are barbed spears, glass bullets, and dum-dum bullets.[25] The whole purpose of using a weapon in a war is to remove an enemy combatant from the fight. The use of a spear would render an enemy harmless; once the spear is used, the purpose of the weapon has been served. But should it be a barbed spear, then even more damage to the enemy would be done when the spear is retrieved. So when a barbed spear is used, the enemy suffers unnecessary injury, because more than minimal harm has been inflicted. Glass bullets do more than minimal harm because glass does not show up on X-rays, so a person wounded with glass bullets would suffer further unnecessary complications. Dum-dum bullets are not fully jacketed, and the jackets help to contain the lead once the bullets hit a body. The exposed lead of dum-dum bullets would expand and distort more on impact and would cause more than the minimal harm possible. When considering the entire menu of weapons systems, very few have been banned by the laws of war. And several weapons banned by conventions and protocols remain in arsenals, including American arsenals. Some warriors ask why the barbed spear is listed as being banned in FM 27-10 when nobody uses barbed spears anymore. Perhaps it has metaphoric and paradigmatic value, illustrating the operative principles. Interestingly, the barbed spear is the symbol of Army Special Forces. This may take on new meaning as the American warlords, among them an Army chief of staff with a special operations background, increase the use of special operations forces in our Global War on Terror. Under the current security regime and with friendly embedded reporters traveling with the military's conventional forces, these conventional forces have very little accountability anymore. If conventional forces have little accountability, then special operations forces have no accountability for their activities. Accountability is a necessary feature of a military if public reason is going to be functioning at all.

While most of the laws pertaining to weapons are informed by the principle of minimal harm, not all of them are, so there are some inconsistencies. Nuclear weapons and chemical weapons, even napalm, cause more harm than necessary. And while these weapons are not used routinely, there are circumstances that would make each of them a legal weapon to be used. Rawls says that inconsistencies would help to justify the principles if we came to believe that we are mistaken about the judgments instead of the principles. In the case of indiscriminate weapons, those that have incredibly excessive destructive capability, there are good arguments that the laws are more probably mistaken than the principle of minimal harm. Another good example of a mistaken law would be that of the use of indiscriminate land mines. The model gives us a way to have a meaningful moral dialogue that would allow us to revise our moral practices so they would be in accordance with the principles. And of course the best recent example of law that contradicts principle is the legislation known as the Military Commissions Act, passed in the fall of 2006, which in essence legalizes torture and denies due process. The fact that Congress passed the legislation does not make it morally legitimate, or even constitutional. In the American system, Congress passes laws, the executive either follows the laws or ignores them, and the Supreme Court decides whether the laws and the executive actions are constitutional. The whole process takes years. It took five years to get a case in front of the Supreme Court for them to decide in favor of the principles of due process and humane treatment that the actions within the executive branch were unconstitutional. It may take several more years for them to do the same with these laws. Principles should prevail.

Now for the second derivation. We can also derive the battlefield principles of the ethics of warfare by employing Rawls' heuristic device of the *original position*. The *original position* for deriving principles of the ethics of warfare would be the idealized initial situation from which relevant moral principles for the ethics of warfare would be chosen.[26] The task at hand then would be to derive a set of principles from within the original position, in this initial situation. One way Rawls helps us to visualize the operation of selecting proper principles in the original position is his application of the metaphor of a veil of ignorance. "I assume that the parties are situated behind a veil of ignorance. They do not know how the various alternatives will affect their own particular case and they are obliged to evaluate principles solely on the basis of general considerations."[27] By applying the veil of ignorance, people in the original position would eliminate any choices they would be tempted to make based on self-interest or personal advantage based on contingent matters that may vary from party to party, group to group. Therefore, in choosing moral principles for conduct on the battlefield, we would not choose any principles that would depend upon giving any advantage to the side that possessed the greater strength, military might, or moral superiority.[28] We would not choose any principles that would allow the side with the greater strength to have a different set of rules for fighting, because, behind the veil of ignorance, we would not know which side we would be on, the stronger or the weaker. We would not want principles that gave special license to fight with greater excess and disregard for the established laws of war or principles of chivalry because of having moral superiority or the greater cause, because we do not know if we would be on the side with the greater or the weaker cause.

Self-interest (the nemesis of morality for Kant) disappears in the original position. The principles that we would choose in the original position would be those same ones derived from the earlier method. We would choose these principles because we might wind up on the weaker side, and we would not want the stronger side to unleash weapons of mass destruction upon us simply because they had the means to do so. If we did wind up on the stronger side, on the other hand, we would not want the weaker side resorting to measures of employing terror tactics simply because they believed they were justified in doing so since they are fighting from a weaker position. The favored operating principle of American exclusionism would disappear from such an ethical method. If self-interest provides no justification for morality for Kant, then a Kantian moral viewpoint would not count national interest as moral justification.

The laws of war exist as a set of considered judgments over particular situations that people find themselves in while fighting. The laws govern the treatment of prisoners as well as the sick and wounded. They govern limita-tions on force and restrictions on weapons. They govern classifications of legitimate targets and illegitimate targets. And they cover the protection of persons from torture and abuse. There are dozens of conventions, hundreds of treaties, and thousands of laws that specify these statutory rules governing the laws of war. These are the considered judgments, more or less, that we have established as a result of attempting to make war more civilized with centuries of experience and hindsight.

THE ETHICAL PRINCIPLES OF WAR

The accepted precepts in our Just War Tradition or just war theory are not adequate. These precepts are usually divided into *jus ad bellum* and *jus in bello* considerations, and sometimes *jus post bellum* ones as well. These considera-tions are usually translated respectively into justice of war, justice in war, and justice after war. Despite the visual similarity of *jus* to the word justice, the original Latin was *ius*, which is more properly translated as "right." So, *jus ad bellum* is more properly translated into "right to war"; *jus in bello* as "right in war"; *jus post bellum* as "right after war." These three categories of considera-tions, based on a belligerent's set of rights before, during, and after war, are in essence enabling criteria, not limiting criteria. Kant does not use the lan-guage of the jurists. He was famously opposed to the project of the just war theorists, "for Hugo Grotius, Pufendorf, Vattel, and the like (only sorry com-forters) . . . are always duly cited in justification of an offensive war . . . there is no instance of a state ever having been moved to desist from its plan by argu-ments armed with the testimony of such important men."[29]

Instead of working with a mosaic of precepts that enabled war by justi-fying it, Kant was more interested in eliminating warfare; he would have been more interested in limiting criteria than enabling criteria. The Enlightenment thinkers thought war to be something bad, bringing much more harm than good. Kant says in "Perpetual Peace" that: "War is bad in that it makes more evil people than it takes away." Kant lays out a set of conditions that must be met for peace to be possible, one being that states have well-formed constitu-tions and another being that states participate in a federation of states, or a league of nations. Kant's coining of the term "league of nations" no doubt influenced Woodrow Wilson and others who were aware of their Enlightenment heritage. The primary goal of the actual League of Nations and later the United Nations was to prevent war, which was consistent with the spirit of Kant's work. This important idea is often lost on those who have criticized both organizations. For Kant, peace is possible when states work together to prevent war and when they have legitimate constitutions. To have a well-formed constitution, a state for Kant has to be both a democracy and a republic. The Enlightenment thinkers thought of republics as being representative democracies, instead of pure democracies or direct democracies. But a republic for Kant also guaranteed the division of what he called plenary power, separating executive power from legislative and judiciary power. Any state in which too much power is located in the executive branch would not be a well-formed republic for Kant because it would allow states to go to war too easily.

The ethical principles of war to be introduced here will not be placed in the traditional categories of *jus ad bellum* or *jus in bello*. Kant did not use these categories, and I believe they have produced precepts that are ultimately incoherent and counterproductive. People can get anything out of traditional just war theory that they put into it. For example, the current war in the Gulf has been found to be both just and unjust by the same theory. All three divisions of the American Philosophical Association—Eastern, Central, and Pacific—have voted on and passed resolutions condemning the war in Iraq based on just war theory. At the same time, the popular just war theorist, Jean Bethke Elshtain, has found the war to be just using the same just war theory, as she argues in her book, *Just War against Terror* (2003). The theory itself is contradictory. The precepts have developed over centuries and do not form a coherent set of principles. The theory was developed by the theologically inclined philosophers and philosophically inclined theologians, and its incoherence is the consequence of the incompatible marriage of religion and philosophy during the Dark Ages. Since religion and philosophy were divorced in the Enlightenment, we should no longer acknowledge the legitimacy of just war theory or any of its offspring. Many people want to keep looking deeper into the theory to find the answers to their questions. If the theory is inconsistent and gives us any conclusion we are looking for, then perhaps it is time to look for a new theory, since anything follows from a contradiction.

Many warriors would recognize the traditional *jus ad bellum* category of just war principles by the name *Weinberger Doctrine*. The elements of the Weinberger Doctrine, which began perhaps with Augustine and were developed throughout the Middle Ages, have for many warriors become too restrictive. When precepts that enable war are considered to be too restrictive, it is time to do some reevaluation. These *jus ad bellum* principles include: just cause, right intention, legitimate authority, last resort, probability of success, proportionality, and comparative justice. These are never used as a set to establish sufficient conditions; any one of them alone is often cited as a sufficient condition for war. Even if they did only collectively establish sufficient conditions, many of them are suspect. Just cause can be established by any number of situations, most frequently that of a state suffering an injury by another. A simple thought experiment can demonstrate that injuries can not only be reciprocally imagined to continue ad infinitum in the future, but can also be recursively traced indefinitely backwards into the past. Legitimate authority is often a chimera, for a population that is already subject to authority can readily be fooled that any war has been begun by that same authority, and no authority would ever admit to being illegitimate. So here we again are faced with the vagaries of moral authority. Consider the criterion of comparative justice. Comparative justice is the idea that all sides in a conflict can have a legitimate cause for entering the war. Are there any cases of any state ever going to war believing that their cause was not just?

These are not the criteria that Kant employs when he is writing about war. Kant's writings on war and politics feature the ideal of cosmopolitanism. Cosmopolitanism is the idea that national and international arrangements and activities are those of peoples, not governments. When one thinks of much of the history of warfare, it is hard to miss the fact that most wars are brought on by leaders and not by the various peoples making up the states that go to war. Governments of states go to war to protect what they believe to be their state's interests. Even supranational organizations, such as the United Nations, represent the narrow viewpoints of those who run the various states. The representatives of the United Nations do the bidding of their respective state leaders. They do not represent the peoples of those states. Sir Michael Howard captures this important distinction when he says, "The complaint often made against both the League of Nations and the United Nations is that these were leagues of *states* and not of *peoples*; and that if only peoples could get together behind the backs of the their governments, they could at least establish peace."[30] So while Kant's theory endorses an international institution such as the UN, the actual UN has not embodied Kant's cosmopolitan ideal.

The ethical principles of war are neither explicitly reflected in the Just War Tradition nor widely accepted throughout the military. All of these principles fall under the category of restraint, applicable to conditions during conflict as well as before and after conflict. If war cannot be eliminated, then any principles that would fit into a Kantian scheme would have to be principles that limit or restrain war rather than enable war. Aggressive war would never be justified in a Kantian scheme, nor would preemptive war, and preventive war, fought for some vague and distant danger, would be out of the question. Under this principle of restraint, then, there would be legitimate occasions of war only to limit or restrain violence that had been started by someone else. Kant cites two examples of justified conflict: self-defense; and defense of others who are beleaguered by their own state. In today's terminology these principles would be self-defense and humanitarian intervention: fighting for defense of the self or for the defense of the other. Defense carries along with it legitimacy. It is important to note that in both cases the object is to restrain and bring to an end the violence that has already breached the peace. I reemphasize that I do not want to put these principles under the category of *jus ad bellum*.

With restraint comes legitimacy. When legitimacy is reinforced by collective restraint and cooperation, then well-formed states can finally achieve a real level of security that in turn promotes the goal of peace. In a Kantian ethical scheme, self-interest cannot be the motive of morality. Yet, at the level of nation-states, self-interest is the prime motivation for state action. The pursuit of naked self-interest does not promote peace; it promotes conflict. We cannot be optimistic about peace when we are in a state of perpetual war. But the pursuit of state interest functions exactly as it is proclaimed. With interest being the operative principle in our foreign policy, war makers clamored for the removal of the military from the Balkans, since that conflict was not directly related to significant American interests. It was largely fought to stabilize the region, preventing large-scale genocide. At the same time American war makers are anxious to remain in the Arabian Peninsula precisely because it is very much in American economic interests to be there. Now, according to a Kantian ethical scheme, these intuitions and desires on the part of American war makers are exactly backwards. The Balkan conflicts we entered in the 1990s were more justified by Kantian moral principles because we were fighting to defend others, those under siege, and our motivation was not based on our own state interest. Operation Iraqi Freedom was not about legitimate self-defense and was very much about state interest. So the ethical principles of war I am arguing for would actually reverse our current judgments about the morality of today's conflicts.

Likewise, I do not want to put the following principles under the category of *jus in bello*. Legal scholars and practitioners will cite three principles that guide the development of the laws of war deriving from the Just War Tradition: unnecessary suffering, military necessity, and proportionality.[31] The last two, military necessity and proportionality, are enabling criteria and superfluous concepts, meaning that a set of moral principles would work without them. The problem with the enabling criteria is this: When military necessity is invoked, the greater the military necessity in a given situation, the less applicable unnecessary suffering becomes. The three principles work together in that unnecessary suffering is inversely proportional to military necessity. In effect, any amount of suffering can be justified if the military objective is absolutely necessary. Military necessity can actually override most of the laws of land warfare. In *Just and Unjust Wars*, Michael Walzer allows military necessity to override other moral and legal constraints in conditions of what he calls "supreme emergency." Most warriors have the intuition, which the military institution reinforces, that warfare is about excess. If there is any doubt, just read anything by the widely read new prophets of realism:

Ralph Peters, Robert Kaplan, Victor Davis Hanson, or Fred Kagan, to name a few of the writers who represent the new conscience of the warriors.

I believe we need to refashion those intuitions away from excess and toward the idea of restraint. These just war principles include: discrimination (discriminating between combatant and noncombatant), minimal force (the avoidance of excessive force), and minimal harm (the avoidance of unnecessary harm). Each of these principles relates to an aspect of restraint: discrimination relates to the *target*, minimal force relates to its *application*, and minimal harm relates to its *effects*. None of these principles are named in the legal statutes: They are not explicitly enumerated in the Army's *Field Manual 27-10: The Laws of Land Warfare* or *The Manual for Courts-Martial*, which the military uses as the statutory document for "war crimes" committed by the American military. Nor are these principles in this country's first codification of the laws of war, *General Orders No. 100*, sometimes known as *Lieber's Code*.[32] *FM 27-10: The Laws of Land Warfare* does mention the "principles of humanity and chivalry,"[33] but there is no enumeration of what these principles of humanity and chivalry may be, and there is no mention of these other specified principles: discrimination, minimal force, and minimal harm.

The principles that we have derived from either a Kantian or a Rawlsian (original) position fall into two categories: the political moral principles of war and the military moral principles of war. Both categories draw upon the regulative idea of restraint. The restraining political principles of war are self-defense and defense of others. The restraining military principles of war are discrimination, minimal force, and minimal harm, limiting harm to the target, application, and effect of military force. These principles are largely consistent with the considered judgments that are embodied in our laws of war. The traditional precepts of just war theory are not consistent with these considered judgments. Rawls says that when we have a situation in which the considered judgments and the principles are essentially consistent, then we have begun to establish what he calls reflective equilibrium:

> By going back and forth, sometimes altering the conditions of the contractual circumstances, at others withdrawing our judgments and conforming them to principle, I assume that eventually we shall find a description of the initial situation that both expresses reasonable conditions and yields principles which match our considered judgments duly pruned and adjusted. This state of affairs I refer to as reflective equilibrium.[34]

We in some ways do exercise this idea of reflective equilibrium, in legal and philosophical circles, while creating and judging cases regarding the laws of war, and while struggling to teach the ethics of warfare. Proper legislative authorities are constantly trying to refine the laws of war, not necessarily intentionally, in a way that would make the laws conform to these principles. For example, the international community is trying to enact legislation that will ban the use of land mines, which may be motivated by the countries' mutual self-interest—their interest in protecting themselves from others who use land mines. However, philosophically, at the level of principle, such a landmine ban would also be in accordance with the principles we have derived in the original position. Banning land mines would be in accordance with the principle of discrimination, since land mines are indiscriminate. Likewise, lawyers and philosophers are constantly trying to refine the principle in its application. It is easy to say that the military should discriminate between combatants and noncombatants. It is quite another matter to establish criteria to distinguish between the two. Partisans, terrorists, guerrillas, military factory workers, armed civilians—it is very hard in these types of cases to determine the combatant status. It is very difficult to establish the criteria to categorize them between the principle and the empirical factors. Somewhere between the principle and empirical facts, though, we are attempting to establish the criteria, thereby refining the application of the principle itself. This refining of both considered judgments and principles is the ongoing process of reaching reflective equilibrium.

Rawls claims that "justice between states is determined by the principles that would be chosen in the original position so interpreted. These principles are political principles, for they govern public policies toward other nations."[35] Rawls mentions that *jus ad bellum* and *jus in bello* principles are just such principles, political principles:

> These principles define when a nation has a just cause in war or, in the traditional phrase, its *jus ad bellum*. But there are also principles regulating the means that a nation may use to wage war, its *jus in bello*. Even in a just war certain forms of violence are strictly inadmissible; and where a country's right to war is questionable and uncertain, the constraints on the means it can use are all the more severe. Acts permissible in a war of legitimate self-defense, when these are necessary, may be flatly excluded in a more doubtful situation. The aim of a war is a just peace, and therefore the means employed must not destroy the possibility of peace or encourage contempt for human life that puts the safety of ourselves and of mankind in jeopardy. The conduct of war is to be constrained and adjusted to this end. The representatives of states would recognize that their national interest, as seen from the original position, is best served by acknowledging these limits on the means of war.[36]

Rawls mentions *jus in bello* principles as being those principles that regulate the means of using force in war. While he essentially shows that *jus in bello* principles can come from the original position, I have specified what some of these moral principles might be. Rawls may have used the terms *jus in bello* and *jus ad bellum*, but Kant did not. In Walzer's framework, *jus ad bellum* and *jus in bello* can be logically separate: It is possible in Walzer's scheme for a military to fight justly in an unjust war or for a military to fight unjustly in a just war. These two categories for the most part remain distinct domains in Walzer's theory, converging only in a marginal way. I think that the political and military ethical domains must be more tightly connected. The medieval days of *invincible ignorance* are over. I prefer not to use the terms from the Just War Tradition because Kant's moral theory falls outside the tradition; Kant worked apart from traditional just war theory, thinking it was not adequate. The political principles of war span the moral boundaries for the political end of war, and the military principles of war do the same for the military means. Means and ends must be connected.

Warriors can come to appreciate these principles by revising their usual conception of reasoning with means and ends, by thinking about means and ends philosophically. Principles will seldom have moral gravity as long as people come to privilege ends over means. Ends will have the priority over means as long as the means are considered to be less important than ends. And people will view ends as being more important than means as long as they think of the relationship between means and ends in an inadequate way. One can think of means and ends and the relationship between them in an adequate way if one were to think of a fully integrated continuum between means and ends. The continuum would be integrated because means would never be considered without ends, and ends would never be considered without means. The integrated continuum would also be reciprocal because ends would regulate means, and means would regulate ends. We would have to view the continuum in both directions, keeping an eye on higher order ends as well as higher order means, making sure they don't truncate the continuum prematurely in either direction. An elevation of the status of principles in our moral thinking will help us to reason better in terms of means and ends.

Awakened warriors demonstrate and embrace restraint at all levels of war: strategic, operational, and tactical. Restraint helps prevent the more dangerous moral error, the Type I error. Had the American warrior embraced the ethical principles of war—self-defense, defense of others, discrimination, minimal force, minimal harm—then we would not be in the dangerous, intractable position we are in early in the twenty-first century.

FROM HETERONOMY TO AUTONOMY: REFORMULATING MORAL INTUITIONS

The pre-reflective views of the warriors—win at all costs; use whatever it takes; attacking axes of evil; the best defense is a good offense, starting wars for fear of vague and distant dangers—are illustrative of an entire body of precepts belonging to *realpolitik* and *realmilitare*. I am arguing that we should replace these inadequate intuitions with better ones. We need to replace the indulgence of excess with the principle of restraint. To emphasize the importance of and the need for the new model, I will describe again the old model in order to highlight the great contrasts, especially in their approaches to moral education. People continue to be at least as interested as ever in ethical matters, perhaps even more so as of late. The current paradigm of doing ethics in the military (outside of the teaching of philosophical ethics at the military academies and a few other military schools) amounts largely to an ideology. This moral ideology is transmitted as I have described in the previous chapters. Take a look at the chief of staff's reading list, a list of books intended to indoctrinate the Army. The dozens of books listed are of the kind I criticize in chapter 2. None of them are critical or deeply introspective. The vast majority of them are comfortable histories. There are no books on the list that are about the process of leadership, no books on ethics, no philosophy, no literature. This would not be so bad if at the same time the Army's senior leaders were not also engaged in the *folie à deux* (shared delusion) that they are developing through this reading program an officer corps that embraces reflection, critical thinking, and imagination. However the ideology is transmitted, it is controlled by authority. While there is no "central committee," and we don't officially have "apparatchiks," this ideology is nevertheless politically controlled and monitored by those in power in the military. The Army's doctrine, including any doctrine dealing with ethics, is fashioned, staffed, and approved under the watchful eye of those in charge. And even though the staffing and approval process is supposed to follow a reasoned process, the process is actually a political process. So, instead of employing well-reasoned arguments using standards of evidence and criteria of rationality that admits of public reason, the process is actually one of manufacturing consent. When those with the power favor tank warfare, for example, the Army winds up with a lot of tank doctrine; when those in charge favor special operations, then that doctrine flourishes.[37] Currently the Army is transforming from a tank-heavy force to a much lighter force, with a larger role for special operations forces. The warlords are driving this change for the sake of readiness, the readiness to move Army units to distant locales within ninety-six hours. Does it make any sense for a free and democratic society to be able to engage its military in any part of the world much faster than the legitimate political process can work? Would this development pass the bar of public reason?

Officership has become a pet project within the Army; many agencies are moving forward to professionalize the Army through its officership project. The project began at West Point. The cadets at the Military Academy have taken a course in military science entitled "Officership."[38] The word "officership" is as lacking in aesthetic value as it is lacking in moral value. This course had replaced a military tactics course, because the leaders at one time at West Point believed that this type of course was more important for the cadets than tactics. The course is another manifestation of the ever-growing effort to emphasize professionalism in the military as the solution to its ethical problems. The course textbook, *West Point's Perspectives on Officership*, as part of this professionalism project, was essentially the core text of a course designed to transmit a predetermined ideology.[39] The book's readings contain a combination of pieces that were designed to indoctrinate, romanticize, and acculturate cadets into the profession. Many of the articles deal with the topic of morality, and the intention was to transmit moral norms to the cadets through these readings. Problems ensue, because those in the institution who propel this project of professionalism actually conflate professionalism with ethics, ideology with morality. There is no discussion of ethics at the normative level, and certainly there is no meta-ethical level of discussion. Ethics remains at the descriptive level.[40] Normative discussions are reduced to prescriptions coming from a communitarian ethic resting upon the members of the military institution who, today in America, make up a nearly homogenous group of people with the same worldview. These ethical dogmas take front and center stage because of the nearly unified worldview that American warriors hold. Political and religious affiliation is overtly flaunted as part of the project, for "ideological self-identification also points to a rise in professed conservatism in the officer corps," as evidenced by the ratio of political conservatives to liberals being "twenty-three to one in 1996."[41]

The textbook has an article by Everett C. Ladd, "American Society: Where Are We Headed."[42] This article is a social scientific study with a heavily biased set of presumptions that help to set the tone for the need for this kind of ideological course, as evidenced when Ladd says that "we are troubled by deficiencies in the moral life of the nation, evident in family break-up, crime, and a degraded television culture."[43] There is a lot of data cited in this study to show the correlation between the alleged decline of morality and the corresponding decline of church attendance and attention to religion. One of the charts displays how attitudes about abortion, for example, have shifted more toward toleration, as if the presumption is that abortion is just *absolutely* wrong in every case. Interestingly, on this same chart there is a comparison of attitudes toward abortion based on education level, and this portion of the chart shows that tolerance of abortion and level of education attained are proportional and correlated. So even though they do not make the claim, an astute observer must conclude that education is part of the problem. One of the agendas of this article, and others in this text, is that a solution to this problem of moral decay of society at large is to turn to the conservative institution of the military, with its conservative, religious moral ideology, to help orient the rest of America back toward the right answers. Naturally, this kind of ideological project is not only dangerous for the military as an institution, but the agendas to impose the military's conservative moral outlook back on the rest of the nation are even more dangerous. There is growing evidence and analysis that shows the opposite is true—that the more religious a nation happens to be, the more societal dysfunction exists, according to all indexes of human progress, development, health, and welfare. The United States is at the top of the list of the top seventeen nations when it comes to religiosity and societal dysfunction.[44] Fundamentalism is not the kind of dogma that will move a free and democratic society toward being a "well-ordered society."[45]

For example, I've already mentioned one of the readings by Roger Nye entitled "The Commander as Moral Arbiter," and the problems that would exist if morality were up to the whim of each commander.[46] Nye's article is in the third of four chapters of the textbook on officership, the third chapter having the title "The Officer as a Leader of Character." The chapter by James Toner in this professionalism book has nearly seventy references to precepts of religious authority, so it fits right in with this professional theme of ethical authority.[47] The cadets in this course also read perhaps the most ubiquitous leadership tract ever published, entitled "A Message to Garcia." *The Future of the Army Profession* also features an article in its "Ethics and the Army Profession" section entitled "A Message to Garcia: Leading Soldiers in Moral Mayhem." This tract is about Lieutenant Rowan, who, during the Spanish-American War was given a message to deliver to one of the guerilla leaders and did so without any hesitation, further guidance, or question, at least according to the tract. Rowan is touted as the exemplar of the good soldier. The small tract is a favorite gift of general officers to their aides.[48]

The most striking feature is that even though "A Message to Garcia" is widely distributed in leadership courses, it is about *followership*, not *leadership*. It has nothing to do with leadership, only blind obedience. Let's look deeper. The tract was written at the turn of the twentieth century as a polemic against socialism. It championed the virtues of capitalism and big business, and eschewed the dignity of independence and the individual. The tract celebrates some of the favored shibboleths of the military: "make it happen," "can do," "stay in your lane." And, of course, these precepts are fraught with the potential to cause moral error. Many leaders want more people in the Army to be like Lieutenant Rowan. The follower who does what he's told without asking questions or thinking it through can very easily commit wrongdoing, even grave wrongdoing. To use a fictional example, Captain Willard, played by Martin Sheen, in *Apocalypse Now* went after Colonel Kurtz, played by Marlon Brando, to assassinate him without any questions. Willard is a Rowan. In the real world, Oliver North is a Rowan. Calley is a Rowan. Sadly, there has been no other publication that has worked more against the idea of acknowledging, let alone celebrating, individual, moral autonomy.

This textbook for the officership course features a speech made by Don Snider on professionalism.[49] He recounts a story when he was a lieutenant serving in Vietnam as a Special Forces officer. He was an advisor on an aircraft that was going to carry a South Vietnamese Special Forces unit so that they could make a jump into Laos. The Vietnamese jumpmaster was using only one hand to make the visual signals to prompt the jumpers through the last few minutes of the jump. Snider was initially stymied by the jumpmaster's use of only one hand, because American jumpmasters always use two hands. Then he noticed that the jumpmaster was using only one hand to make the signals because he had his pistol drawn in the other hand. Snider conjectured that he had his gun drawn in order to threaten his jumpers, helping to ensure that they would actually make the jump. Snider concluded that he was proud to be part of an Army that did not need to threaten its soldiers at gunpoint to jump out of an aircraft. The point of the story is to demonstrate the professionalism of the United States Army, compared to the lack of professionalism of the South Vietnamese Special Forces, thereby showing our alleged moral superiority. And here professional superiority entailed moral superiority, due to the better character that the American soldiers ostensibly had. What Snider fails to acknowledge, or perhaps even realize, is that the illegal nature of jumping into Laos makes the entire episode morally suspect, since they were jumping—secretly and unwelcome—into a neutral country that was not at war with us. Were the American jumpers really more professional because they were more willing to make an illegal jump?

And if it is necessary to be moral to be professional, then there is another contradiction operating here as well. In the speech Snider described, and even emphasized, the covert nature of the jump—the "sanitization" of the aircraft so that the government could claim "plausible deniability." Special Operations units, also known as "black ops" units, routinely operate with unmarked uniforms and equipment, so much so that few people think twice about it. The laws of war forbid the sterilization of equipment and uniforms and go so far as to expressly deny prisoner of war status to those who do not identify themselves clearly on the battlefield.[50] This story demonstrates that "professionalism" can be logically separate from legality or morality, and at a minimum the two concepts do not have to have a necessary connection. It also points out the danger in conflating professionalism with ethics. What good does it do to claim professional, and even moral, superiority when one is engaged in an illegal or immoral activity? What happens to our special forces if our enemies set aside international customary law? By the way, the Geneva Conventions and Protocols are established enough now to be considered customary law, which means that they are in effect for those who have not signed or ratified the treaties and even for those who try to rewrite the laws.

There is much talk in the military about "moral ascendancy," which is both a nonsensical term as well as a dangerous one, much like the term "moral toughness." Military leaders now tout the importance of moral ascendancy, which has even worked its way into military doctrine.[51] Ever since J. F. C. Fuller outlined what he called the principles of war, there have been nine of them: maneuver, offensive, speed, security, mass, objective, unity-of-command, surprise, and economy of force. But he did not pick them arbitrarily or by using factor analysis; he picked them based on some categorical thinking. The one main category, the whole that comprises the parts, is that of *control*. The two main categories that compose control are *pressure* and *resistance*. The nine principles of war are those principles that a military commander should think about in order to control the battlefield through pressure and resistance, and they fall under those categories.[52] General Montgomery Meigs (Ret.), when he was the commander at Ft. Leavenworth and responsible for Army doctrine, made the decision, arbitrarily—and certainly in a manner not consistent with Fuller's original scheme—to add a tenth principle of war: morale. What he had in mind, of course, is *morale* in the sense of psychological spirit and enthusiasm, a feature that he believes is necessary for success in military operations—*morale* as a kind of *psychological ascendancy*. Meigs instructed the authors of the Army's operational doctrine to say something about some *moral* aspects of war in the section of the doctrine that covered *morale*, undoubtedly because of the resemblance of the two words. In the same paragraph the term "moral ascendancy" is used in two different ways. The operational doctrine started by talking about moral ascendancy as psychological superiority and moved very subtly to talking about moral ascendancy as ethical superiority, thereby conflating the psychological with the ethical. Talk of ethical superiority is not only nonsensical, but also dangerous. It reappears constantly.

Michael Walzer writes about the concept of moral equality in his still widely read *Just and Unjust Wars*. Moral equality is a concept that enables soldiers to view their enemy as their moral equals, equals who are entitled to all of the rights to humanity and personhood that they themselves are entitled. The concept would prevent the widespread practice of using propaganda to demean the enemy and to think of them as less than human, as we did when we dehumanized the Germans, the Japanese, the Vietnamese, the Iraqis, Arabs, and Moslems.[53] J. Glenn Gray reminds us in his classic 1959 work, *The Warriors*, that: "Most soldiers are able to kill and be killed more easily in warfare if they possess an image of the enemy sufficiently evil to inspire hatred and repugnance."[54] Despite Walzer's fairly wide readership in the military, most people either miss his discussion of moral equality or do not like it, for a number of reasons, none of which are justifiable. Early drafts of the Army's 1999 leadership manual included the notion of moral equality of the enemy when discussing the value of respect; in fact, the key feature of respect was that of respecting the enemy on the battlefield. That idea did not survive the staffing process, and even a cursory check of the manual today will reveal that only Americans are mentioned as being recipients of this important value of respect. The White House and Congress have bolstered this immoral view.

The problem I am describing is one of justification. Those who oppose philosophical ethics want to indoctrinate people into an ideology, but how do we know if the content of the ideology is rationally and morally justifiable? In chapter 2, I argued that the military should be careful of the narratives it tells. Here is yet another example of a narrative that can do damage. The fictional account is the widely read and discussed *Defense of Duffer's Drift* (1905), a novella about Lieutenant Backsight Forethought, who has a series of dreams the night before his unit has to prepare a defense to ward off an attack. In these dreams, the lieutenant is able to refine the defensive position that he was intending to prepare, because the consecutive dreams point out the results of his decisions along the way. After the seventh dream, he has worked out all of the tactical problems, has completely changed his plan, and by the time he awakens, he is prepared to set up a sound defense. The dream sequences, though, give advice that a young officer should not follow. Unfortunately, the dreams give some advice that would be both illegal and immoral. For example, in one of the dreams, the leader abducts civilians who live in a nearby house and extorts them under duress to obtain vital information about the local population, holding them against their will to prevent any possible contact with the enemy and forcing them to work as a labor force.[55] All these actions today, while consistent with a warrior consciousness, are violations of the laws of war. Do warriors ever address these moral problems as they discuss the tactical lessons in the book? So the book transmits perhaps some good tactical lessons at the expense of some very bad moral lessons. What justifies the stories? Which stories, studies, novels, shibboleths, and methods are justified? Can we justify them using public reason? While they may remain justified to the limited audience of the military, they should not be. In addition, I do not think they would be justified to the wider public, at Kant's "bar of reason," because of the violation of the principles of battlefield morality. The ideological project of indoctrinating moral norms in the guise of professionalism is a dangerous one, as I've argued. Is indoctrination bad in itself? Can we ever escape it? There is little or no effort or interest to publicly scrutinize the content of that which is being indoctrinated.

I have argued that an ideological approach, based on indoctrination and authority, with ethical norms issuing from a completely opaque black box, is not sufficient for professional ethics, especially for military ethics, or for the more broad subject of the ethics of warfare. Many warriors have challenged me as I have made this argument, for, they ask, how else can the military impart its ethical standards and norms? Is it appropriate to be teaching philosophy to everyone in the military? What other options do we have?

I think we have many options. The military can formalize a model of military ethics. For after all, the issue at hand is that of moral education. The moral education of the military can be set up so that there are different levels of moral education, and they may roughly parallel the three levels of ethics: descriptive, normative, and meta-ethics. The first level of moral education for the military may very well have to be that of indoctrination and ideology, transmitting the requisite ethical conception through the means and methods I've critiqued throughout. Military members, upon entry into the Armed Forces, would at this level be introduced to the ethical norms, standards, and principles of the profession. We already do this. So what is different about the new model? At this point we have not sufficiently examined the unreflective ideology to see if it could be adequately defended at the bar of reason. The new model would have two additional levels, and each of these two additional levels would be philosophical. The second level, the normative level, would engage members in the normative, philosophical realm of moving beyond the descriptive level and moving into the realm of possibility. This second level would move beyond what happens to be the case, beyond what *is*, beyond the givens, and move toward what *ought* to be. This already happens in a limited way, when warriors study philosophical ethics in college. The military can expand the exposure to philosophical ethics by introducing it into the curricula in the Army schools. For officers, this should occur at every school, since they have in many cases already been exposed to it in college. For noncommissioned officers, this should occur at some point in their education, since many of them now have some college, and their promotion potential is already now enhanced by college education. The second level of moral education would bring those members into the wider audience of public reason concerned about the moral dimension of the military. The use of public reason would allow them to personally ratify and justify the moral norms, traditions, customs, and doctrines that exist and should exist for the military—thereby establishing and exercising their moral autonomy. They will, in this way, be able to reformulate for themselves better moral intuitions. Right now there are perhaps dozens of people within the military who have the education, interest, and ability to engage in this dialogue concerning the philosophical justification of military ethics, to the extent there is concern and dialogue (this would include some philosophical and legal circles as well as faculty at the military schools). Energetic interest in helping to formalize this second level of moral education could bring hundreds and perhaps even thousands into this conscious level of public reason, instead of merely dozens. But having people exposed to this second level is not completely adequate; teaching faculty, decision-makers, policy makers, and doctrine writers need some grounding in the third level of moral education.

The third level of moral education would entail more study of philosophical ethics, including the analytical acumen, linguistic abilities, and awareness of concepts within meta-ethics, and philosophic ethics would be a requirement for those on the staffs of strategic leaders and those who are responsible for establishing policy and doctrine. This third level of moral education would be available to those in the military who get advanced degrees in civilian institutions and those who are attending the senior service schools within the military school system. This level of education would empower people within the institution to do the work to publicly engage in the dialogue required to give moral justification to the public regarding its norms, traditions, customs, doctrines, and precepts in the first two levels of moral education. Networks among philosophers teaching ethics in the military have already been created. There is one network that connects all the service academies. There is another that connects the schools of higher learning in the military: staff colleges, war colleges, and advanced war fighting schools. The faculty in these networks collaborate on the best teaching practices to provide their students a philosophical ethics education. Admittedly, this kind of education is not available for the vast majority of warriors. However, the students from these schools in the second group listed will be the ones promoted to the highest levels of command and staff responsibility. They will have the greatest influence in improving the political-military levels. A Kantian or Rawlsian project of public reason would be appropriate for this level. Since there would be a number of people involved at this level, they could employ the method to ensure that institutional ethical norms are justified. If the military institution has justified moral norms, then the military will be a just institution as part of the basic structure of a just society. The ends, methods, narratives, and doctrines would follow from this set of justified moral norms. In this way, Rawls' philosophical method could be an important part of the moral education for the military, and could be part of the system of education that would guarantee moral autonomy within the military.

These three levels do not divide the subject of morality cleanly, just as no system of categorization can cleanly "cut nature at its joints." There is mutual reinforcement among these three levels, and there is great overlap among the levels. For example, people engaged in the study of normative ethics (the second level) are also engaged in many of the concepts within meta-ethics (the third level). The study of normative ethical theories naturally involves employing analytical acumen and paying attention to language as well as considering other concepts as well. The third level could be reached without ever delving into the irresolvable quagmires of metaphysics and epistemology, except to the degree necessary to have enough understanding to recognize these issues, so that they could be avoided. John Rawls develops the normative theory of what he calls "Kantian constructivism,"[56] without Kant's metaphysics, but he does so while being fully conscious of Kant's metaphysics, and epistemology as well—features that may contain aspects that fall within the category of meta-ethics. So sometimes it is very hard to engage in normative ethics without paying attention to meta-ethical aspects at the same time. However these different levels may be interrelated, the fact remains that in order to engage in moral discourse we should incorporate philosophical ethics. Philosophical ethics can help set the conditions so that people can exercise their moral autonomy. Philosophical ethics can help the military move away from the project of establishing a moral foundation and toward the project of justifying adequate modes and methods of ethics, through public reason and through an empowered agency, moral autonomy. Philosophical ethics can help us to develop military ethics without the metaphysics, morality without fixed metaphysical or epistemological presumptions. Philosophy may not be necessary for a warrior to be autonomous, but there is a role for philosophy to help set the stage and set the conditions so that warriors can become morally autonomous.

MORAL AUTONOMY: CREATING BETTER UNDERSTANDING AND MOTIVATION

Autonomy often refers to independence. In this context, though, an autonomous person would be one who is capable of more than independent thought and action, more than mere freedom from constraints, negative freedom. An autonomous person would be one who is self-governed, governed by rules of action and maxims that he can freely give himself, exercising positive freedom. Jean-Jacques Rousseau carries out a nascent project of autonomy and refers to it as "virtuous self-legislation." Immanuel Kant carries out Rousseau's project and "invents" the concept of moral autonomy.[57] Kant refers to any other authority, outside the individual freely giving himself rules according to reason, as being "heteronomous," or one who is subject to external moral laws or authority.

Another term describing a heteronomous edict in philosophical literature would be an instantiation of *ipse dixit*, Latin for "he himself said it." In this context, *ipse dixit* would refer to a heteronomous edict, such as an order that someone follows merely because it comes from a superior *à la Rowan.*

Does free independent thinking out there in the armed services scare some people? Of course it does, and probably more so than we would like to admit. To establish the requirement of autonomous thinking in our leaders, we need to take a look at the type of world we would have to live in for autonomous, free-thinking leaders to be ineffectual. What assumptions would we have to assent to in order to think it would be enough for leaders to simply follow orders, without thinking for themselves, without being autonomous?

Do perfect organizations exist? Only in our imaginations. Assuming the existence of a perfect organization entails several contradictions. Either the military is such an organization, or we would need autonomous thinkers. All we would have to do is follow orders, because we would know that everything coming down to us is correct. However, the military is not a perfect organization. By *reductio ad absurdum* these contradictions tell us that perfect organizations do not exist. Since it is not such a corporation, then we do need autonomous thinking in our leaders. Warriors pretend that operational leaders are handed good strategies and that they in turn create good campaign plans for tactical leaders to execute. All of it requires revision all the time. Instead of being logical and sequenced, the reality is more like a Tarantino movie, where we start in the middle and move back and forth freely from top to bottom and back, beginning to end and back again—all of it requiring autonomous moral agency on the part of all leaders.

Does this mean that everyone in the military is out there doing whatever he or she wants to do? Hardly. The best leaders who do not feel threatened welcome discussion and questioning of their orders, at the right place and time. Many strong, reflective leaders understand that despite the questioning and discussion there comes a point in time in which the questioning and discussion are over and the soldiers have to carry out the orders, given that the orders are legal and moral. Unfortunately, we have too many leaders and soldiers who feel that they should never question orders. Many soldiers and leaders do not understand that not only do they have a right to disobey illegal orders, but they also have a duty to disobey illegal orders. Leaders also have the institutional responsibility to fix the system so that orders given are not illegal.

America shifted from actually targeting and bombing oil targets in Desert Shield and Desert Storm to protecting oil targets in Operation Iraqi Freedom. During all the targeting meetings that took place prior to the air strikes for Desert Shield, one prominent set of targets involved Iraqi oil wells and oil fields. We actually attacked some oil fields and wells, but then stopped after recognizing the long-term damage. This is significant because of the moral high ground the United States was able to take, branding Saddam Hussein as an international ecological terrorist, once he also torched his own oil wells. Had everyone gone along with keeping the oil wells on the target

lists for a prolonged period of time, then we would have been ecological terrorists ourselves. At the time they nominated the wells as targets, it probably
made sense to some, in the name of military expediency. However, fully
reflective dialogue through a process of public reason could have prevented
the bombing of oil assets, or even their nomination as targets. Could other
ethical conceptions have generated the same conclusions? If we had turned
to virtue theory, could any of the values or virtues have informed the warriors? What would Jesus bomb? Virtue theory doesn't inform us here; neither
do religious precepts. Which values would prohibit such a mistake? What
about consequentialist considerations? Instrumental utilitarian thinking can
be reflective, or as Rawls would call it, *rationally autonomous* thinking.
Consequentialist thinking brought the warriors to bomb the oil assets
because, tactically, the confusion resulting from the smoke and fire was a
great distraction and favors an attacking force. Only a Kantian approach,
which is fully reflective, or *fully autonomous*, would lead the military to fore-
stall the attack on oil assets altogether from the beginning. Now that we
have examined our world and found that leaders are not perfect and need to
be questioned and checked and held accountable, we can turn to another
aspect of autonomy. What kind of intellectual, psychological, and moral
conditions do soldiers require before they can be autonomous?

Remember, an autonomous warrior has to have the moral courage[58] to
stand up to seniors, peers, and juniors alike, should his own opinion differ
with the current wisdom. If being autonomous indicates an independence of
mind, then a lack of autonomy, or heteronomy, would indicate dependence.
A heteronomous leader would be dependent on another person, a text, a
law—something other than a rule or principle he could freely give himself
and then justify with reason. If a person is dependent on a moral authority,
that authority could be wrong. If he is dependent on a text, that text could
be interpreted in different ways. If a person is dependent on a law, that law
may not even be moral, or the law could change. On the other hand, if the
person is autonomous and can give reasons for what he thinks is right, then
he can substantiate and justify what a person, text, or law might be dictating
with good reasons. There are good reasons for some of the things that we find
leaders saying, or that we find in texts, or in laws. However, without reason
to provide a justification for these edicts and laws, to follow them blindly
would be *ipse dixitism*. How do we as leaders get to the point where we can
think for ourselves?

Rousseau devises a distinction that separates a good type of self-esteem
from a bad type.[59] In his work *Emile: Or, On Education* he provides a major
critique of society, claiming that society unwittingly fosters the bad type of
self-esteem while neglecting to nurture the good type as they raise children.
The distinction is informative because the military mimics society in that

they also advance the bad type at the expense of the good type. Rousseau would classify the type of self-esteem based on the good opinions of others as a bad type of emotion, based on illegitimate grounds. He refers to this type of self-esteem as *amour-propre*, a good feeling about the self due to the fulfilling of expectations of others. He views this as harmful and at the same time as the type of self-esteem that most people actually base their ego development upon. "This is how the gentle and affectionate passions are born of self-love, and how the hateful and irascible passions are born of *amour-propre*."[60] This bad type of self-esteem we can contrast with the good type, which is dependent on skill development, self-assurance, and confidence in one's own abilities. We can only achieve the correct type of ego development by concentrating on and emphasizing development and honest critique, understanding that this is a long-term and painful investment. Training and critique employ this good type of ego development at the Training Centers. However, nobody "enjoys" the training at these centers, and the centers are the only places one will find such "no-holds-barred" training and evaluation. While some operational training admits of these "playing fields," where one can develop, there are no corresponding training fields for ethics.

Rousseau is engaging in a branch of philosophy we now call moral psychology. Rawls also spends considerable time writing about our moral psychology, as do many other philosophers: Martha Nussbaum, Gabrielle Taylor, and David Sachs, to name a few. It is very important to these theorists that our emotional life is coherently connected to a highly developed ethical understanding. The appropriate affectations of pride, shame, and guilt would be indications of a properly developed ethical understanding, since emotions and the propositional attitudes that make up our beliefs are connected. We would not want leaders who have an unhealthy moral psychology. Such a leader may be absolutely shameless about their mistakes, for example.

People who grow up and develop their self-esteem based on the approval of others are constantly looking to others for this approval. If they do not get this approval, then their self-esteem diminishes. They often need positive feedback from juniors, peers, and seniors; they constantly seek to be "patted on the back." These people need positive reinforcement, even when they do not deserve it. Many warriors are of this type, which in turn encourages leaders to constantly tell their people that they are doing a good job, even when they are not doing a good job. These leaders fall into the trap of thinking it is more important to make their people feel good, and they engage in the process of *cheerleadership* at this point. That is why there is usually a euphoric atmosphere whenever senior leaders address a subordinate audience. They know that their audience is not truly thick-skinned enough to take much criticism, if any at all. We can all think of a time when we received undeserved praise. In our honest moments this undeserved praise made us feel cheap and dishonest, rather than proud. Morally autonomous action, motivated properly, would make for a healthier military.

A healthy military would be one in which the leadership, as one went up in rank, would be more and more critical of the military's capabilities. Such an approach would require honest assessments at each level, no one leader at any level being unable to handle bad news. Our military leadership, on the other hand, becomes more and more positive as we go up in rank until we have our military overburdened and overstretched beyond any measure of good sense. This abject optimism indicates an inability along the way to accept bad news or to consider failure. At times we need honest, open criticism instead of cheerleading and victory videos.

Another example highlighting our dependence upon each other is our overreliance on the metaphor of sports and teamwork as a paradigm for the military. Team sports rely not on genuine self-esteem but group-esteem based on peer approval, *amour-propre*. Historians and psychologists tell us that the only thing that propels soldiers in combat is the feeling they get when they are not alone; they must be surrounded by comrades in order to be motivated. Is this something to relish or should we be dissatisfied with this phenomenon? Should we accept this? To accept this psychological description as a moral prescription, to move from what "is" the case to what "should be" the case is to the commit the normative fallacy. Soldiers need others primarily because they have developed too much of the bad type of self-esteem and not enough of the good type of self-esteem. Do soldiers really need to be self-reliant? Self-reliance has become more and more important over the decades as we become increasingly isolated on the battlefield. We have recognized for decades that soldiers have to be able to operate more and more in isolation. How have we solved this problem? We have approached this problem by promoting teamwork more and more. Does this make sense? I don't think so. I would say that teaching soldiers how to be more self-reliant and self-sufficient would prepare them for isolation rather than emphasizing teamwork. To promote teamwork instead of self-reliance as a solution to the problem of isolation is a little like promoting more running instead of strength training as a solution to the problem of lack of upper-body strength. Building cohesion into military units without also building self-reliance can have disastrous effects. Compare the Rangers with Delta Force when things went bad in Somalia in October of 1993. The Delta soldiers were able to function autonomously, cut off, without orders from higher or assistance from others. The Rangers nearly fell apart in this chaotic environment, precisely because of their extreme cohesion and attendant dependence upon each other.

Being self-reliant due to proper ego development and the accrual of the right type of self-esteem, *amour-de soi*, is important for soldiers, but exponentially so for leaders as they increase in rank. As leaders go up in rank, they have fewer and fewer *peers of agency*. The loneliest man in a division is the division commander and the loneliest man on a ship is the ship's captain. They have no peers and no seniors at hand to constantly stroke them and make sure they are doing the right thing all the time. How do these lonely leaders make decisions that might be unpopular? How could they do unpopular things that their juniors, peers, or seniors might not like? The only way leaders can do so is to have enough *amour-de soi* to be able to withstand the attendant pressure or criticism.

Even on a battlefield that is linked together by layers of nested synchronization matrixes, leaders make innumerable decisions on their own in order to make the whole operation work. As a military, we admire the concept of mission-type orders, *Auftragstaktik*. But we are far from understanding what the concept really means. American military leaders talk about this type of tactic, but they also try to maintain command and control. *Normaltaktik* was about command and control: giving orders, maintaining control, maintaining *order*. The German Army during the nineteenth century developed *Auftragstaktik* as an alternative to *Normaltaktik*. Auftragstaktik was about relinquishing command and control. True mission-type orders require autonomy for them to work. As individuals and units began to work in a more and more isolated and separated manner on the battlefield, leaders recognized the value of operating in a decentralized manner with mission-type orders. We are in danger of not being able to operate at all in a decentralized manner. Technology and digitization on the battlefield will allow more synchronized control at higher levels. Leaders today strive to realize a common operating picture. The danger is that we will forget the lessons of tying an operation together with units being decentralized to handle all of the unforeseen contingencies, yet accomplishing the mission because of understanding the commander's intent at all levels. Army and theater commanders tomorrow will be able to control dozens of individual units, just as Frederick the Great did in his time. The danger is that because they will be able to, they will think they ought to in order to make their plan and their synchronization matrixes work. Likewise, moral autonomy would help to empower soldiers to understand morality and act ethically on their own, without external controls and sanctions. We should replace the current model of moral authority and control with moral autonomy and empowerment.

Embracing philosophical ethics can enhance understanding, which in turn will positively affect motivation and action. Philosophical ethics may even require paying attention to theory. Many people in the moral ideology camp are skeptical about theory. This skepticism is primarily due to misunderstanding. But moral theory at some level may be an important aspect of a moral education, if not for some of the individual members, at least for the framers of the institutional conception of ethics. As Kant argued, when there are problems between theory and practice, the problem is not too much theory but that "the fault is that there is *not enough* theory." Kant gives an example of responding to an artilleryman who is ridiculing the difference between theoretical prediction and empirical experience by replying that "if mechanics were supplemented by the theory of friction and ballistics by the theory of air resistance, in other words if only more theory were added, these theoretical disciplines would harmonize very well with practice."[61] As Kant argued, the solution to the problem is not to discard theory, but to turn even more toward theory. The word "theory" can refer to many things, including the idea of a structured way of thinking requiring a set of principles.[62] Theories help us to do many things: to understand, to explain, and to judge. Theory helps us accomplish these goals through conceptual exploration, criticism, and imagination.[63] In addition, theory also needs to be self-conscious, disclosed, articulated, and transparent—not opaque. In other words, one should be able to "see through it." It cannot contain unarticulated, undisclosed doctrines. This requirement rules out dogma as a possible source of morality.

The moral dialogue need not dogmatically privilege any particular theory, either. The dialogue should move freely in the theoretical realm. "It is the function of the philosopher to be able to theorize about all things."[64] Several philosophers, such as Edmond Pincoffs, argue that theory does not possess the negative qualities that some philosophers claim.[65] Theory simply does not do what the antitheorists claim it does; it is not hopelessly abstract, reductivist, and hierarchical.[66]

Many people, even friends of ideology, talk about moral principles. Only principles and perhaps the theories that ground those principles make *principled* moral thinking a possibility. This may be an obvious tautology, but what is not obvious is the obverse proposition, that moral practice using indoctrination, particularism, and instrumental moral methods are by definition *unprincipled*. So, one of the major outcomes of using theory in ethics is that of obtaining principled moral thinking. Principled moral thinking is preferable for many reasons. Morality does not need a foundation; justification is enough. Moral judgment requires a justification, a rational justification. Thinking can then be consciously consistent. The principles help us to organize, understand, and explain the particulars that we are confronted with continuously. Our practices can be informed when backed by principles that are tied together with theory. Theory can be an aid even at an unconscious level. It will inform and reformulate our intuitions as well. The principles that make up the theories will be those features that we tend away from while we tend to make judgments. There is much in moral philosophy about *pre-theoretic intuitions* being woefully misguided. This explains why our pre- and post-theoretical moral beliefs can be so radically different after spending time with philosophy. Empirical research bears out the notion that education is far more effective than indoctrination when it comes to the realm of ethics. The Defining Issues Test (DIT) is a common instrument to measure moral judgment and its development. The most powerful factor in DIT scores is not religion or authority, but education, which can improve scores by a factor of 250.[67]

An example of this is the effect that the study of formal logic has on a philosopher. Many philosophers claim that the study of logic changed their thinking, at least in the way they saw and thought about things from that point forward. To study formal logic is to study a theory about how we should reason; it is theory, based on a set of principles. Most philosophers do not deliberately spend time using logical tools to assess all their thoughts. And it may take years for them to recognize much application for the logical principles they learned. But what does change is the way they recognize good and bad forms of thinking, and they can eventually do much of this at a tacit level, once so educated in logic. Their post-theoretic ability to think logically has increased, even if they rarely use the language of logic, such as the terms of art *validity* and *soundness*. They tend away from the particulars they studied and are able simply to tend to make the intuitive judgments with far more accuracy and efficacy.

Likewise, moral philosophy can improve a person's moral judgment. Just as grammatical correctness will tacitly develop after the formal study of grammar, or logical judgment will tacitly develop after the formal study of logic, a person's moral judgment will tacitly develop after the formal study of moral theory. The effect of studying moral philosophy is not immediate. Those interested in quick payoffs will more likely turn to ready-made decision-procedures and any number of techniques that are readily available, described in the early chapters. Training has immediate payoffs that can be measured. Education is different because so much of what we learn through education is not immediate or measurable. The deep understanding that comes from reflective study happens over a long period of time. A person who has reflected deeply or studied moral philosophy will simply see moral situations much more differently than someone who is merely applying common sense or a folk-ethical moral approach of their youth. A philosophical ethics education will revise the warrior's pre-theoretic intuitions arrived at through the methods critiqued prior to this chapter.

IS MORAL AUTONOMY POSSIBLE?

Engaging people in philosophical ethics will simply help warriors to reason better, and this will enable them to reduce the moral error in their moral lives. For example, warriors should understand the laws of war better if they have greater moral understanding. It is far easier to learn and think about a few principles than it is to learn and think about dozens, hundreds, or thousands of laws, or competing sets of rules of engagement. And principles have to be derived and justified through conscious and sound theory. For decades people relied on farmer's almanacs to predict the weather so that they could get the most out of the cycles of nature, but they really did not understand weather or climates. It was not until they theorized about the weather that they came to understand it better. When they finally theorized at the level of pressure systems and fronts, they had reached a level of understanding where they could explain and predict at a much more sophisticated level. This level of understanding, explaining, predicting, and judging did not come from relying on common sense, tending to the particulars, staying in the world of appearances, and following the shadows on the wall. It came from reliable theory. Common sense did not teach us about weather fronts. Common sense did not tell us that the earth goes around the sun. Common sense did not tell us about the structure of the atoms that make up our physical being. Common sense did not teach us about evolution. Common sense did not produce mathematics or logic. Common sense does not provide the most defensible theories that inform our practices. If common sense did not aid us in these common endeavors, why should we rely on common sense in ethical matters, especially in professions engaging in activities that are anything but common? Commonsense morality in the military has led us down the wrong path, a path I have described in the first several chapters. Philosophical ethics can help to set the stage so that soldiers as morally autonomous agents can think through these issues, reformulating their intuitions. Right now the common intuitions in the military are the wrong ones. In time, I do think this could change. I'm hopeful that the common intuitions in the military will someday change to be morally justifiable ones.

Indoctrinators assume that moral problems are simply matters of the will—warriors simply *know* the difference between right and wrong; they just *do* the wrong thing for one reason or another. In actuality, the more significant problems are problems of the understanding. These problems can only be correctly sorted out through the deliberate use of moral philosophy. We can go farther than attending to only those moral issues that deal with the voluntary actions of the agent. We can examine and attend to those aspects that deal with the structure (culture, climate, etc.). How do we improve judgment, perception, understanding? By theorizing. There is a gap between theory and practice, and it should neither be kept too large nor bridged too abruptly. Moral autonomy will require that we treat each member of the profession as a thinking being capable of rational thought and logical thinking.

Many criticize philosophy because they think it is too abstract and doesn't adequately connect to reality. Some of these criticisms come from a misunderstanding of philosophical ethics. In chapter two I mentioned, for example, that many ethicists mistakenly inflate the normative force of ethical principles by mistaking universal claims as absolute ones. Absolute claims apply at all times in all places for all people. Universal claims, the type Kant's theory defends, apply to classes of people in particular times and particular places. This more refined philosophical view of ethical principles makes a big difference in being able to better understand ethics. I would not want to rule out any type of philosophical theory or inquiry. There is room in the pursuit of military ethics for some of the better, highly contextualized moral theories, such as Walzer's just war theory. Contextualism is not just a recent development in ethics, and it has some promise and could contribute to the theoretical pursuit of adequate applied ethics. In actuality, the major theoretical traditions, including Kant's and Aristotle's, can be highly contextualized. Their theories are not guilty of much of the criticism that the antitheorists want to attribute to them.

Moral philosophy and the enterprise of theoretical reflection can contribute in an important way to the understanding and practice of a professional ethic, for the other approaches have some deep problems that reflection can help to fix. There has not been a sustained philosophical critique of applied or professional ethics to date as they relate to the military enterprise. As much as ethical theory is shunned, feared, avoided, and watered down, there is a great need to embrace theory and explore the relationship between theory and practice even further, for "the general topic of theory and method in moral philosophy is large, important, and underexplored."[68]

My proposals for philosophical ethics have not been modest ones in this chapter. I have tried in previous chapters to show how and why the military has erred in its approach to ethics. I have also tried to show some of the work that needs to be done. The military has navigated poorly through the moral jungle—it has lost its ability to use its *moral compass*. I propose that we move from heteronomy to autonomy as a model for military ethics, a radical departure, to be sure. The military culture will have to adapt and evolve to embrace new norms of operating. In order for true dialogue to occur leaders will have to possess enough self-esteem to allow juniors to disagree with them, to be accountable as leaders for their decisions, and to be able to justify their actions with reasons. I propose that we pay attention to philosophical ethics in the military and engage the institution further in disclosing, analyzing, and justifying an ethical understanding that would be adequate. I propose that paying attention to philosophical ethics in the military will help to refashion our moral intuitions, making them sound and compatible with ethics at large. And I propose that soldiers going about their business autonomously, empowered through the public use of reason, will be adequately motivated by a better ethical understanding.

6

The Fully Reflective Life and Military Ethics

THE POSSIBILITY OF MORAL PROGRESS

Many within the war machine will not agree with the bulk and thrust of my argument, especially those whose work requires that they be mouthpieces for policy. My critics must remember, though, that the leaders of the war machine are responsible for creating, sustaining, or changing the policies; they are not merely passive executors of policy. Luckily there are real academic schools within the military institution that value academic freedom and free inquiry, not political pressure and information management to protect a public image. The academy (the professoriate pursuing the free exchange of ideas in an atmosphere of academic freedom bounded only by logic and reason) has traditionally been critical of governmental institutions *when warranted*. For the last half century a counter-academy has blossomed, though, populated by a counter-intelligentsia, a term they have coined for themselves, no doubt motivated by their contempt for the intelligentsia that makes up the academy in the world of the university. The counter-academy began with huge grants from tycoons such as John M. Olin and William E. Simon, and over the decades these corporate sponsors with governmental affiliations have built corporate think-tanks, such as the Olin Foundation, the Heritage Foundation, the American Enterprise Institute, and their offshoots and affiliates. University schools of government, even those at Harvard and Johns Hopkins, with the help of governmental monies and oversight, are also at times part of the counter-academy. The counter-academy has its own presses and paper mills, as their work in the main would not survive the peer review guided by free inquiry in mainstream academic university presses, free from

177

Political correctness with a capital "P." Insofar as I critique the ethics center at West Point in an earlier chapter, it is no accident that the William E. Simon Center for the Professional Military Ethic (SCPME) enjoys the patronage of one of the original founders of the counter-academy.

This issue concerning the academy and the counter-academy is not about being fair and balanced, as Fox News or David Horowitz will couch the argument, as they pretend, mistakenly and misleadingly, in their more honest moments that each side is equally ideological. On the contrary, if the conclusions are derived through a process of free inquiry, then it cannot by definition be ideological. Let's look at the intelligent design controversy as an example. Intelligent designers want to claim that evolution is equally ideological, so why not expose students to both ideologies? Those in favor of putting intelligent design in science classes within the public school system argue from this false construction. But this debate does not depend on left versus right, one ideology versus another. It depends upon whether the inquiry is free or not, bounded only by logic and reason. The bottom line is that *science is already free*, and science itself rejects intelligent design as a scientific theory. To impose intelligent design instruction on a community whose intellectual standards reject such an idea is the opposite of academic freedom—it would be forced, not free. The key distinction in question whether we are concerned with evolution or the ethics of warfare is about whether the inquiry is free or not. Inquiry is free if it privileges argument over status, reason over rank. My argument in this book emerges from the school of free inquiry. While my harsher critics will be from the counter-academy, I do welcome philosophical critique from the academy itself. The counter-academy often argues from a set of errors in reasoning: the normative fallacy, seeing description as prescription, and so on as I have argued in the first critical chapters of this book.

As this book goes to print, there is a lot of discussion within the war machine about how what I refer to as the academy is hurting the war effort. But honest critique should not threaten the war effort unless there is something wrong with the war effort to begin with. The American people and the world community would be supporting America if the current Long War, especially the one in Iraq, were justifiable. For example, one hears a lot about the negativity of the current critique. The warriors want to know why there isn't equal time given to all the good that the war machine is doing in the Fertile Crescent and the Hindu Kush. From a particular point of view, there are some good things happening. There is a scene in the movie *Platoon* where the soldiers in the platoon are doing good things. The camera captures the humanity of Chris Taylor (Charlie Sheen) when he caringly carries a child from a burning village and stops a rape in progress. These are good things. But the platoon had just finished burning the village and killing many of the parents. There is a difference in kind and degree (of logarithmic scale) between the grave harm this unit did and the paltry good it did. No measure of proportionality could find a positive balance of good over harm in this case. I'm afraid the same general problem of proportionality is operative in the current war. Building schools and securing voting machines do not compare to flattening cities and bringing long-term instability and violence to an entire region. Even if we could add up all the good particular acts that warriors are doing in this war, they would pale in comparison to the great harm that has been done from the strategic down to the tactical level. The American war machine is keeping track of its own casualties. War deaths now exceed the toll on 9/11. General Tommy Franks said, "We don't do body counts." This is unfortunately another violation of international law. By law we should be doing so. The most conservative body count in Iraq alone is over 40,000 and the most liberal over 600,000. The sad part of this count is that most of them are considered to be collateral damage. The moral error we have exacted on the Iraqi population can no longer be considered "collateral," unless we have abandoned the meaning of the term. If so, then our entire linguistic construction for this war should be suspect. This war would fail any proportionality test of even the most instrumental nature.

When I claim philosophy has a role in moral education, I am not suggesting that the military issue each of its members a copy of Kant's *Groundwork*. Would they benefit from reading this work? Possibly. But as a practical matter, no institution has the resources to adequately teach Kant's works in a way that may give an accurate enough account with any appreciable benefit. However, while the students receiving the moral education may not benefit from reading Kant, the teachers within such a system would benefit, and the framers of the substance and content of that moral education would certainly benefit tremendously from Kant's work, if only to serve as background for any justifiable principled thinking. But teachers of ethics should read more than Kant's *Groundwork*; they will do a disservice to Kant if they rely only on this work. The Rawlsian derivation is more understandable and justifiable when taking Kant's philosophy into account as background for Rawls, since Rawls' Kantian constructivism figures heavily here. Philosophy is important not only for the students of this system of moral education, but also for the framers and the teachers. I find that teachers are good learners. But many people obtain bachelor's or master's degrees without really having their convictions or world view challenged or affected. The vast majority of people who struggle hard and long enough to earn their doctorate have developed habits of mind that enable them to grow intellectually. I find cadets in their undergraduate years to be good learners. And majors in their mid-thirties are very good learners as well. But colonels are typically not as good when it comes to learning. Their curiosity is replaced with the certainties they have acquired through their experience. In general, reflection challenges us to change, and it is harder to change the older and more entrenched we become.

Moral education in the military can benefit from philosophical reflection. The problem remains that the military has the wrong precepts, is ignorant of or resistant to more proper precepts, or even if they are aware of proper, justifiable precepts they are not inclined to heed them. Philosophy can help sort out all of these problems. A principled approach to ethics can increase understanding of principles. Philosophical argument can give people reasons for adhering to moral principles. And philosophical argument can help to revise existing precepts that are in error.

Military ethics, and professional ethics in general, will improve drastically when we can view morality as the first philosophy, if we can move ethics away from the received metaphysical and epistemological dogmas and toward reason, away from a project of moral *foundation for* morality and toward a project of moral *justification to* the military of its proper moral principles. Changing military ethics so that it embraces autonomy rather than authority is no small challenge. This change will not be easy because all of the inertial forces will continue to move the military in its present trajectory, away from a moral "center of gravity." It is important to attempt to redirect the military toward morality. In the near future, however, the picture may not change much.

I have established in chapter 2 the phenomenon of the military teaching ethics through authority and indoctrination. The military will continue to teach the dogmatic, ideological precepts of professionalism. Soldiers will learn these precepts and may continue to do immoral things that at the same time may also seem *professional*. The chaplains will continue to teach ethics, and the institution will continue to go to them for moral advice, as the ancients went to the oracles for advice. The unreasoned faith in moral authority is potentially the most dangerous and most ubiquitous threat in the world today—abroad and at home. Our moral discourse has to evolve beyond the medieval, theological language of good and evil. People who think of morality in these terms are at an adolescent stage of moral development, (see Peter Singer, *President of Good and Evil*, Dutton, 2004). As dangerous as moral authority can be in either a religious or political context, it is ten-fold more dangerous when political and religious authority combine. I have also established in chapter 2 the practice of employing particularism as a means of ethical instruction. The apparatchiks of ideology will transmit this moral ideology through narrative. The military will continue to transmit its own history, and its own moral history, through narratives, through stories, both good and bad. These narratives are employed because stories sell. These stories will be popular, but will continue to contain unreflective lines of thought that will defy moral reasoning.

Henry Fleming was happy that he did not have to experience a barbaric, "Greeklike struggle." He had concluded before he tasted battle in Crane's novel, which depicts what later became to be known as Chancelorsville, that his despair over Homeric warfare was misguided, for "such would be no more." Far from the destructive barbarity that existed in the ancient world, he thought he was about to experience more civilized warfare: "Men were better, or more timid. Secular and religious education had effaced the throat-grappling instinct." The remainder of Henry's experience proved that his early conclusion had been mistaken. The American Civil War had turned out to be every bit as Homeric as his worst fears had imagined. This ninteeenth-century conflict, as horrific as it was, only presaged the horrors of twentieth-century conflict. We have regressed again, confronting the ghost of Achilles yet once more, the ghost in the war machine.

In chapters 3 and 4 I demonstrated the inadequate consequentialist approach that the military employs when it comes to reasoning about means and ends. The military will continue to search for more efficient means to achieve the end of victory. When they do employ ethical decision-procedures, these procedures will not stand up to reason. And they will be directed to the end of victory, without much deliberation over new ends. When people do view the ends and the means together, they will have an incomplete picture, an incomplete grasp of the chain of human activity and of the moral dimension. As this book goes to print, the ghost in the war machine seeks only victory in the so-called Long War or Global War on Terror. We have handicapped ourselves if we continue to call it a war, for that language conditions us to seek victory. Using counterinsurgency operations and irregular warfare tactics will most certainly guarantee failure, for their illegitimacy will work counter to any legitimate political goals. If the war machine prosecutes a Long War, they will fall into a Long Sleep. A revolution in mindset seems far away.

We have to seriously, perhaps even painfully, examine the complex relationship between what we normally think of in terms of cause and effect. The days of simple, linear models of cause and effect should be ancient history today, but many of today's political and military leaders have no more sophistication when it comes to thinking about cause and effect than did the Neanderthals. A deeper understanding may help ward off our own extinction. Causation is the wrong philosophical study; the appropriate philosophical study is that of human action. Causation presumes a behaviorist model of cause and effect. As Arthur Koestler says in his book *The Ghost in the Machine*, (1967) behaviorism is the flat-earth view of human activity. Behavioral theory should be retired to make room for action theory. The current war-making elite believe that if we fight evil hard enough good will triumph. If we can root out and destroy every terrorist then we can win the war on terror. If we can increase the mentality and actuality of a national security state then we will be safe from attack. If we can scare our potential enemies out there then they will leave us alone. Cause and effect are just not so naively simple. I suggested in the introduction to this book that Lieutenant Calley was not simply a defective human being, but that the Army helped to create him. And just as the military helped to create Calley, American policies and actions helped to create Saddam Hussein, especially in the 1980s. We cannot simply attribute Hussein's crimes to his evil nature any more than we can attribute Calley's crimes to his bad character. Sartre's mature philosophical work took a more systemic than individualistic approach to moral questions: *what should we do* gave way to *what do we make of what others have made of us.* And, yes, America's realist foreign policies and unreflective intrusion into the Islamic world has helped to create Osama Bin Laden. We should take him seriously when he says that he considers America his enemy because of our influence in the Arabian Peninsula, our decade-long war against Iraq, and our unflinching and unquestioned support of Israel's occupation. From his point of view, Bin Laden views American and Israeli occupation of Islamic territory as the modern-day occupation of Jerusalem by the Crusaders, beginning in 1099. And he views his role as that of Salah al-Din (Saladin), who expelled the Crusaders in 1187, after nearly one hundred years of occupation. From a strategic point of view, he has us just where he wants us, and he is taking the long view.

We have to reflect deeply about this problem, from all angles and points of view. History has shown that terrorism cannot be solved in kind, by fighting fire with fire, terror with terror. What we fail to acknowledge in act after act of unself-consciousness is that counterterrorism is terrorism; counterinsurgency doctrine is a doctrine of terror. Had we learned this insight by paying attention to Algiers in the mid-to-late 1950s, America could have saved a lot of trouble by avoiding Vietnam. Terrorism cannot be solved in the long run by violence. The Israelis have yet to come to grips with this idea, and it appears that America will spend years before we are struck by this blinding flash of the obvious. The way to deal with terrorism is to deal with the legitimate concerns that the terrorists may have. This is the only legitimate way to lower the tensions and solve the problem at its root. The recent findings of the Iraq Study Group suffer the same defect as most other group findings. They make a lengthy assessment of the current situation, and then they make even lengthier recommendations. What is the problem? How do we fix it? Two parts: simple. They answered the *what* question and then the *how* question. The problem with this ubiquitous problem-solving method is that it skips over the *why* question. Why is there terrorism?

It's all about legitimacy. Without legitimacy, there is no hope. When Napoleon extended his empire, he believed that he was doing the right thing, bringing the revolutionary ideal to the rest of Europe, freeing them from monarchic, autocratic tyranny. His occupation of Spain lasted for many years, long enough for Goya to capture the images of the atrocities of both the French and the Spanish guerillas. The French Army was beleaguered by guerilla activity from the beginning, but the guerilla movement took two years to mature into the indomitable resistance that it became. The French occupation never had legitimacy in the eyes of the Spanish. Are we going to face the same situation as America continues to build its own occupation of another part of the world that does not recognize American legitimacy? Have we seen the peak of the resistance movement, or has it not even yet begun to organize? Are we in any better position than France was in Spain, or France in Algieria? I had mentioned already that the basic manuscript for this book was finished before the current Long War. So our current failings are not merely the consequence of an inadequate understanding right now or the consequences of the present circumstances. The current moral failings are the same failings we have always had, and they are the consequence of the inadequate understanding that we have always had. It is hard to keep up with the bad news, which we have been increasingly receiving. This bad news—evidence of moral error—is the consequence of a failed understanding. H. R. McMaster writes convincingly about the failings of the political and military leaders who enabled and sustained the debacle that was Vietnam, (*Dereliction of Duty*, Harper, 1998). With all due respect to Heraclitus, haven't we stepped into the same river twice?

These questions will only get worse with time. Why? Perhaps Socrates laid out the master moral narratives upon reflection on the Peloponnesian War. Socrates described three moral conceptions for his three divisions of society: the working class, the military class, and the ruling class. Each moral conception for each class is relevant today, and his social critique as well as his skepticism remains unchanged over the millennia. The moral conception of the working class was expressed by the merchant Cephalus as "to each his own," or by Polemarchus, his son, as "to each his due." The business world has kept this moral conception alive and well through the centuries. The moral conception of the military class was defended by Thrasymachus as "might is right," and that moral conception still describes as trenchantly the logic of force as it has remained unchanged. The current Army advertising campaign uses the slogan: *Army Strong*. All of these moral conceptions are dismantled by Socrates because of the harm they bring to people. And none of these moral conceptions is appropriate for the ruling class to apply to society as a whole. Since these conceptions are precisely the ideas that guide the moral thinking of the ruling class, such social critique was very likely as ironic in ancient Athens as it is in contemporary America. Socratic morality amounted to the very simple notion that it is better to suffer harm than to do harm. The Kantian principles outlined in chapter 5 reflect a Socratic moral-ity; on the contrary, current warrior ethics is some combination of the busi-ness and military moral schemes. Of course, Socrates is right, but try selling that idea to a military audience. If the predominantly Christian American military were more Christ-like, Socrates' idea would resonate through Jesus' injunction to "turn the other cheek," but the more theologically minded mil-itary Christians tell me that we were meant to turn it once, at tops twice (the exegetical rationalizations are infinitely ambiguous).

So, how can we create the conditions for moral progress? In chapter 5, I outlined the approach that would help to bring about effective change—a change from moral heteronomy to moral autonomy. And this change would be greatly facilitated through philosophy. The trajectory can change if people continue the hard work of bringing the cases of military ethics to the *bar of reason*. It can change if people in the military can be empowered to employ public reason in moral matters. When people in the military start thinking for themselves about morality, then they can start to change the direction of movement. When they can start to think beyond the level of moral doctrine to the level of moral principle, the military will start to change. Illegal orders will not stand up to scrutiny. People will think through the ideology and nar-ratives they are given. They will think through their ends and means more adequately. And, most importantly, they can come to appreciate the moral principles associated with the battlefield.

In the end I argue for the Kantian conception as being the most robust, but I have also shown how other moral schemes can make a contribution. Moral autonomy is a key idea in this process. In order for this moral education to take place, each warrior must be empowered to use his or her own reason. Each warrior must seek moral justification through the public use of reason. If the warriors do not come to see these arguments for themselves, and are not genuinely persuaded by the arguments in their own minds, then they will not genuinely believe the conclusions of these arguments. In addition to the class-rooms throughout military schools, this change can potentially take place in the ethics centers at each of the three major military academies. Each of the services, the Army, the Navy, and the Air Force, will draw heavily upon the work of these ethics centers, which should be networked with the academic departments, not only within but also outside of the academies. They should especially be working with the philosophy departments. The ethics centers will be useful to the degree they belong to the real academy rather than the counter-academy. These centers can be a great asset in the education of some future military leaders. If they too are engaged in the project of moral auton-omy instead of moral authority, public reason instead of ideology, and moral justification instead of foundation, then they can be help move the military toward a better peace.

I have essentially made a revolutionary proposal including important justifiable moral principles of war under the regulative idea of restraint. The political principles are self-defense and the defense of others, and the military principles are discrimination, minimal force, and minimal harm. These principles have already been recognized by those who understand that terrorism is a crime. There are many commanders who talk about the need for the military to engage in police work to combat terrorism. Perhaps someday the nation's leaders will realize that we should approach terrorism with a crime model, not a war model. Acts of terror are criminal acts, not acts of war, and they are properly proscribed by international criminal law. Many of us in the academy stated as much from the beginning. These principles, then, should become a part of every aspect of moral education in the military, at all of the levels. They should be part of the indoctrination, instead of other competing principles. They should be well understood by the Army's leadership, so that the authoritarian nature of military ethics will at least propel morally justifiable principles. The principles should be part of the narratives that the military uses to impart moral instruction. The principles should act as constraints while employing methods to achieve the ends. And they should be considered with deliberating new ends. Finally, the principles should be part of the public reason that informs military ethics so that a just military can be part of the structure of a moral American society. Other professions may benefit from a similar analysis of their institutional conception of ethics. They may have parallel challenges within their methods of moral education. Likewise, they may benefit from a similar derivation and justification of their moral principles. A justified set of moral principles derived through public reason for each of the institutions that help to make up the basic structure of a just society could only be an improvement.

I end with guarded optimism, for the warrior is awakening. Some warriors are beginning to think about war and morality in a serious way. Some are even thinking about means and ends in a more intellectually robust way. For example, planners who were involved in the current war in Iraq, who had been graduates of the School of Advanced Military Studies, such as Colonel Kevin Benson, had done some serious planning for the phase of the operation after the kinetic phase. And some commanders knew beforehand that the mere taking of Baghdad was just the beginning of something much harder. We need a dialogue to redefine the avenues of dissent when things are going wrong. Young officers are speaking out. Several members of the Judge Advocate General Corps, some retired, are speaking out. Increasingly retired generals are speaking out: Major General (Ret.) Charles Swannack, Jr., Major General (Ret.) John Batiste, Lieutenant General (Ret.) Gregory Newbold, to name a few. But since the days of *invincible ignorance* are gone (the medieval separation between the political and military spheres), we need a revolution in discourse so there are legitimate avenues of public reason and disagreement, dissent, and disobedience within the war machine. We need a healthier culture so that people know when and where they can speak out, disobey, walk away, or even resign in protest. The price of failure now can be in the trillions of dollars and millions of lives; we can no longer afford such costly errors—literally and figuratively. Wisdom begins with doubt and learning begins with failure. Those warriors who are willing to see things for what they may be and who are willing to learn give me the hope that the war machine could someday become fully conscious. An exciting new idea is emerging to think about military operations in a new way, Systemic Operational Design (SOD), developed by the Israeli warrior, historian, and philosopher, Shimon Naveh. SOD is difficult to understand and is countering the more dominant doctrine of Effects Based Operations (EBO). Systemic Operational Design leaves room for moral considerations in a way that Effects Based Operations never could, for it enables reasoned upward influence in an unprecedented manner. EBO's flat-earth assumptions that rely on teleology and behaviorism will prevent the doctrine from ever being able to even consider deep moral concerns; it will remain bereft of any moral quality or possibility. On the other hand, SOD will allow moral dialogue and has potential in allowing the war machine to follow a moral compass. It's enough just to mention these concepts now. The promising alternative is a reasoning process rather than a decision procedure. Reason falls still born from our current abortive decision making process, for argument gives way to status, reason gives way to rank. The teleological focus on the end state and desired effects we currently have sets the moral default to consequential-ism—the end justifies the means. Morally it's about the path we take, what we do that matters. It's not about effects, but evolving conditions. It's not about cause and effect, but actions and conditions. More to follow—I will pursue the pitfalls and potential of these emerging doctrinal approaches in a future work.

We must guard our optimism with the greatest vigilance, however. Re-naming "The Long War as "Persistent Conflict" does not move us out of the current, inadequate framework. For example, Emma Vialpando of the Center for a New American Security (CNAS) insightfully asks what the disturbing rise in post-traumatic stress disorder means in the context of Persistent Conflict. No society in the history of the world has ever embraced a permanent war footing. Do we need to change PTSD to stand for persistent-traumatic stress disorder?

I have two final thoughts. First, there is good work going on that argues for the possibility of moral warriors by Shannon French and Martin Cook. I don't think this book detracts from or conflicts with their fine work. I use both of their books in the classroom, and they get good reviews. However, I don't think the term "moral warrior" is redundant. Finally, I have no doubt that many people will not agree with or like my argument. As I often have to remind my students, the philosophical enterprise is not about agreeing or disagreeing, liking or disliking the works they encounter. It is about engaging them and maybe understanding them.

Notes

1. THE UNREFLECTIVE LIFE: THE SLEEP OF REASON

1. Colin Powell, with Joseph E. Persico, *My American Journey* (New York: Random House, 1995), 144. Reportedly, Major Colin Powell as the assistant G3 in December 1967 had responded to allegations of the massacre from Tom Glen by saying that nothing happened.

2. Powell, *My American Journey*, 143.

3. William R. Peers, *My Lai Inquiry* (New York: Norton, 1979), 208.

4. Karen J. Greenberg and Joshua L. Dratel, eds., *The Torture Papers: The Road to Abu Ghraib* (Cambridge, UK: Cambridge University Press, 2005).

5. Harry G. Frankfurt, *On Bullshit* (Princeton, NJ: Princeton University Press, 2005).

6. Roger Spiller, *An Instinct for War* (Cambridge, MA: Harvard University Press, 2005), 386.

7. "Shock and Awe" is a term that gained currency in 1996 due to a book published by a retired Naval officer, Harlan K. Ullman, and a retired Army officer, James P. Wade, *Shock and Awe: Achieving Rapid Dominance* (Washington, DC: National Defense University Press, 1996). The book is now out of print, but the text is in the public domain and available for perusal on the National Defense University Web site.

8. Grotius worked against the skeptics to ground morality in a *sensus communis*; Hume worked against a popular religious morality to establish secular ethics grounded in human nature; Bentham worked to improve the poor state of affairs in England; and Kant worked to defeat the problems associated with any heteronomous moral system, creating a sophisticated justifiable morality, grounded in reason and available to everyone. "But one cannot require pure practical reason to be subordinate to speculative reason and so reverse the order, since all interest is ultimately practical and

even that of speculative reason is only conditional and is complete in practical use alone." Kant, *Critique of Practical Reason,* ed. Mary Gregor (Cambridge, UK: Cambridge University Press, 1997), 102, 5:121.

9. John Rawls uses the term "moral error." "Fifty Years after Hiroshima," *John Rawls: Collected Papers* (Cambridge, MA: Harvard University Press, 1999),572. "It is sometimes said that questioning the bombing of Hiroshima is an insult to the American troops who fought the war. This is hard to understand. We should be able to look back and consider our faults after fifty years. We expect the Japanese and the Germans to do that—'*Vergangenheitsverarbeitung,*' as the Germans say. Why shouldn't we? It can't be that we think we waged the war without *moral error.*" [Emphasis on "moral error" mine.]

10. William Bennett, *Why We Fight: Moral Clarity and the War on Terrorism* (New York: Doubleday, 2002).

11. Edward Said, *Orientalism* (New York: Vintage Books, 1978), 25.

12. *Field Manual 1, The Army* (Washington, DC 2001).

13. Leonard Wong and Douglas Johnson II, "Serving the American People: A Historical View of the Army Profession," *The Future of the Army Profession,* eds. Don M. Snyder and Gayle Watkins, (Boston: McGraw-Hill Custom Publishing, 2002), 70.

14. The Army's foundational field manual states, "The ability to close with and destroy enemy forces, occupy territory, and control populations achieves moral dominace over enemy will and destroys means to resist." *FM 1, The Army* (Washington, DC, 2001). In a section on building trust, the context of morals is emotional or psychological when it says that soldiers develop trust when they "know their commander will support their decisions physically and morally." *FM 6-0, Mission Command, Command and Control of Army Force* (Washington, DC, 2003). It was vital for the American military to "gain moral ascendancy over Noriega's forces." From *FM 3-0, Operations,* (Washington, DC 2001).

15. President Bill Clinton, the Army Chief of Staff's Command Sergeant Major Gene McKinney, Army Major General Hale, the Air Force chief of staff, and Air Force bomber pilot Kelley Flynn are some of the key figures here.

16. The error of hanging an innocent person can be called a Type I error, similar to the usage in the natural and social sciences, the mistake being the ascription of a false positive (a phrase used in this context is in the movie *Minority Report*), or, in ordinary language, seeing something that is not there. The error of letting a guilty person go free can be called a Type II error, the mistake of missing what is actually there. Michael Meyerson, *Political Numeracy: Mathematical Perspectives on our Chaotic Constitution* (New York: Norton, 2002), 39.

17. "Then General Westmoreland showed me a copy of a letter from Ron Ridenhour, an ex-GI who had been in Vietnam in 1968. This letter had triggered the Army's decision to look into the My Lai incident." W. R. Peers, *My Lai Inquiry* (New York: Norton, 1979), 4.

18. "What happened at My Lai was neither a unique nor an isolated incident." Joanna Bourke gives evidence for this claim in *An Intimate History of Killing: Face to Face Killing in the Twentieth-Century Warfare* (New York: Basic Books, 1999), 166–70.

19. Powell, *My American Journey*, 144.

20. Alan Donagan, *The Theory of Morality* (Chicago: University of Chicago Press, 1977), 135.

21. Robert S. McNamara, *In Retrospect: The Tragedy and Lessons of Vietnam* (New York: Vintage Press, 1995).

22. Christopher Hitchens, *The Trial of Henry Kissinger* (London: Verso, 2001). The Roger Morris quotation is from the documentary also by Christopher Hitchens, *The Trials of Henry Kissinger*, released in 2002.

23. The idea of the split between our Enlightenment and Romantic heritage is explored in the book by the legal scholar George P. Fletcher, in *Romantics at War: Glory and Guilt in the Age of Terrorism* (Princeton, NJ: Princeton University Press, 2002).

24. Michael J. Sullivan III, *American Adventurism Abroad: Thirty Invasions, Interventions, and Regime Changes since World War II* (London: Praeger, 2004), 9.

25. J. B. Schneewind, *The Invention of Autonomy: A History of Modern Moral Philosophy* (Cambridge, UK: Cambridge University Press, 1998).

26. President Truman's executive order enacting racial integration occurred in 1948. Mark Osiel, *Obeying Orders: Atrocity, Military Discipline & the Law of War* (Piscalaway, NJ: Transaction Publishers, 1999), 29. Congress mandated the admission of women into the United States Military Academy in 1976. Literally days before the this mandate, I remember as a cadet our superintendent, Lieutenant General Sidney B. Berry, a consummate warrior, announcing to the Corps of Cadets that women would enter the Academy over his dead body. He commanded V Corps afterward, so their entrance did not kill his career.

27. The legislative, executive, and judicial branches of government are all involved in these moral issues within the medical and law enforcement professions, for example. In contrast, the military has relatively little oversight in their moral matters, or even legal matters, especially when it comes to enforcing established laws and then judicially punishing violations of those laws. The Supreme Court, for example, routinely decides cases that have an impact on the moral questions in the medical and law enforcement professions, but it normally stays out of the military's business.

2 . THE PSEUDO-REFLECTIVE LIFE: BATTLE SLEEP

1. "There have been some great movies recently—I think of *Saving Private Ryan*, *Schindler's List*, and *Glory*—but so much of what appears is trash, or worse." James H. Toner, "A Message to Garcia: Leading Soldiers in Moral Mayhem," in *The*

Future of the Army Profession, eds. Don M. Snider and Gayle L. Watkins (Boston: McGraw-Hill Custom Publishing, 2002), 315.

2. Carl von Clausewitz, *On War* (New York: Alfred A. Knopf, 1993), 189.

3. Christopher Browning, *Ordinary Men: Reserve Police Battalion 101 and the Final Solution in Poland* (New York: Harper, 1992).

4. The oath of enlistment is as follows: "I, _____, do solemnly swear (or affirm) that I will support and defend the Constitution of the United States against all enemies, foreign and domestic; that I will bear true faith and allegiance to the same; and that I will obey the orders of the President of the United States and the orders of the officers appointed over me, according to regulations and the Uniform Code of Military Justice. So help me God." (Title 10, U.S. Code; Act of May 5, 1960, replacing the wording first adopted in 1789, with amendment effective October 5, 1962). In contrast, the oath of office is as follows: "I, _____ (SSAN), having been appointed an officer in the Army of the United States, as indicated above in the grade of _____ do solemnly swear (or affirm) that I will support and defend the Constitution of the United States against all enemies, foreign or domestic, that I will bear true faith and allegiance to the same; that I take this obligation freely, without any mental reservations or purpose of evasion; and that I will well and faithfully discharge the duties of the office upon which I am about to enter. So help me God." (DA Form 71, August 1, 1959, for officers.)

5. Robert B. Louden, *Morality and Moral Theory: A Reappraisal and Reaffirmation* (Oxford: Oxford University Press, 1992), 91.

6. Annette Baier, "Doing without Moral Theory," *Anti-Theory in Ethics and Moral Conservatism*, eds. Stanley Clarke and Evan Simpson, (Albany: State University of New York Press, 1989),36.

7. Baier, "Doing without Moral Theory," 37.

8. *FM 22-100, Army Leadership*.

9. Karel Montor, *Ethics for the Junior Officer* (Annapolis: Naval Institute Press, 1993).

10. I will make rough distinctions among practical, applied, and professional ethics, because of the usages of these terms as they have emerged in the literature. I believe it is largely true that every type of ethics can in some way be practical. People usually speak of applied ethics when they are talking about pressing philosophical problems, including the death penalty, abortion, euthanasia, or distributive justice. Professional ethics can overlap with applied ethics as stipulated above, but normally is a little narrower because it refers to the practical or applied ethical problems of a particular institution. At the same time, I do not want to create distinctions that do not hold among all legitimate usages, thereby making the distinctions a great distraction. Some may use the terms "applied," "practical," and "professional" interchangeably when talking about ethics, and they may be justified in doing so.

11. Shannon French, *The Code of the Warrior: Exploring Warrior Values Past and Present* (New York: Rowman & Littlefield, 2003), 60.

12 Aristotle, *The Rhetoric and Poetics of Aristotle*, ed. Friedrich Solmsen (New York: Random House, 1954), *Rhetoric*, Book II, Chapter 12, 1389^{a}13, p. 122.

13. Aristotle, *Rhetoric*, Book III, Chapter 15, 1416b 26,207.

14. General Paul Aussaresses, *The Battle of the Casbah: Terrorism and Counter-Terrorism in Algeria, 1955-1957* (New York: Enigma Books, 2002).

15. Roger Trinquier, *Modern Warfare: A French View of Counterinsurgency* (Fort Leavenworth, KS: U.S. Army Command and General Staff College, 1985).

16. Bernard Williams, "The Scientific and the Ethical," *Anti-Theory in Ethics and Moral Conservatism*, eds. Stanley Clarke and Evan Simpson, (Albany: State University of New York Press, 1989), 73.

17. General William T. Sherman, *Memoirs of General William T. Sherman* (New York: De Capo Press, 1984), volume ii, p. 126.

18. Thucydides, *The History of the Peloponnesian War* (New York: Penguin Books, 1972), 404.

19. Douglas MacArthur, in a Speech to the Corps of Cadets at West Point, 1962. Interestingly, many have searched for this sentiment in Plato's works and have not found it. I'm hesitant to conclude that MacArthur either made it up or stretched something else Plato said, even if it were to his advantage to describe necessity and realism, because I may not have looked well enough.

20. J. Glenn Gray, *The Warriors: Reflections on Men in Battle* (New York: Harper Torchbooks, 1959), 51.

21. Brigadier General Mark Welsh, Commandant of Cadets at the United States Air Force Academy, in his first speech as the commandant given on August 26, 1999. The text of his remarks indicates that he is self-conscious of the suspect moral nature of his actions and so gives military realism as a moral justification.

22. Martin L. Cook and Major Phillip A. Hamann, USAF, "The Road to Basra," in *Ethics for Military Leaders*, eds. George R. Lucas, Jr., and Paul E. Roush, (New York: Simon and Schuster, 1998), 538.

23. Russell Weigley, "A Strategy of Annihilation: U. S. Grant and the Union," *The American Way of War* (Bloomington: Indiana University Press, 1973), 128–52.

24. A term propelled into the modern philosophical lexicon by Thomas Hobbes, who may have seen the power of the idea when he translated Thucydides himself. There has yet to be a prominent humanist or ironic interpretation of Thucydides.

25. The conclusions of a typical study advocate the following to enhance ethical behavior in an organization: leaders who model ethical behavior, reward and punishment systems, and a focus on adherence to the law and professional standards.

Such studies do not mention anything about moral education or character develop-
ment, and they will never mention anything as immeasurable as intention, desire,
belief, understanding—the very topics of a moral education. Linda Klebe Trevino,
Kenneth D. Butterfield, and Donald L. McCabe, "The Ethical Context in
Organizations: Influences on Employee Attitudes and Behaviors," *Business Ethics
Quarterly*, Special Issue on Psychology and Business Ethics, Oct. 1996.

26. Alexander Rosenberg, *Philosophy of Social Science*, 2d. ed. (Boulder, CO:
Westview Press, 1995), 35.

27. Plato, *Euthyphro, in The Trial and Death of Socrates* (Indianapolis: Hackett,
1975),12.

28. General Norman Schwarzkopf, with Peter Petre, *It Doesn't Take a Hero*
(New York: Bantam Books, 1992), 542.

29. Ramsey Clark, *The Fire This Time: U.S. War Crimes in the Gulf* (New York:
Thunder's Mouth Press, 1994), 52.

30. Martin Cook and Major Phillip A. Hamann, "The Road to Basra," 533.

31. Clark, *The Fire This Time: U.S. War Crimes in the Gulf*, 50-51.

32. Schwarzkopf, *It Doesn't Take a Hero*, p. 554. Major Tim Brotherton recalls
General Schwarzkopf's rhetoric when addressing the 24th Division before the battle.
Schwarzkopf was telling each of the branches what their job was to be as they
destroyed the Iraqi Army. He told the infantry that it was their job to carve the V for
victory into the foreheads of the dead Iraqis. The archetypal defiling of the dead from
the time of Homer remains with us to this day, if even in just our rhetoric.

33. Seymour Hersh, "Overwhelming Force," *The New Yorker* (May 22, 2000),
49–82.

34. For an eye-opening account of the extent of propaganda used during Gulf
I, see John R. MacArthur's *Second Front: Censorship and Propaganda in the Gulf War*
(Berkeley: University of California Press, 1993).

35. Robert Audi, "The Separation of Church and State and the Obligations of
Citizenship," *Philosophy and Public Affairs* 18, no. 3. (1989).

36. John Rawls, "The Idea of Public Reason Revisited," in *The Law of Peoples*
(Cambridge: Harvard University Press, 1999), 166.

37. FM 22-100, *Army Leadership* (Washington, DC: HQ, Department of the
Army, Aug. 1999).

38. *The Future of the Army Profession*, eds. Don M. Snider and Gayle L.
Watkins (Boston: McCraw-Hill Custom Publishing, 2002).

39. Official military functions (parades, award ceremonies, promotions, and
graduation ceremonies at military academies as well as virtually all military schools)
often feature some form of sectarian prayer or observance. Military commanders (who
have captive audiences) are witnessing to their troops. Military dentists (who also

have captive audiences) are proselytizing. Some military leaders are engaging in the so-called secular war against Christmas, spreading a specific brand of holiday cheer. Voice mail messages and e-mail messages contain religious allusions. Strangers identify themselves as being believers upon introduction, much like secret handshakes of old, only they are not secret anymore. Invitations to social functions contain explicit religious messages. Religious metaphor suffuses the language: People are often referred to as "brother" and are often said to be doing the "lord's work." Everyone knows who the believers are.

40. Sam Harris, *The End of Faith: Religion, Terror, and the Future of Reason* (New York: Norton, 2004), 155–56.

41. The Army's weekly newspaper ran a front-page headline, "Army Chaplains Always Have Been a Source of Counseling and Spiritual Guidance for Soldiers. In the wake of Aberdeen, their services may be needed now more than ever." *Army Times*, Army Times Publishing Co., May 19, 1997, front page.

42. Alan Donagan, *The Theory of Morality* (Chicago: Chicago University Press, 1977), 147.

43. Alan Donagan, *The Theory of Morality*, 62

44. Paul Christopher, *The Ethics of War and Peace: An Introduction to Legal and Moral Issues*, 3rd ed., (Upper Saddle River, NJ: Prentice Hall, 2003).

45. Immanuel Kant, *The Conflict of the Faculties* (New York: Abaris Books, 1979), 115.

46. Michael Martin, *The Case against Christianity* (Philadelphia: Temple University Press, 1991), 15.

47. Sam Harris, *The End of Faith*, pp. 171–72.

48. Homer, *The Iliad*, trans. Robert Fagles (New York: Penguin Books, 1990), 554, 22–466.

49. Homer, *The Iliad*, Book 22, 554, lines 467–72.

50. Eric Havelock, *Preface to Plato* (Cambridge, MA: Harvard University Press, 1963), 6.

51. Arrian, *The Campaigns of Alexander* (New York: Penguin Classics, 1971), 215.

52. Quintus Curtius Rufus, *The History of Alexander* (New York: Penguin Classics, 1984), 179–80.

53. Seneca, p. 179.

54. Seneca, p. 245.

55. Percy Bysshe Shelley, "A Defence of Poetry," in *Romantic Poetry and Prose*, eds. Harold Bloom and Lionel Trilling (New York: Oxford University Press, 1973), 750–51.

56. Walter Sinnott-Armstrong, "Some Varieties of Particularism," *Meta–philosophy* (Oxford: Blackwell Publishers, 1999), 9. Sinnott-Armstrong is arguing against particularism in this journal article.

57. Sinnott-Armstrong, "Some Varieties of Particularism," p. 1

58. Dwight Furrow, *Against Theory* (New York: Routledge, 1995), xiii.

59. Michael Polanyi, *The Tacit Dimension* (Gloucester, MA: Peter Smith, 1983) and *Personal Knowledge: Towards a Post-Critical Philosophy* (Chicago: University of Chicago Press, 1958).

60. "I shall be calling the two levels the intuitive and critical. . . . " R. M. Hare, *Moral Thinking* (Oxford: Oxford University Press, 1981), 25.

61. The list includes Bentham, J. S. Mill, and Sidgwick. J. B. Schneewind, *Sidgwick's Ethics and Victorian Moral Philosophy* (Oxford: Oxford University Press, 1977).

62. J. B. Schneewind, *Sidgwick's Ethics and Victorian Moral Philosophy*, 178.

63. William J. Bennett, *The Book of Virtues* (New York: Simon and Schuster, 1993), pp. 514–16. The speech has served as a model for many military leaders and statesmen, including Patton, Montgomery, and Churchill.

64. Michael Walzer, *Just and Unjust Wars* (New York: Basic Books, 1992), 17–18.

65. Walzer, *Just and Unjust Wars*, 17.

66. Wristbands with WWJD (What Would Jesus Do?) inscribed on them are very popular today.

67. Stephen Crane, *The Red Badge of Courage* (New York: Pocket Books, 1996), xvi.

68. Stephen Crane, *The Red Badge of Courage*, A Norton Critical Edition, 3d Edition (New York: Norton, 1994), 27

69. "Habit should have been translated as habitus, because habit carries with it the connotation that the act is an unconscious one when exercised. Habit relieves us of the need to think; but habitus makes us think creatively." Yves R. Simon, *The Definition of Virtue* (New York: Fordham University Press, 1986), 60.

70. Robert M. Gordon, *The Structure of Emotions: Investigations in Cognitive Philosophy*, Cambridge Studies in Philosophy (Cambridge, UK: Cambridge University Press, 1987), 7.

71. This may be an original interpretation of Crane's novel, one suggested by Tim Brotherton, who taught years ago in the English Department at the Military Academy. I have looked over the years but have not found any critical work on Crane's novel that tries to make the same connections to Homer. Much of the literature makes connections between the novel and many other previous works, however.

72. Jonathan Shay writes extensively about the moral consequences of fighting as berserkers in *Achilles in Vietnam* (New York: Simon and Schuster, 1994).

73. Sidney Axinn, *A Moral Military* (Philadelphia: Temple University Press, 1989), 29.

74. Tariq Ali, *The Clash of Fundamentalisms: Crusades, Jihads and Modernity* (London: Verso, 2002).

75. Sam Harris, *The End of Faith*, 67.

76. Major Carl Bradshaw argued that it would be much more expedient to assassinate heads of state in an article, "Taking Out Saddam Could Work" in *Army Times* (January 12, 1998): 63.

77. Antonin Scalia, *A Matter of Interpretation* (Princeton: Princeton University Press, 1997), 23.

78. Ronal Dworkin's comment in Scalia, *A Matter of Interpretation*, 115.

79. Alasdair MacIntyre, *After Virtue*, 2nd ed., (Notre Dame: University of Notre Dame Press, 1984), 257.

80. Aristotle, *Nicomachean Ethics*, trans. Terence Irwin (Indianapolis: Hackett, 1985), 1142a27, 161.

81. Julia Annas, *The Morality of Happiness* (Oxford: Oxford University Press, 1993), 90.

82. Aristotle, *Nicomachean Ethics*, 418.

83. Annas, *The Morality of Happiness*, 94.

84. Nussbaum, *The Fragility of Goodness: Luck and Ethics in Greek Tragedy and Philosophy*, (Cambridge: Cambridge University Press, 1986), 291.

85. Annas, *The Morality of Happiness*, 94.

86. Richard Rorty, *Philosophy and Social Hope* (New York: Penguin Books, 1999), xxx.

87. Rorty, *Philosophy and Social Hope*, xxxi.

88. Joseph Margolis, *Life without Principles* (Oxford: Blackwell Publishing, 1996), note 2, 239–40

89. Furrow, *Against Theory*, 36.

90. Martha Nussbaum, *The Fragility of Goodness: Luck and Ethics in Greek Tragedy and Philosophy* (Cambridge: Cambridge University Press, 1986), 302.

91. Nussbaum, *Fragility of Goodness: Luck and Ethics in Greek Tragedy and Philosophy*, 304.

92. Jonathan Dancy, "Ethical Particularism and Morally Relevant Principles," *Mind*, 92, no. 368, (October, 1983): 530.

93. Dancy, "Ethical Particularism and Morally Relevant Principles," 534.

94. Martha Nussbaum, *For Love of Country: Debating the Limits of Patriotism* (Boston: Beacon Press, 1996), 3–17, 131–44.

95. Ian Hacking describes this subtle yet important shift in meaning in his book about the emergence of social science, *The Taming of Chance* (Cambridge, UK: Cambridge University Press, 1990), 160–64.

96. R. M. Hare describes this problem when he talks about any normative (prescriptive) conclusion being unwarranted if is based on a descriptive premise, unless there is also a prescriptive premise. *Language of Morals* (Oxford: Oxford University Press, 1952), 46.

97. Alan Donagan, *The Theory of Morality* (Chicago: Chicago University Press, 1977), 201.

98. Donagan, *The Theory of Morality*, 201. Isaac Asimov, *The End of Eternity* (New York: Signet, 1955), 12.

99. Dancy, "Ethical Particularism and Morally Relevant Principles," 534.

100. Sinnott-Armstrong, "Some Varieties of Particularism," 5.

101. Pizer, "*The Red Badge of Courage*: Text, Theme, and Form," in *The Red Badge of Courage*, 26–64.

102. Pizer, "*The Red Badge of Courage*: Text, Theme, and Form," in *The Red Badge of Courage*, 264.

103. Dancy, "Ethical Particularism and Morally Relevant Properties," 531.

104. Dancy, "Ethical Particularism and Morally Relevant Properties," 532.

105. James D. Wallace, *Ethical Norms, Particular Cases* (Ithaca: Cornell University Press, 1996), 31.

106. Immanuel Kant, *The Metaphysics of Morals* (Cambridge, UK: Cambridge University Press, 1996), 17.

107. Onora O'Neill, *Acting on Principle: An Essay on Kantian Ethics* (New York: Columbia University, 1975), 132–37.

108. The Air Force Academy uses a philosophical anthology entitled *Moral Dimensions of the Military Profession: Readings in Morality, War, and Leadership*, 3d ed. (New York: American Heritage, 1997). The Naval Academy uses a philosophical anthology entitled *Ethics for Military Leaders*, eds. George R. Lucas, Jr., and Paul E. Roush (New York: Simon and Schuster, 1998). And West Point has used a philosophical anthology entitled *A Modern Symposium on Military Ethics as an Introduction to Philosophy*, ed. Tim Challans (Cincinnati: Wadsworth/Thomson Publishing, 2000).

109. Roger H. Nye, "The Commander as Moral Arbiter," in Major Christopher C. Starling, USMC, *West Point's Perspectives on Officership* (Cincinnati: Thomson Learning Custom Publishing, 2001), 271–82. It also exists as chapter 6 in Roger H. Nye, *Challenge of Command: Reading for Military Excellence* (Wayne, NJ: Avery Publishing Group, Inc., 1986), 99-114. The tactics course is once again a tactics course. However, the emphasis on professionalism continues to thrive.

110. "In 1917, the fundamentalist preacher Billy Sunday summed it all up when he announced that Christianity and patriotism were synonymous, as were hell and traitors. Jesus was no pacifist, thundered pious war mongers." Joanna Bourke, *An Intimate History of Killing*, 259.

111. Karen J. Greenberg, ed., *The Torture Debate in America* (Cambridge, UK: Cambridge University Press, 2006), 3; Joyce S. Dubensky and Rachel Levery, "Torture: An Interreligious Debate," 162–82.

112. John Dewey distinguishes between apprehension and comprehension in *How We Think* (Buffalo: Prometheus Books, 1991). He says that this distinction is like the one between *können* and *wissen*, practical knowledge and theoretical understanding.

113. West Point has a multimillion-dollar endowment to sustain a Center for the Professional Military Ethic. The center belongs to the commandant, the general in charge of discipline, training, and indoctrination—not education. The center is not connected to the academic departments under the dean. In contrast, the Center for the Study of Professional Ethics at the Naval Academy has several advantages over the center at West Point: It focuses on studying and understanding the subject of ethics, it is under the Naval Academy's superintendent, has been explicitly separated from the clerics, and therefore is properly plugged into the academic community.

3. THE SEMI-REFLECTIVE LIFE: INSTRUMENTAL MEANS

1. Henry Richardson, *Practical Reasoning about Final Ends* (Cambridge, UK: Cambridge University Press, 1997), 14.

2. Gregory R. Beabout and Daryl J. Wennemann, *Applied Professional Ethics: A Developmental Approach for Use with Case Studies* (New York: University Press of America, 1994), 75.

3. Logicians give this fallacy various names. Irving Copi calls it simply the "dilemma," in *Introduction to Logic, 10th ed.* (Upper Saddle River, NJ: Prentice-Hall, 1998), 330. Patrick Hurley calls it the "false dichotomy," the "false bifurcation," or the "either-or fallacy," in *A Concise Introduction to Logic* (Belmont, CA: Wadsworth, 1997), 161.

4. Daniel Statman, *Moral Dilemmas* (Amsterdam: Rodopi Press, 1995), 8-14.

5. This is the problem of relevant descriptions, discussed in Onora O'Neill's *Acting on Principle* (New York: Columbia University Press, 1975), 12–31.

6. Rush Kidder, *How Good People Make Tough Choices: Resolving the Dilemmas of Ethical Living* (New York: Simon and Schuster, 1995), 118–45.

7. Alan Donagan, *The Theory of Morality* (Chicago: University of Chicago Press, 1977), 149.

8. Following O'Neill's analysis in *Acting on Principle* (New York: Columbia University Press, 1975), 10-11.

9. Department of Defense Joint Ethics Regulation and Executive Order 12674, April 12, 1989, as amended by Executive Order 12731 55 Federal Register 42547, Washington, DC: August 30, 1993, pp. 157–59. The Ethical Decision-Making Procedure is also in the Department of Philosophy and Fine Arts, United States Air Force Academy, *Moral Dimensions of the Military Profession: Readings in Morality, War, and Leadership, 3d ed.*, (New York: American Heritage, 1997), 7–8.

10. Descartes, *Rules for the Direction of the Mind*, in *The Philosophical Writings of Descartes*, eds. John Cottingham, Robert Stoothoff, and Dugald Murdoch, Volume I, (Cambridge, UK: Cambridge University Press, 1985), 9–76.

11. Joint Ethics Regulation, pp. 155–57.

12. Major General Chilcoate, the Commanding General of the War College at the time it was attempting to influence the Army's set of values, vetoed the inclusion of the value of *wisdom* as an Army value on the grounds that he claimed that young people could not be wise. While not conscious, perhaps, of these metaphors, he was very likely thinking of a value as establishing an ethical or behavioral "floor" rather than a "ceiling."

13. At the War College, there was a discussion that lasted for hours about a "moral compass." Liking our inclusion of the term "moral compass" into a draft of the leadership manual, the War College wanted to graphically depict this very compass. Led by MG Chilcoate, the participants of this particular conference quickly overextended the metaphor and tried to reify the compass. They wanted the values to represent compass points. They asked several questions: What does magnetic north represent? Truth? God? Since the values at these different points look as if they point in different directions, does that mean that the different values direct us to act differently? Won't soldiers be confused if loyalty is pointing to the east and integrity is pointing to the west? As one would gather (and hope), the graphical representation of the Army's moral compass never made it past the drawing board. As a result, Kant's useful and modestly employed metaphor of a compass from the first section of the *Groundwork* was unusable and was eventually lost due to the Army's penchant for reifying metaphors. Of course, attaching values to the points on the compass completely changes Kant's idea of the metaphor, which for him was to represent the functioning of the Categorical Imperative as an aid to navigate through moral problems:"Here it would be easy to show how common human reason, with this compass in hand, knows very well how to distinguish in every case that comes up what is good and what is evil, what is in conformity with duty or contrary to duty, if, without in the least teaching it anything new, we only, as did Socrates, make it attentive to its

own principle; and that there is, accordingly, no need of science and philosophy to know what one has to do in order to be honest and good, and even wise and virtuous." Immanuel Kant, *Groundwork of the Metaphysics of Morals* (Cambridge, UK: Cambridge University Press, 1997), 16.

14. "Speech of the Reichsfuehrer—SS at the meeting of SS Major-Generals at Posen, October 4th, 1943," Document 1919-PS. *Nazi Conspiracy and Aggression*, Vol. 4 (Washington, DC: Office of the United States Chief of Counsel for Prosecution of Axis Criminality, 1946), 558–72.

15. "Let us articulate this new demand: We need a critique of moral values, the value of these values themselves must first be called in question." Friedrich Nietzsche, *On the Genealogy of Morals* (New York: Vintage, 1969), 20.

16. "For a survey of the current literature of the subject discloses that views on the subject range from the belief, at one extreme, that so-called 'values' are but emotional epithets or mere ejaculations, to the belief, at the other extreme, that *a priori* necessary standardized, rational values are the principles upon which art, science, and morals depend for their validity." John Dewey, *Theory of Valuation*, in *John Dewey: The Later Works 1925-1953*, Vol. 13, 1938–1939 (Carbondale: Southern Illinois University Press, 1988), 191.

17. Aristotle, *Nicomachean Ethics*, trans. Terence Irwin (Indianapolis: Hackett, 1985), 1094b24, 4.

18. James R. Schlesinger, *The Schlesinger Report*, in *The Torture Papers: The Road to Abu Ghraib*, eds. Karen J. Greenberg and Joshua L. Dratel (Cambridge, UK: Cambridge University Press, 2005), 975.

19. "Ethos, character, a person's nature or disposition...the characteristic spirit, prevalent tone of sentiment, of a people or community." *The Oxford English Dictionary*, 2nd ed., (Oxford: Clarendon Press, 1989), 426.

20. "As he becomes more virtuous he understands the basis of and reasons for bravery; so he can explain to others why one should do this rather than that. So the criterion for right action is indeed what the virtuous person would do." Julia Annas, *The Morality of Happiness* (Oxford: Oxford University Press, 1993), 110. There is still the challenge put to virtue theorists to fully develop a theory of right action. "An act-centered morality will naturally welcome the virtues, construed in its own way, as subordinate to the explicit rules or laws that require specific actions. So if a virtue-centered ethic is to be significantly different from an act-centered ethic, it needs to show that the virtues which are most important to morality have a life of their own, which is independent of rules or laws." J. B. Schneewind, "The Misfortunes of Virtue," in *Virtue Ethics*, eds. Roger Crisp and Michael Slote (Oxford: Oxford University Press, 1997), 180.

21. "Nor could anything be more fatal to morality than that we should wish to derive it from examples." *The Fundamental Principles of the Metaphysics of Morals*, based on the translation by T. K. Abbott, with emendations by Daniel Kolak. Electronic HyperText Markup Language Version Copyright 1999 by Daniel Kolak.

All rights reserved, on Compact Disc, (Wadsworth/Thomson Learning, 1999). The Abbott translation uses the language "fatal to philosophy." Another translation is, "What is more, we cannot do morality a worse service than by seeking to derive it from examples." In Immanuel Kant, *Groundwork of the Metaphysics of Morals*, trans. H. J. Paton (New York: Harper Torchbooks, 1964), 76. Mary Gregor translates the passage as, "Nor could one give worse advice to morality than by wanting to derive it from examples." In Kant, *Groundwork of the Metaphysics of Morals* (Cambridge, UK: Cambridge University Press, 1997), 21. The passage in German is, "Man könnte auch der Sittlichkeit nicht übler rathen, als wenn man sie von Beispielen entlehnen wollte." Immanuel Kant (1724–1804) GRUNDLEGUNG ZUR METAPHYSIK DER SITTEN. Rescogitans Philosophical Library Electronic edition, 1997, http://www.rescogitans.it/sitenew/ita/SalaLettura/003/Zweiter.htm.

22. Michael Slote, *From Morality to Virtue* (Oxford: Oxford University Press, 1992), 89, 93.

23. Martha Nussbaum, *The Therapy of Desire* (Princeton: Princeton University Press, 1994), 68.

24. Justin Oakley, *Morality and the Emotions* (New York: Routledge, 1992), 81.

25. Aristotle, *Nicomachean Ethics*, in *The Basic Works of Aristotle*, ed. Richard McKeon (New York: Random House, 1941), 1103a33, 952.

26. Yves R. Simon, *The Definition of Moral Virtue* (New York: Fordham University Press, 1986), 55–61.

27. Michael Slote, *From Morality to Virtue*, 91.

28. These are the virtues considered throughout Michael Slote's *From Morality to Virtue*.

29. A useful term from Susan Wolf, "Moral Saints," *The Journal of Philosophy*, 79, no. 8 (August 1982).

30. I take this distinction between honor and integrity from Gabriele Taylor, *Pride, Shame, and Guilt: Emotions of Self-Assessment* (Oxford: Oxford University Press, 1985), 108–14.

31. Taylor, *Pride, Shame, and Guilt: Emotions of Self-Assessment*, 108 ff.

32. For the Army's leadership doctrinal manual, I originally conceived of the value of respect as being primarily about treating the enemy with moral equality, following Walzer. The doctrinal editorial process dropped any reference to the enemy, and respect is now only operative for friendly forces in the doctrinal leadership manual. Would Guantanamo or Abu Ghraib have turned out differently if the Army had included respect for the enemy in its definition?

33. In "Crisis of Conscience," *Government Executive*, October 1995, 18.

34. Raymond Smullyan, *The Tao is Silent* (San Francisco: Harper, 1977), 69.

35. "Thus, for example, guilt is relieved by reparation and the forgiveness that permits reconciliation; whereas shame is undone by proofs of defects made good, by a

renewed confidence in the excellence of one's person." John Rawls, *A Theory of Justice* (Cambridge, MA: Belknap Press, 1971), 484.

36. John Dewey, *Theory of Valuation*, in *John Dewey: The Later Works, 1925-1953*, Vol. 13: 1938–1939, (Carbondale: Southern Illinois University Press, 1988), 229.

37. Carl von Clausewitz, *On War* (New York: Alfred A. Knopf, 1993), 165.

38. Michael Howard, quoted by Williamson Murray, in *Military Innovation in the Interwar Period*, eds. Williamson Murray and Allan Millet (Cambridge, UK: Cambridge University Press, 1998), 301.

39. Dewey's language of values includes intrinsic and instrumental value; I am using "innate" instead of "intrinsic" because the word can be ambiguous. Dewey, *Theory of Valuation*, p. 216.

40. Dewey, *Theory of Valuation*, p. 213. I am also employing his distinction of us prizing ends but appraising means. *Theory of Valuation*, 213.

41. John Rawls, "Fifty Years after Hiroshima," in *John Rawls: Collected Papers*, ed. Samuel Freeman (Cambridge, MA: Harvard University Press, 1999), 567.

42. Rawls, "Fifty Years after Hiroshima," 571.

43. Rawls, "Fifty Years after Hiroshima," 570.

44. The main difference between the military decision-making process (MDMP) and the deliberate military decision-making process (DMDMP) is that the deliberate process involves much more time. When there is enough time before a military operation, the deliberate process can take hours or even days. If the process is not deliberate, usually because there is not enough time, then the same process is supposed to occur, only compressed. The military's conception of ends, ways, and means is reminiscent of the governmental usage of ends, ways, and means. *ST 100-9, The Tactical Decision-Making Process* (Fort Leavenworth, KS: CGSC Press, 1993), 1–1 to 1–5 and 7–4 to 7–5. See also FM 5-0, *Army Planning and Orders Production*, (Washington, DC: Headquarters Department of the Army, 2005), 3–33.

45. *ST 100-9, The Tactical Decision-Making Process*, 7 4. Also in FM 5-0, 3–153.

46. Geoff Simons, *The Scourging of Iraq*: Sanctions, Law and International Justice, 2d ed. (New York: St. Martin's Press, 1998), 4. The list of questionable targets include: electric power stations, and relay and transmission systems; water treatment facilities, reservoirs, and water distribution systems; telephone exchanges and relay stations; radio exchanges, and transmission systems; food processing plants, food warehouses, food distribution facilities, infant milk formula factories, and beverage factories; irrigation sites; animal vaccination facilities; buses, bus depots, trains, and railways; bridges, roads, and highway overpasses; oil wells, oil pumping systems, pipelines, oil refineries, oil storage facilities, petrol stations, and fuel delivery systems; textile factories; automobile assembly plants; universities and colleges; hospitals and clinics; places of worship; and archaeological sites. Simons, 12.

47. "In the early 1980s, during a Navy exercise code-named *Hey Rube*, long strands of rope chaff—glass filaments in which metal shards were embedded—had

been dropped over the Pacific Ocean as part of a standard tactic to befuddle an oppo-
nent's radar. An unexpectedly stiff westerly wind carried some of the chaff ninety
miles to the coastline, where it got draped across power lines, shorting out transform-
ers and causing power failures in parts of San Diego. The Navy quietly settled for
damages—while carefully noting the effects of its unintended attack.... The State
Department also worried about unforeseen consequences for Iraqi society if the lights
went out indefinitely. But at the Pentagon Richard Cheney urged, 'Let's give them
the full load the first night.' Anything less smacked of escalation, of the stench of
Vietnam. Consequently, on the American attack list were twenty-eight electrical
sites, many of them, particularly around Baghdad, targeted with Kit 2s." In Rick
Atkinson, *Crusade: The Untold Story of the Persian Gulf War* (New York: Houghton
Mifflin, 1993), 30–31.

48. Michael Ignatieff, *Virtual War: Kosovo and Beyond* (New York:
Metropolitan Books, 2000), 199. Kant also comments on the propensity of the lawyers
to act as apologists, "For Hugo Grotius, Pufendorf, Vattel and the rest (sorry com-
forters as they are) are still dutifully quoted in *justification* of military aggression,
although their philosophically or diplomatically formulated codes do not and cannot
have the slightest legal force, since states as such are not subject to a common external constraint." *Perpetual Peace*, in *Kant: Political Writings*, ed. Hans Reiss (Cambridge,
UK: Cambridge University Press, 1991), 103.

49. Many of the ideas for the set of virtues as values found here were put for-
ward in a paper, Tim Challans, "A Strategy for a Military Ethic," and delivered at the
Cantigny Conference for Professional Military Education: An Asset for Peace and Progress,
Robert R. McCormick Tribune Foundation and the Center for Strategic and
International Studies, March 13, 1996.

50. Gabrielle Taylor compares the virtues of honor and integrity. She talks of
them as being overarching virtues that encompass other virtues. The main difference
between them in her view is that honor is tied to public codes and integrity is tied to
personal codes. If it makes any sense to speak of personal integrity, then the virtue has
to be tied to personal codes. Honor, on the other hand, is dependent on the codes of
a group. *Pride, Shame, and Guilt: Emotions of Self-Assessment* (Oxford: Clarendon
Press, 1985), 108–41. The Army leaders did not like this distinction, even though it
seemed useful in marking the distinction between the two. They felt that it made
honor relative to different societies. So, while suicide is not acceptable in Western
societies, *seppuku* was honorable in feudal Japan. Interestingly, the Japanese do not
consider *seppuku* to be suicide, even though outsiders tend to conflate the two. This
made integrity even more relative—relative to each individual. One of the more
humorous episodes involved the Judge Advocate General's office calling me to find
the exact title and number of the *public code* to which honor was tied.

51. Interestingly, Army leaders were adamant against having fairness as an
Army value, even though it was an important feature in the tradition of chivalry. The
first basic principle of the laws of war is that law restrains violence and restricts combatants so that "they conduct hostilities with regard for the principles of humanity
and chivalry." FM 27-10, *The Law of Land Warfare*, p. 3. The values of honesty, fairness, and respect are often taught at West Point as the positive prescriptive correlates

to the proscriptions contained in the Honor Code, a code that specifically forbids cadets from lying, cheating, or stealing. Perhaps fairness is not the moral justification for proscribing cheating; perhaps the Army and West Point really care nothing about fairness. It is possible that the operative principle that forbids cheating is something like competence. If it is competence rather than fairness that the military is concerned about, then this is consistent with the idea that the military is mostly concerned about practical matters, which can be completely separate from moral matters, even though they should not be separate.

52. I resisted the use of the acronym because of the conceptual relationship among the values. When the chief of staff (CSA) mandated the acronym, the conceptual relationship was destroyed. Afterward, the CSA, GEN Reimer, was disturbed about the apparent lack of conceptual coherence, the coherence his very decision destroyed.

53. Alan Donagan makes this distinction in *The Theory of Morality*, pp. 112–42.

54. Lyndon Johnson said, "It's not doing what is right that's hard for a President. It's knowing what is right." In James R. Rest and Darcia Narváez, eds., *Moral Development in the Professions: Psychology and Applied Ethics* (Mahwaha, NJ: Lawrence Erlbaum Associates, 1994), x.

55. The Golden Rule turns out to fall short of giving guidance on at least three counts: People may have different tastes (there are many masochists out there); people should be treated differently based on age, position, education, situation (a judge would not rule in the case of a minor or incompetent based on how he wants to be treated); and the rule says nothing about how we should treat ourselves. Donagan, *The Theory of Morality*, 57–66.

4, THE QUASI-REFLECTIVE LIFE: INADEQUATE ENDS

1. Bernard Williams, "A Critique of Utilitarianism," in *Vice and Virtue in Everyday Life: Introductory Readings in Ethics*, 5th ed., ed. Christina Sommers and Fred Sommers, (New York: Harcourt, 2001), 129.

2. "And through all this welter of change and development, your mission remains fixed, determined, inviolable—it is to win our wars. Everything else in your professional career is but corollary to this vital dedication. All other public purposes, all other public projects, all other public needs, great or small, will find others for their accomplishment; but you are the ones who are trained to fight; yours is the profession of arms." Douglas MacArthur, speech to the Corps of Cadets upon acceptance of the Sylvanus Thayer Award, United States Military Academy, West Point, New York, May 12, 1962, in Lieutenant Colonel Lawrence P. Crocker, *The Army Officer's Guide*, 42nd ed., (Harrisburg, PA: Stackpole Books, 1983), ix.

3. Harry Summers, "Leadership in Adversity: From Vietnam to Victory in the Gulf," *Foundations of the Military Profession*, eds. Charles Krupnik and Richard Workman (New York: American Heritage), 526. Also in Harry Summers, *On*

Strategy: The Vietnam War in Context (Washington, DC: U.S. Government Printing Office, 1981), 1.

4. Summers, "Leadership in Adversity: From Vietnam to Victory in the Gulf," 526.

5. "Combat experience in the jungles of Vietnam was the common thread that bound all of the senior U.S. commanders in the Persian Gulf War, from Chairman of the Joint Chiefs of Staff (CJCS) General Colin Powell to General H. Norman Schwarzkopf, the U.S. commander in the field, to the senior Army, Navy, Air Force, and Marine Corps generals, to their colonels commanding the regiments and brigades." Summers, 525.

6. Norman Schwarzkopf, "General H. Norman Schwarzkopf Defends Strategy and War Aims, 1992," in *Major Problems in American Military History*, ed. John Whiteclay Chambers II and G. Kurt Piehler (New York: Houghton Mifflin, 1999), 462.

7. Geoff Simons, *The Scourging of Iraq: Sanctions, Law and Natural Justice*, 2nd ed. (New York: St. Martin's Press, 1998), 35.

8. Simons, *The Scourging of Iraq*, 48.

9. The UN Food and Agriculture Organization made this estimate. Simons, *The Scourging of Iraq*, 215.

10. Noam Chomsky, "Rogue States," in *Acts of Aggression: Policing "Rogue" States* (New York: Seven Stories Press, 1999), 22. Security Council Resolution 687, dated April 3, 1991, states "that Iraq shall unconditionally accept the destruction, removal, or rendering harmless, under international supervision of: (a) all chemical and biological weapons and all stocks of agents and all related subsystems and components and all research, development, support, and manufacturing facilities." Appendix 3, Simons, *The Scourging of Iraq*, p. 262.

11. Robert S. Litwak, *Rogue States and U.S. Foreign Policy: Containment after the Cold War*, (Baltimore: Johns Hopkins University Press, 2000), 241.

12. Michael Walzer, *Just and Unjust Wars* (New York: Basic Books, 1992), xiii.

13. Cadet Third-Classman William Wadzinski asked me this question while discussing Iraqi suffering in philosophy class, March 13, 2001. I give him credit for being ahead of many of his peers by being able at least to recognize it as a moral issue.

14. "This arbitrary selection of some one part of the attained consequences as *the* end and hence as the warrant of means used (no matter how objectionable are their *other* consequences) is the fruit of holding that *it*, as *the* end, is an end-in-itself, and hence possessed of 'value' irrespective of all its existential relations." Dewey, *The Theory of Valuation*, 228.

15. After the battle of Asculum, "The two armies disengaged and the story goes that when one of Pyrrhus' friends congratulated him on his victory, he replied, 'One more victory like that over the Romans will destroy us completely!'" Plutarch, "Pyrrhus," in *The Age of Alexander* (New York: Penguin Books, 1973), 409.

16. Dewey, *The Theory of Valuation*, 228.

17. Dewey, *The Theory of Valuation*, 227.

18. Simone Weil in Sissela Bok, *A Strategy for Peace: Human Values and the Threat of War* (New York: Vintage Books, 1989). 11.

19. Dewey, *The Theory of Valuation*, 229.

20. "Classic philosophy identified *ens*, *verum*, and *bonum*, and the identification was taken to be an expression of the constitution of nature as the object of natural science." Dewey, *The Theory of Valuation*, 192.

21. Richardson, *Practical Reasoning about Final Ends*, 54.

22. Richardson, *Practical Reasoning about Final Ends*, 163.

23. Dewey thinks that the notion of objects being ends-in-themselves is a dangerous idea when he says, "If the notion of some objects as ends-in-themselves were abandoned, not merely in words but in all practical implications, human beings would for the first time in history be in a position to frame ends-in-view and form desires on the basis of empirically grounded propositions of the temporal relations of events to one another." *The Theory of Valuation*, 229.

24. Dewey, *The Theory of Valuation*, 229.

25. Hart and Honoré lay out these two extremes and argue that causal responsibility lies somewhere between the minimal and maximal view. "The answer we suggested was to reject causal minimalism without embracing causal maximalism." In H. L. A. Hart and Tony Honoré, *Causation in the Law* (Oxford: Oxford University Press, 1985), xxxv. It is safe to say that both countries can share in the blame for bringing about the current state of affairs. Hart and Honoré continue: "Though causal maximalism goes too far, we think it is a moral and legal principle of central importance that people are responsible for the harm they cause, where 'cause' is understood not as *sine qua non* but in the sense in which ordinary people understand it. It is true merely to cause harm is not generally sufficient for liability. Normally, we hold people responsible for causing harm only when they do so by their wrongful or unlawful conduct and when other considerations of policy do not require the limitation of responsibility," lxxvii.

26. Dewey, *The Theory of Valuation*, 222.

27. Stanley Milgram, *Obedience to Authority* (New York: Harper, 1969), 186.

28. This statement can be found in many sources. A previous Army Chief of Staff, General Dennis Reimer, said it in his speeches as well as his letters, including the General Dwight D. Eisenhower Speech given to the Association of the United States Army (AUSA) on October 15, 1996. General Eric Shinseki, the former chief of staff, stated it in his letter of intent, which he signed when he took office on June 23, 1999. The current chief, General Peter Schoomaker, continues this hypertradition.

29. FM 22-103, *Leadership and Command at Senior Levels* (Washington, DC: Department of the Army, 1987), 21.

30. Lawrence Crocker, *The Army Officer's Guide*, 42nd ed., (Harrisburg, PA: Stackpole, 1983), 21.

31. FM 22-103, *Leadership and Command at Senior Levels*, 22.

32. Interviews with Admiral Leighton Smith, in the BBC documentary, "The Rules of Engagement," by Michael Ignatieff, 1997.

33. George C. Wilson, "Land Mine Opinion Not a Done Deal," *Army Times* (June 22, 1998).

34. Wolfgang Schivelbusch explores the paradoxes of victory and defeat in his book, *The Culture of Defeat* (New York: Metropolitan Books, 2003).

35. Richardson, *Practical Reasoning about Final Ends*, 59.

36. Dewey, *The Theory of Valuation*, 215.

37. Richardson, *Practical Reasoning about Final Ends*, 164.

38. Richardson, *Practical Reasoning about Final Ends*, 85.

39. Julia Annas, *The Morality of Happiness* (Oxford: Oxford University Press, 1993), 34.

40. General Dennis Reimer's speech to the Association of the United States Army (AUSA), October 15, 1996. Tony Hartle was a long-time professor of philosophy at West Point, and as a member of the West Point class of 1964 was present at MacArthur's speech. As he recalled the event, in characteristically witty fashion, he said that had he known it would have turned out to be so important, he would have paid more attention to the speech.

41. General Douglas MacArthur, "Speech before the Joint Session of Congress," April 19, 1951.

42. Daniel W. Christman, Lieutenant General, Memorandum, MAOR, Subject: "Superintendent's Intent Concerning Competitive Athletics," June 1, 2000.

43. Telford Taylor, *Nuremberg and Vietnam: An American Tragedy* (New York: New York Times Book Company, 1970), reprinted as chapter 24 in Malham Wakin, ed., *War, Morality, and the Military Profession* (Boulder: Westview Press, 1986), 373.

44. Michael Reisman and Chris T. Antoniou, *The Laws of War: A Comprehensive Collection of Primary Documents on International Laws Governing Armed Conflict* (New York: Vintage Books, 1994), 36-37.

45. Taylor, *Nuremberg and Vietnam: An American Tragedy*, 376.

46. "Physics cannot tell us when it is permissible to use the weapons it has enabled us to create: biology cannot tell us how to distribute the medicines it has us develop. Moreover, it is often held that people do not need scientific qualifications to give informed and well-grounded answers to fundamental questions of what is right or good. But this issue is highly controversial, and the controversy is pure philosophy." Alexander Rosenberg, *Philosophy of Social Science, 2nd ed.*, (Boulder: Westview Press, 1993), 2.

47. Bill Joy, "Why the Future Doesn't Need Us," *Wired* (April 2000); also quoted inTheorore Schick, "The Cracks of Doom: The Threat of Emerging Technologies and Tolkien's Rings of Power," *The Lord of the Rings and Philosophy*, eds. Gregory Bassham and Eric Bronson (Chicago: Open Court Press, 2003), 26.

48. Immanuel Kant, *The Metaphysics of Morals* (Cambridge, UK: Cambridge University Press, 1996), 123.

49. Henry Richardson, *Practical Reasoning about Final Ends*, 59.

50. Immanuel Kant, *Critique of Pure Reason* (New York: St. Martin's Press, 1929), A644/B672, 533.

51. Clausewitz talks about the end of military activity as being peace. Military victory is merely a means to that end. *On War*, 165.

52. Peter Paret, *Clausewitz and the State* (Princeton: Princeton University Press, 1976), 154.

53. Francis Lieber, *General Orders No. 100*, in *Lieber's Code and the Law of War* ed. Richard Shelly Hartigan, (Chicago: Precedent, 1983), 50.

54. *FM22-100, Army Leadership*, 1–18.

55. Mohammed Hafez, "Suicide Terrorism in Iraq," *Studies in Conflict and Terrorism*, (London: Routledge, 2006), 29:591–619.

56. I was the author of this article in my last few months wearing a uniform. Two general officers in my chain of command heavily edited my paper, for they wanted the article to appear in one of the Army's most widely read journals, *Military Review*, and they wanted my bad news story to be a good news story. The generals lost interest in the article after they were reassigned away from Ft. Leavenworth. But the colonel who was my boss at the time, Colonel Mike Flowers, was intent upon getting it published. As the author of the article, I refused to send it to the journal for publication since the editing process changed my ideas so drastically, in some cases even reversing my conclusions. The judgment of the use of proxy forces in the main text is one such example. Colonel Flowers published my article under his name. Mike Flowers is now a general officer.

57. Annette Baier, "Trust and Distrust of Moral Theorists," in *Applied Ethics: A Reader*, eds. Earl R. Winkler and Jerrold R. Coombs (Oxford: Blackwell, 1993), 133.

58. General Charles C. Krulak, USMC (Ret.), "The Debate on Ethics Must Continue," *Proceedings*, December 2000, 96.

5. THE FULLY REFLECTIVE LIFE: AUTONOMY FOR AUTOMATONS

1. Shakespeare's treatment of the epic battle between Achilles and Hector in *Troilus and Cressida* is illustrative here. Achilles is tired when he fights Hector. Hector bests Achilles first and shows mercy to Achilles by offering him the chance to rest.

Hector wants to have Achilles at his best, in the purest spirit of chivalry, regarding his enemy more as a comrade-in-arms than as a foe.

> "HECTOR: Pause, if thou wilt.
> ACHILLES: I do disdain thy courtesy, proud Trojan. Be happy that my arms are out of use. My rest and negligence befriends thee now; But thou anon shalt hear of me again. Till then, go seek thy fortune.
> HECTOR: Fare thee well."

After fighting all day, Hector disarms himself and Achilles reappears.

> "ACHILLES: Look, Hector, how the sun begins to set, How ugly night comes breathing at his heels. Even with the veil and dark'ning of the sun to close the day up, Hector's life is done.
> HECTOR: I am unarmed. Forgo this vantage, Greek.
> ACHILLES: Strike, fellows, strike! This is the man I seek."

William Shakespeare, *Troilus and Cressida*, in *The Norton Shakespeare*, ed. Stephen Greenblatt, Walter Cohen, Jean E. Howard, and Katharine Eisaman Maus (New York: Norton 1997), 5.6.14–19 and 5.9.5–10, 1907, 1909.

2. Some studies indicate that the Naval practice of reasoned dialogue and questioning—a practice that very closely follows the principle of individual, reasoned, autonomy—actually enhances efficiency and reduces error in ship operations. E. Hutchins, *Cognition in the Wild* (Cambridge, MA: MIT Press, 1995) and T. R. La Porte and P. M. Consolini, "Working in Practice but Not in Theory: Theoretical Challenges of High-Reliability Organizations," *Journal of Public Administration Research and Theory* (1991): 19–47.

3. "Public reason, then, is public in three ways: as the reason of citizens as such, it is the reason of the public; its subject is the good of the public and matters of fundamental justice; and its nature and content is public, being given by the ideals and principles expressed by society's conception of political justice, and conducted open to view on that basis." John Rawls, *Political Liberalism* (New York: Columbia University Press, 1993), 213. Rawls acknowledges that his description of public reason is not exactly like Kant's description; however, it may still be thought of as being Kantian in that it operates in the spirit of Kant's moral philosophy.

4. "Kant holds that everyone can use the categorical imperative to reason out what they ought to do in particular cases, and to see also why they ought to do it." J. B. Schneewind, *The Invention of Autonomy* (Cambridge, UK: Cambridge University Press, 1998), 522.

5. "Those of us who hope to see the development of a fully secular under-standing of morality need not have any interest in some of the problems Kant tried to solve. Ignoring them, we of course pay no heed to the conditions they impose on what can count as a satisfactory moral philosophy. If, for instance, we do not think that a prime task for moral philosophy is to show that God and we belong to a single moral community, then we will not have Kant's reason for insisting that our theory show how there can be moral principles necessarily binding on all rational beings. There may be other reasons for holding that there must be such principles, but we will not think the requirement self-evident. Principles for humans may be enough." J. B. Schneewind, *The Invention of Autonomy*, 554.

6. Immanuel Kant, "What Is Enlightenment," in *Kant: Political Writings*, ed. Hans Reiss (Cambridge, UK: Cambridge University Press, 1991), 55.

7. Kant, "What Is Enlightenment," 55.

8. Onora O'Neill, *Constructions of Reason: Explorations of Kant's Practical Philosophy* (Cambridge, UK: Cambridge University Press, 1989), 34.

9. I use the term "critical method" to refer to an open-ended, self-conscious, reflexive philosophical investigation into a certain topic. I mean to juxtapose that with a decision-procedure, which can have none of the features of a critical method. Decision-procedures are often associated with preference-based models of rational decision making.

10. John Rawls, "Kantian Constructivism in Moral Theory," in *John Rawls: Collected Papers*, ed. Samuel Freeman (Cambridge, MA: Harvard University Press, 1999), 305.

11. "Outline of a Decision Procedure for Ethics," in *John Rawls: Collected Papers*, ed. Samuel Freeman (Cambridge, MA: Harvard University Press, 1999), 1–19. His method is a decision procedure in the broad sense that the method does aid one in making decisions. However, it is not a decision-procedure in the stricter sense, the sense I am arguing against, the sense that it is a decidable, closed, and complete system to evaluate calculable, quantifiable courses of action.

12. Rawls, p. 2. Rawls goes on to say that "since a competent judge is not required to have a special training in logic and mathematics, an explication either must be formulated or formulatable in ordinary language and its principles must be capable of an interpretation which the average competent man can grasp." "Outline of a Decision Procedure for Ethics," p. 7. While the competent moral judge may not be a philosopher, and the people who engage in the public dialogue need not be philosophers, it may be philosophers (such as Rawls, for example) who are designing and justifying the critical methods that everyone should be employing.

13. Rawls, "Outline of a Decision Procedure for Ethics," 6–7.

14. Rawls, "Outline of a Decision Procedure for Ethics," 7.

15. Rawls, "Outline of a Decision Procedure for Ethics," 10.

16. Rawls, "Outline of a Decision Procedure for Ethics," 11.

17. Richard Hartigan, *Lieber's Code and the Laws of War*, 45.

18. *FM 27–10, Laws of Land Warfare*, iii.

19. *FM 27–10, Laws of Land Warfare*, 36, paragraphs 89 and 90.

20. *FM 27–10, Laws of Land Warfare*, 84, paragraph 215.

21. *FM 27–10, Laws of Land Warfare*, 31, paragraph 75.

22. Don Snider, "USMA Class of 2000. 100th Night Banquet Remarks," also in *West Point's Perspectives on Officership* (Cincinnati: Thomson, 2001), 98.

23. Lieutenant Siebert's letter came to the department in January of 1991.

24. "Members of the medical personnel and chaplains while retained by the Detaining Power with a view to assisting prisoners of war, shall not be considered as prisoners of war." FM 27–10, *Laws of Land Warfare* (Washington, DC: Department of the Army, 1956), 28.

25. FM 27–10, *Laws of Land Warfare*, 18, paragraph 34.

26. "The concept of the original position, as I shall refer to it, is that of the most philosophically favored interpretation of this initial choice situation for the purposes of a theory of justice." John Rawls, *A Theory of Justice* (Cambridge, UK: Cambridge University Press, 1971), 18.

27. Rawls, *A Theory of Justice*, 136–37.

28. "First of all, no one knows his place in society, his class position or social status; nor does he know his fortune in the distribution of natural assets and abilities, his intelligence and strength, and the like." Rawls, *A Theory of Justice*, 137.

29. Immanuel Kant, *Toward Perpetual Peace*, in *Practical Philosophy*, trans. and ed. Mary J. Gregor (Cambridge, UK: Cambridge University Press, 1996), §8:355, 326.

30. Michael Howard, *The Invention of Peace* (New Haven: Yale University Press, 2000), 103.

31. W. Michael Reisman and Chris T. Antoniou, *The Laws of War: A Comprehensive Collection of Primary Documents on International Laws Governing Armed Conflict* (New York: Vintage Books, 1994), 36–37.

32. FM 27-10, *Laws of Land Warfare* (Washington, DC: Department of the Army, 1956), *The Manual For Courts-Martial*, United States, 1998, *General Orders No. 100*, in *Lieber's Code and The Laws of War*, by Richard Hartigan (Chicago: Precedent Publishing, 1983).

33. FM 27–10 *Laws of Land Warfare*, 3.

34. Rawls, *A Theory of Justice*, 20.

35. Rawls, *A Theory of Justice*, 378.

36. Rawls, *A Theory of Justice*, 379.

37. When General Don Starry (Ret.) was in charge of the Army's Training and Doctrine Command (TRADOC), there was a proliferation of armor-based doctrine, for he favored and gave the Army an articulation of what he called the "Air-Land Battle" doctrine. This doctrine preceded and occurred in conjunction with the Army's modernization in the 1980s, which gave us the heavy Army we went to war with in the Gulf in the early 1990s. Contrast that doctrine with the current preference for doing away with tanks. The Army's current leadership favors a lighter force, and recent pronouncements informed the Army of its decision to replace tanks with wheeled vehicles. This change occurred without any debate or dialogue over the options—except at the highest levels—and gives evidence for my claim that decisions in the Army largely revolve around the "machinery of political consensus." This is perhaps the largest and quickest change the Army has ever undergone, at

least over the last two decades, that I have witnessed. Interestingly, this change had been eclipsed by the recent controversy over the adoption of the beret for all soldiers to use as headgear. The Army has seemingly lost sight of this huge transformation in the way we fight and has focused its attention on the dissatisfaction of the Army's elite forces over the fact that everyone in the Army will now be allowed to wear berets that were once reserved for only those who had qualified to be members of the Army's elite forces.

38. "Officership" as a word that strikes many as odd, even given that the military is notorious for abusing the English language. I'm not sure of the origin of the word, although I suspect it may be a good example of what has come to be known as "Haigspeak." Haigspeak is of course a self-consciously chosen word to describe the peculiar usage of words that reached its peak during the time when General Alexander Haig (Ret.) became a public figure as the White House chief of staff. Haig, being perhaps the best exemplar of the phenomenon, had imported the military's practice of this form of language into the political arena. Haigspeak is a highly jargonized mixture of bellicose metaphors, with parts of speech transformed into other parts of speech, such as nouns used as verbs and verbs used as nouns, or nouns transformed into more complicated nouns (from office to officer to officership). It may parallel leadership (lead, leader, leadership), but this conversion would be odd in most other contexts (play, player, playership or drive, driver, drivership). John Petrik talks of Haigspeak when he discusses avoiding clichés in "Writing Philosophy," *Symposia: Readings in Philosophy* (Boston: Pearson, 2001), 4.

39. Colonel Don Snider (Ret.) was the main force behind this course. He had done a lot of work in the Army's ethics projects and he remains a major force in the ethics business at West Point, now promoting the utility of religious spirituality through the Cadet Prayer. Major Christopher C. Starling was the course director for *West Point's Perspectives on Officership*, Department of Military Instruction (Cincinnati: Thomson Custom Publishing, 2001).

40. Philosophers remain aware of these different levels of ethics: descriptive ethics, normative ethics, and meta-ethics. William Frankena describes these three levels in *Ethics*, 2nd ed., (Englewood Cliffs: Prentice-Hall, 1973), 4. While I agree with Frankena that these distinctions are important to keep in mind, his book is not entirely reliable. For example, he gives a heteronomous reading of Kant.

41. Marybeth Peterson Ulrich, "Infusing Civil-Military Relations Norms in the Officer Corps," in *The Future of the Army Profession*, eds. Don Snider and Gayle Watkins (New York: McGraw-Hill, 2000).

42. Everett C. Ladd, "American Society: Where Are We Headed?", *West Point's Perspectives on Officership*. This article originally appeared in *The Public Perspective* (March 1997): 1–30. Reprinted by permission of the Roper Center: Hall and Bill Printing Company.

43. Ladd, in *West Point's Perspectives on Officership*, 12.

44. Gregory S. Paul, "Cross-National Correlations of Quantifiable Societal Health with Popular Religiosity and Secularism in the Prosperous Democracies," *Journal of Religion & Society* 7 (2005).

45. *John Rawls: Collected Papers*, 308.

46. Roger Nye, "The Commander as Moral Arbiter," in *West Point's Perspectives on Officership*.

47. James Toner, "A Message to Garcia: Leading Soldiers in Moral Mayhem," in *The Future of the Army Profession*.

48. I have been a general's aide, and I have known many aides over the years.

49. Don Snider, "USMA Class of 2000, 100th Night Banquet," February 26, 2000, in *West Point's Perspectives on Officership*, 97-102. I also attended the banquet and heard the speech first-hand.

50. *FM 27–10, Laws of Land Warfare*, 31.

51. Major General Nash spoke of it during the Bosnian peacekeeping mission. Lieutenant General (Ret.) Cavasos, who is big on the speaking and mentoring circuit in the military, speaks of the importance of "moral ascendancy" in many of his speeches. The term has even worked its way into the Army's operational doctrine over the years, *FM 100-5, Operations*.

52. See also "The Categorization of Conflict," by David Fastabend, *Parameters* 27, no. 2 (1997): 75–87. This article describes the process that Fuller used to think about the concepts of war in terms of categories, which is, interestingly, too abstract, philosophical, and theoretical for most people's taste. Instead of thinking about the principles of war in this way, the Army teaches them through the use of an acronym: MOSSMOUSE (ordered above by the acronym). By using the acronym instead of thinking about them in a more theoretical way, it renders the list arbitrary, and people will be tempted to add or take away from the list based on arbitrary whims instead of according to the original categorical conception.

53. J. Glenn Gray discusses this phenomenon in his chapter "Images of the Enemy," in *The Warriors: Reflections on Men in Battle* (New York: Harper & Row, 1959). Gray recounts a comment found in *The Caine Mutiny* about the battle of Kwajalein and the indifference the Navy had toward enemy suffering. "This cold-bloodedness, worthy of a horseman of Genghis Khan, was quite strange in a pleasant little fellow like Ensign Keith. Militarily, of course, it was an asset beyond price. Like most of the naval executioners at Kwajalein, he seemed to regard the enemy as a species of animal pest. From the grim and desperate taciturnity with which the Japanese died, they seemed on their side to believe they were contending with an invasion of large armed ants. This obliviousness on both sides to the fact that the opponents were human beings may perhaps be cited as the key to the many massacres of the Pacific War"(149).

54. J. Glenn Gray, *The Warriors: Reflections on Men in Battle*, 133.

55. "It is not business to allow lazy locals (even though they be brothers and neutrals) to sit and pick their teeth outside their kraals whilst tired soldiers are break-ing their hearts trying to do heavy labour in short time. It is more the duty of a soldier to teach the lazy local the dignity of labour, and by keeping him under guard to pre-

vent his going away to talk about it." E. D. Swinton, *The Defense of Duffer's Drift* (Wayne, NJ: Avery Books, 1986), 25.

56. John Rawls, "Kantian Constructivism in Moral Theory," in *John Rawls: Collected Papers* (Cambridge, MA: Harvard University Press, 1999), 303–58. When Rawls says that "Kantian constructivism holds that moral objectivity is to be understood in terms of a suitably constructed social point of view that all can accept" (307), he is employing one feature of Kant's moral theory (that of intersubjective agreement) but not relying on Kant's metaphysical distinction between the phenomenal and the noumenal realms.

57. "Kant invented the conception of morality as autonomy." J. B. Schneewind, *The Invention of Autonomy: A History of Modern Moral Philosophy* (Cambridge, UK: Cambridge University Press, 1998), 3.

58. Moral courage is not an explicit feature of Kant's idea of autonomy. However, it does appear to be a requirement for such a moral conception to exist.

59. Jean-Jacques Rousseau, *Emile: Or, On Education* (New York: Basic Books, 1979), 3–27.

60. Rousseau, *Emile*, 214.

61. Immanuel Kant, "On the Common Saying: 'This May Be True in Theory, but It Does Not Apply in Practice,'" in *Political Writings*, ed. Hans Reiss (Cambridge, UK: Cambridge University Press, 1991), 61–62.

62. Kant, "On the Common Saying," 61.

63. Robert B. Louden, *Morality and Moral Theory: A Reappraisal and Reaffirmation* (Oxford: Oxford University Press, 1992), 143–52.

64. Aristotle, *Metaphysics*, 1004a35-b1.

65. Edmund L. Pincoffs, *Quandaries and Virtues: Against Reductivism in Ethics* (Lawrence: University of Kansas Press, 1986).

66. Louden, *Morality and Moral Theory*, 97.

67. James R. Rest and Darcia Narvaez, *Moral Development in the Professions* (Mahwaha, NJ: Lawrence Erlbaum Associates, 1994), 14.

68. Dale Jamieson, "Method and Moral Theory," in *A Companion to Ethics*, ed. Peter Singer (Oxford: Blackwell, 1991), 486.

Bibliography

Anderson, David L., ed. *Facing My Lai: Moving beyond the Massacre.* Lawrence: University of Kansas Press, 1998.

Aristotle. *Nicomachean Ethics.* Translated by Terence Irwin. Indianapolis: Hackett, 1985.

Audi, Robert. *Religious Commitment and Secular Reason.* Cambridge, UK: Cambridge University Press, 2000.

Axinn, Sidney. *A Moral Military.* Philadelphia: Temple University Press, 1989.

Baier, Annette. "Doing without Moral Theory." In *Anti-Theory in Ethics and Moral Conservatism.* Stanley Clarke and Evan Simpson, eds. Albany: State University of New York Press, 1989.

Best, Geoffrey. *War and Law Since 1945.* Oxford: Oxford University Press, 1994.

Bohman, James, and Matthias Lutz-Bachmann, eds. *Perpetual Peace: Essays on Kant's Cosmopolitan Ideal.* Cambridge: MIT Press, 1997.

Bourke, Joanna. *An Intimate History of Killing: Face-to-Face Killing in Twentieth-Century Warfare.* New York: Basic Books, 1999.

Browning, Christopher R. *Ordinary Men: Reserve Police Battalion 101 and the Final Solution in Poland.* New York: Harper Perennial, 1992.

Christopher, Paul. *The Ethics of War and Peace: An Introduction to Legal and Moral Issues.* Englewood Cliffs, NJ: Prentice Hall, 1994.

Clausewitz, Carl von. *On War.* New York: Alfred A. Knopf, 1993.

Cook, Martin. *The Moral Warrior*. Albany: State University of New York Press, 2005.

Dewey, John. *Theory of Valuation*. In *John Dewey: The Later Works 1925-1953*, Volume 13, 1938–1939. Ed. Jo Ann Boydson. Carbondale: Southern Illinois University Press, 1988.

French, Shannon. *The Code of the Warrior*. New York: Rowman & Littlefield, 2003.

Gray, J. Glenn. *The Warriors: Reflections on Men in Battle*. New York: Harper Torchbooks, 1959.

Greenberg, Karen J. ed., *The Torture Debate in America*. Cambridge, UK: Cambridge University Press, 2006.

Harris, Sam. *The End of Faith*. New York: W. W. Norton, 2004.

Homer. *The Iliad*. Trans. Robert Fagles. New York: Penguin Books, 1990.

Kant, Immanuel. *Political Writings*, ed. Hans Reiss. Cambridge, UK: Cambridge University Press, 1991.

———. *The Metaphysics of Morals*. Trans. Mary Gregor. Cambridge, UK: Cambridge University Press, 1991.

Korsgaard, Christine M. *The Sources of Normativity*. Cambridge, UK: Cambridge University Press, 1997.

Louden, Robert B. *Morality and Moral Theory: A Reappraisal and Reaffirmation*. Oxford: Oxford University Press, 1992.

Lucas, George R., Jr., and Paul E. Roush, eds. *Ethics for Military Leaders*. New York: Simon and Schuster, 1998.

Milgram, Stanley. *Obedience to Authority*. New York: Harper & Row, 1974.

O'Neill, Onora. *Acting On Principle*. New York: Columbia University Press, 1975.

———. *Constructions of Reason: Explorations of Kant's Practical Philosophy*. Cambridge, UK: Cambridge University Press, 1989.

———. *Towards Justice and Virtue: A Constructive Account of Practical Reasoning*. Cambridge, UK: Cambridge University Press, 1996.

Plato. *The Republic of Plato*. Trans. Francis MacDonald Cornford. London: Oxford University Press, 1945.

———. *Euthyphro, in The Trial and Death of Socrates*. Indianapolis: Hackett, 1975.

Rawls, John. *A Theory of Justice*. Cambridge, MA: Belknap Press, 1971.

———. *Political Liberalism*. New York: Columbia University Press, 1996.

———. *John Rawls: Collected Papers*. Cambridge, MA: Harvard University Press, 1999.

———. *The Law of Peoples*. Cambridge, MA: Harvard University Press, 1999.

Schneewind, J. B. *The Invention of Autonomy: A History of Modern Moral Philosophy*. Cambridge, UK: Cambridge University Press, 1998.

———. "The Misfortunes of Virtue." In *Virtue Ethics*, edited by Roger Crisp and Michael Slote. Oxford: Oxford University Press, 1997.

———. "The Divine Corporation and the History of Ethics." In *Philosophy in History*, ed. Richard Rorty, J. B. Schneewind, and Quentin Skinner, Cambridge, UK: Cambridge University Press, 1984.

Spiller, Roger. *An Instinct for War*. Cambridge, MA: Harvard University Press, 2005.

Walzer, Michael. *Just and Unjust Wars: A Moral Argument with Historical Illustrations*. New York: Basic Books, 1992.

Wolf, Susan. "Moral Saints." *The Journal of Philosophy*. Vol. 79, No. 8. (August 1982).

U.S. Department of the Army. *Field Manual 27-10, The Law of Land Warfare*. Washington, DC, 1956.

About the Author

Tim Challans is a native of Colorado. A West Point graduate, he earned his master's and doctorate degrees in philosophy at The Johns Hopkins University. For more than ten years he has taught more than a thousand military students from the rank of cadet to colonel, at West Point (USMA), the Command and General Staff College (CGSC), and the School of Advanced Military Studies (SAMS). He has spoken widely and presented many papers on the ethics of warfare. Notably, he was the principal author for the Army's 1999 doctrinal manual on leadership, *FM 22–100, Army Leadership*. A career infantry officer, Challans has had troop experience in the 172nd Infantry Brigade at Ft. Richardson, Alaska; the 10th Mountain Division at Ft. Drum, New York; and the 101st Airborne (Air Assault) Division at Ft. Campbell, Kentucky. His military training and education include Airborne School, Ranger School, Infantry Officer's Basic Course, Infantry Officer's Advanced Course, Combined Arms Services Staff School, and the Command and General Staff College. He retired from the Army in 2002 and now lives an autonomous life as a "citizen of the universe" (as Kant would put it), following whatever path his Harley takes him.

Index

Abu Ghraib, 3, 6, 7, 35, 90, 146
academy v. counter-academy, 177–178
Achilles, 34, 37, 40, 49, 50, 51, 55, 56,
    71, 138, 181
After Virtue (MacIntyre), 60
Alexander the Great, 38, 50, 51
Ali, Tariq, 57
    Clash of Fundamentalisms, 57
American Enterprise Institute, 177
amour de soi v. *amour propre*, 168–171
Annas, Julia, 61, 62, 127
Apocalypse Now, 112, 160
Aristotle, xi, 34, 61, 62, 63, 67, 82, 85,
    90, 92, 113, 127
    logic, xi
    paralogism, xi
Arnold, Benedict, 57, 58, 68
Athenians, 36
    Melian Dialogue, 36
Audi, Robert, 42, 43
Aussaresses, General Paul, 35
authority (*see* authority under moral)
autonomy (*see* autonomy under ethics)
    full v. rational, 168
Axinn, Sidney, 57
    Moral Military, A, 57
Azimov, Isaac, 65

Baars, Bernard, 38
    Cognitive Revolution in Psychology, The,
    38

Band of Brothers, 30
Batiste, General John, 185
Battle of the Casbah, 35
battle sleep, ix, xvi, 29–31, 60, 72, 112
behaviorism, 38
    operant conditioning, 38
    Pavlovian conditioning, 38
Bennett, William, 54
    Book of Virtues, The, 54
Benson, Colonel Kevin, 185
Bible, The, 37, 47, 48
Boykin, General William, 44, 45
Breaking the Spell (Dennett), 48
Browning, Christopher, 32
    Ordinary Men, 32
bullshit, 5, 6, 16, 31
Bush, George W., 45, 84

Calley, Lieutenant William, 3, 18, 19,
    21, 182
Cambodia, 22
Carlyle, Thomas, 51
Catch-22 (Heller), 30, 71
causation, x, 113
chaplains, 42, 43, 46, 69, 70, 138
    spiritual fitness, 43
Chomsky, Noam, xi
Christopher, Paul, 47
    Ethics of War and Peace, The, 47
civil war
    American Civil War, 36, 37

Clark, Ramsey, 40
  Fire This Time, The, 40
Clausewitz, Carl von, 31, 95, 131
Code of Conduct, 10
cognitive science, 38
common sense, 174
communism, 17
constitution
  Center for Constitutional Rights, 4
  U.S. Constitution, 2, 32, 44, 58, 104,
    118, 146
constructivism (*see* constructivism under
  Kant)
contextualism, 175
Cook, Martin, 44, 186
cosmopolitanism, 153
Crane, Stephen, 55, 56, 60, 181
  Red Badge of Courage, The, 55, 56, 60,
    66

Dancy, Jonathan, 63, 66, 67
Dawkins, Richard, 38, 48
  Selfish Gene, The, 38, 48
Declaration of Independence, 104
democracy, 24
Dennett, Daniel, 48
  Breaking the Spell, 48
Descartes, René, ix, 80, 109
  innovation, x
  Meditations, ix
Dewey, John, 93, 112, 113, 114, 126
Dienbienphu, 36
dogma, 38, 48
Donagan, Alan, 19, 46, 64, 79
Dönitz, Admiral Karl, 77
Dörner, Dietrich, 104
  Logic of Failure, The, 104
Dworkin, Ronald, 60

education, x, xi
effects-based operations (EBO), 9, 109,
  110, 186
Ellsberg, Daniel, 22
Elshtain, Jean-Bethke, 152
Emile (Rousseau), 168
empiricism, x, 12

End of Faith, The (Harris), 45, 48, 57
ends, 16, 25, 93–101
  deliberating new ends, 127–133
  disregarding ends, 93–101
  inadequate, 25, 105–136
  presumed, 116–126
  telos, 113, 127
  telos v. skopos, 127
  victory, 96, 99–101, 111, 117–118,
    123–124, 128–129, 132, 134
Enlightenment, ix, 8, 23, 35, 70, 151,
  152
  endarkenment, x, 48
error, ix, 18
  moral error, ix, x, 9, 19, 23, 25, 31–38,
    74–77, 106–110, 136
  theory, 17
error theory, 17
  Type I and Type II errors, 17, 76–77,
    96, 101, 115, 120, 133, 157
ethical interoperability, 34, 140
ethical principles of war (restraint),
  151–157
  defense of others, 153, 155, 157
  defense of self, 153, 155, 157
  discrimination, 155, 157
  minimal force, 155, 157
  minimal harm, 155, 157
ethics
  absolutes v. universals, 46, 175
  consequentialism, 74
  decision procedures, 25, 26, 82, 101
  descriptive ethics, 16, 164
  dilemma, 78
  ethical interoperability, 34, 140
  ethics of warfare, 7
  ethos, 8, 10, 11, 12, 15, 23
  foundation, x, 41 42, 104, 141, 184
  integrating means and ends, 120–123
  intuition, 157–166
  jus ad bellum, 6, 147, 151, 152, 154,
    156, 157
  jus in bello, 6, 147, 151, 154, 156, 157
  jus post bellum, 151
  justification, 141, 184
  levels, 16, 164–166

meta-ethics, 16, 159, 164
normative ethics, 16, 164, 166
philosophical ethics, 26, 52, 69, 71, 82–93, 136, 138, 141–151, 164, 166, 171
possible v. actual, 140, 144
principles, 62–64, 68, 69, 115, 116, 120–123, 141, 150–157
professional ethics, 33, 42
right action, 61
systemic level, 4, 76
values, 46, 60, 77–82, 102–103, 116, 117
virtue ethics, 82–93, 102
work ethic, 11, 14
Ethics of War and Peace (Christopher), 47
Euthyphro (Socrates), 39

Fallujah, 98
falsification (see scientific theory under theory)
Few Good Men, A, 29
first philosophy, x
Fishback, Captain Ian, 22
Flowers, General Mike, 134, 207n56
FM 22-100 Army Leadership (see manual under leadership)
Fort Leavenworth, 35, 162
Frankfurt, Harry, 5, 6, 8
On Bullshit, 5 (see On Bullshit)
Franklin, Benjamin, 39
Poor Richard's Almanac, 39
freedom, xi
academic, xi (see academic freedom)
French, Shannon, 34, 186
Code of the Warrior, 34
Fromm, Lieutenant Colonel Peter, 36
Thin Red Line, The, 36

genocide, 10
Global War on Terror (GWOT), 128, 135, 149, 181
God, 32, 41, 42, 47, 71, 138
Golden Rule, The, 103
Goya, Francisco, xvi, 64, 183
Grant, General Ulysses, 37, 124, 125

Gray, J. Glenn, 162
Warriors, The, 162
Greenberg, Karen J. and Dratel, Joshua L.
Torture Debate, The (Greenberg), 70
Torture Papers, The, 4, 6, 70, 82
Greene, Graham, 30
Quiet American, The, 30
Guantanamo, 90, 146

Hafez, Mohammed, 133, 207n55
Haig, Alexander, 21
Hanson, Victor Davis, 155
Hare, R. M., 52
Harris, Sam, 45, 48, 57
End of Faith, The, 45, 47, 57
Havelock, Eric, 50
Heller, Joseph, 30, 71
Catch-22, 29
Heritage Foundation, The, 177
History of the Peloponnesian War, The, 36
Hitchens, Christopher, 22
Hobbes, Thomas, 138
Homer, 34, 36, 49, 55, 138
Iliad, 34, 38, 49, 56
Horowitz, David, 178
Howard, Sir Michael, 7, 152
human nature, x

Iliad (Homer), 34, 38, 49, 55
impeachment, 5
indoctrination, 15, 25, 29–31, 102, 158, 164, 174, 185
induction, ix, x
Instinct for War, An (Spiller), 7, 8
intentionality, 39
intersubjectivity, 140
invincible ignorance, 185
Irwin, Terence, 61

Johnson, Chalmers, 132
Jones, James, 71
jus ad bellum (see ethics)
jus in bello (see ethics)
jus post bellum (see ethics)
just war theory, 147, 157, 175
Just War Tradition, 147, 153, 154, 157
justification (see justification under ethics)

Kagan, Fred, 155
Kant, Immanuel, x, 15, 24–26, 47, 64,
    68, 84, 90, 131–135, 139–144,
    150–155, 157–172, 179, 184
  constructivism, 166
  logic, xi
  moral progress, x
  paralogism, xi
  systems, x
Kaplan, Robert, 137–138, 155
Kendrick, LT, 29
Kidder, Rushworth, 78
Killer Angels, 30
Kissinger, Henry, 21–22, 134
Koestler, Arthur, 181
  Ghost in the Machine, The, 181
Kolenda, Christopher, 51
  Warrior's Art, The, 51
Koran, The, 47
Krulak, General Charles C., 135
Kubrick, Stanley, 71

Laconia, 77
Laos, 16, 134, 161
law, 2, 59
  international law, 6, 115
  laws of war, 145, 146, 154, 155
  rule of, 2, 7 (*see* rule of law)
leadership, 33
  manual, 33, 132 (see FM 22-100 *Army*
    Leadership)
Lee, General Robert E., 57, 58, 124
Lemon Test, 43, 59
Lieber, Francis, 145, 155
logic, ix
  deduction, ix
  fallacy of appeal to ignorance, 108
  induction, ix, x
  paralogism, xi
  reduction ad absurdum, 167
Logic of Failure, The (Dörner), 104
Long War, 27, 54, 96, 181

MacArthur, General Douglas, 36, 106,
    107, 127, 128, 129
MacIntyre, Alisdair, 60
  After Virtue, 60

Malick, Terence, 71
Margolis, Joseph, 63
Mattox, Mark, 44
McCaffrey, General Barry, 40, 41, 59
McMaster, H. R., 183
  Dereliction of Duty, 183
McNamara, Robert, 21
means, 16, 93–101
  disregarding means, 110–116
  instrumental means, 25, 73–77,
    110–116
Meditations (Descartes), ix
Meigs, General Montgomery, 162
Melians, 36
  Melian Dialogue, 36
meme, 38, 40, 48, 64, 138
method, 24, 25
  critical, 26
  decision procedure, 25–26, 74, 77–82,
    98
  instrumental, 25, 73–77
  philosophical, 82–93
Middle East, 1, 13, 70, 128, 133
Milgram, Stanley, 31, 32
  Obedience to Authority, 32
military ethics, 7
  military ethics v. ethics of warfare, 7
Mill, John Stuart, 53
moral, ix
  action, x
  agency, 20
  ascendancy (*see* superiority under
    moral)
  authority, 15, 29, 41, 46, 164
  autonomy, 24–26, 139, 141–151,
    166–176, 184
  certainty, 11
  character, xi
  clarity, 11, 13
  compass, 81, 198n13
  consequences, xi
  critique, xi
  education, ix
  error, ix, 10, 17, 19, 23, 25, 31–37,
    74–77, 106–110, 188n9
  evaluation, xi

ideas, 2
judgment, 2
moral v. morale, 14
normativity, xi, 16, 164, 166
practice, 2
principles (*see* principles under ethics)
problem of the understanding, 4, 18, 103, 174
problem of the will, 4, 103
progress, ix, xi, 1, 11
psychology, 92, 168–171
public v. private morality, 15
revolution, 27
superiority, 11–14, 118, 162
theory, x, 33, 52, 142
truth, x
understanding, 2, 4, 20–22,
moral error (*see* error under moral)
John Rawls on moral error, 188n9
Moral Military, A (Axinn), 57
moral v. morale, 14
moral progress, ix, 1, 11
myth of, 1–27
moral understanding, ix, 2, 4, 20–22
dupes, 20–22
knaves, 20–22
knights, 22
morale, 14
Morris, Roger, 22
My Lai, 3, 4, 6, 7, 18, 19, 21, 22
myth
Masada Myth, 37
myth of moral progress, 1–27

narrative, 15, 29–34, 38, 52, 53, 55, 64–68
National Military Strategy, 8
nationalism, 23
Naveh, General Shimon, Ph.D., 100, 186
Newbold, General Gregory, 185
Nietzsche, Friedrich, 60, 81
normative ethics, 16
normative fallacy, 64
North, Oliver, 134, 161
Nuremberg trials, 23, 77
Nussbaum, Martha, 62, 63, 64, 84, 169

oath of office, 32, 190n4
Obedience to Authority (Milgram), 32
Odysseus, 34
officership, 158, 159
Olin Foundation, The, 177
Olin, John M., 177
Once an Eagle, 30
O'Neill, Onora, 68, 143
Operation Desert Shield, 41, 167
Operation Desert Storm, 11, 39–41, 95, 99–100, 106–107, 147, 167
Operation Iraqi Freedom (OIF), 41, 105, 114, 154m 167
Ordinary Men (Browning), 32
Orientalism, 13
  Orientalism (Said), 188n11
Orwell, George (*1984*), 128
Osama bin Laden, 77, 182

particularism, 31, 33, 38, 52, 53, 55, 56, 59, 61–69
Patton, General George, 51
Pentagon Papers, 6
perpetual war, 9
Peters, Ralph, 137, 138, 155
philosophy, x
  epistemology, x, 41, 42, 78, 104
  ethics, x (*see* ethics)
  logic, x (*see* logic)
  metaphysics, x, 41, 42, 78, 104, 166
  moral philosophy, x, 104
  moral theory, x
Pincoffs, Edmond, 172
Plato, 36, 50, 51, 60, 61, 62, 69
Poor Richard's Almanac (Franklin), 39
Powell, Colin, 3, 5, 9, 20–21, 37–39, 107, 133–135
pragmatism, 15
preemptive war, 5, 9
preventive war, 5, 9
problem of the understanding, 4, 18
problem of the will, 4
professional ethics, 33, 42
professionalism, 159, 161
progress, ix, x, 13
  actual v. possible, 13
  moral progress, ix, xi

Quiet American, The (Greene), 30

Rawls, John, 43, 133, 140–151, 152–157, 158–173, 179, 188n9
  Rawls on moral error, 188n9
realism, 24
  military realism, 24, 37, 137, 139
  political realism, 24, 137, 139
reason, ix
  sleep of reason, ix, 1 (*see* sleep of reason)
Red Badge of Courage, The (Crane), 55–56, 60, 66
reflection, xi, 34, 70, 71
  no reflection (unreflective life), 1–27
  pretended reflection (pseudo-reflective life), 29–72
  semi reflection (semi-reflective life), 73–104
  strained reflection (quasi-reflective life), 105–136
  total reflection (fully reflective life), 137–175
regime change, 23
Reimer, General Dennis, 120, 127
religion, 33, 57, 70
  Abrahamic, 70
  clash of fundamentalisms, 46, 57
  faith-based intelligence, 45, 48
  faith-based morality, 48
  religious authority, 32, 41
  religious endorsement, 45
  religious establishment, 45
  religious fundamentalism, 44, 45, 160
  religious relativism, 42
  religious test, 44
revolution, 8
  moral revolution, 8 (*see also* moral revolution)
Richardson, Henry, 113, 125, 126, 131
Ridenhour, Ron, 18
Right Stuff, The (Thomas Wolfe), 30, 71
Ritter, Scott, 22
Roberts, Kenneth, 58, 68
Rogers, Robert, 58
Romantic era, 23

Rorty, Richard, 63, 64
Rousseau, Jean-Jacques, xi, 166, 168, 169
  Emile, 168
rule of law, 2, 7
Russell, Bertrand, xi, 48

Sachs, David, 169
Said, Edward, 13, 188n11
  Orientalism, 13, 188n11
Sartre, Jean-Paul, xii, 182
Sassaman, Lieutenant Colonel Nate, 75, 93
Scalia, Justice Antonin, 59, 60
Schneewind, J. B., xv, 189n25, 194n62
School of Advanced Military Studies (SAMS), 185
Schoomaker, General Peter, 117
Schwarzkopf, General Norman, 40, 106
Selfish Gene, The (Dawkins), 38, 48
separation of church and state, 43, 59
Shakespeare, William, 54, 68
Sharon, Ariel, 35, 37
Shaw, George Bernard, 103
Shelley, Percy Bysshe, 52
Sherman, General William, 36, 37, 59
shock and awe, 9
Simon, William E., 177, 178, 197n113
Singer, Peter, 180
  President of Good and Evil, 180
Sinnott-Armstrong, Walter, 66
sleep of reason, ix, 1
Snider, Don, 44, 161, 211n39
Socrates, 39, 183, 184
Spiller, Roger, 7, 8
  Instinct for War, An, 8
spiritual fitness, 43
Summers, Colonel Harry, 106
Supreme Court, 2, 43, 59, 149
  Katkoff v. Marsh, 43
  Lemon Test, 43, 59
Swannack, General Charles, 185
systemic level of ethics, 4, 18

tacit knowledge, 52
Taylor, Gabrielle, 169
Taylor, General Telford, 130

terrorism, 17
theory, x, 172
  action theory, x, 39, 181
  Auftragstaktik v. *Normaltaktik*, 171
  error theory, 17
  moral theory, x, 33
  pre-theoretic intuitions, 18
  scientific theory, 109
telos (*see* end)
Thin Red Line, The, 30
Thompson, Hugh, 22
Thucydides, 36
  History of the Peloponnesian War, The,
    36
Toner, James, 44
torture, 75
Torture Debate, The (Greenberg), 70
Torture Papers, The (Greenberg and
  Dratel), 4, 6, 70, 82
tradition, 36
  hypertradition, 36, 38, 64
training, x, xi
Trinquier, Roger, 35
Troy, 36

Ulmer, General Walter, 39
United Nations, 24, 106, 107, 108, 151
U.S. Air Force Academy, 39, 69
U.S. Army, 38
U.S. Military Academy, 19, 36, 39, 69
U.S. Naval Academy, 33, 69, 91, 135

victory (*see* ends)
Vidal, Gore, 69
Vietnam, 16, 18, 22, 23, 31, 39, 106,
  132, 133–134, 161
virtue
  courage, 49, 56, 67, 84, 90
  honesty, 41, 52, 84, 85
  honor v. integrity, 88, 89, 91
  justice, 52
  loyalty, 91
  other-regarding and self-regarding,
    86–90

respect, 85
selflessness, impossibility of, 87, 88
shame v. guilt, 92
virtue ethics, 82–93, 102
virtue theory, 56, 61, 91, 168

Wallace, James D., 68
Walzer, Michael, xi, 6, 54, 109, 123,
  133, 154, 157, 162–163, 175
war, 4
  American way of war, 37
  destructive, 10
  indiscriminate, 10, 119
  intervention, 6 (*see* intervention)
  Long War, 27, 54, 96, 181
  military necessity, 130, 154
  perpetual war, 9 (*see* perpetual war)
  preemptive war, 5, 9 (*see* preemptive
    war)
  preventive war, 5, 9 (*see* preventive
    war)
war machine, ix, xi, 27, 143
warrior, xi, 8, 12, 32, 48, 147, 184
  cult of the warrior, 12
  warrior ethos, 9, 10, 12, 14, 15, 23,
    112, 117
  warrior spirit (*see* warrior ethos)
Warriors, The (Gray), 162
Warrior's Art, The (Kolenda), 51
We Were Soldiers Once and Young, 30
weapons of mass destruction (WMD),
  107, 108, 131, 149
Weil, Simone, 112
West, Lieutenant Colonel Allen, 35,
  75–80, 90, 93
West Point, 19, 36, 39, 42, 57, 69, 80,
  85, 106, 116, 128–129, 147–148,
  158–159, 178
Westmoreland, William, 4
Williams, Bernard, 105
Wolfe, Thomas, 30, 71
  Right Stuff, The, 30
work ethic, 11, 14